Annexation Hawaii

Thomas J. Osborne

Island Style Press
Waimanalo, Hawai'i

Previously published as "Empire Can Wait," under:
Library of Congress catalog card 81-8156
ISBN 0-933484-1-8
Manufactured in the United States of America
Cover Design Doug Behrens
Cover Photo Kimo Kahoano by Michael Dougherty

Library of Congress Cataloging In Publication Data

Osborne, Thomas J., 1942 -
Annexation Hawaii. (See listing "Empire Can Wait")
Bibliography: p
Includes index.
1. Hawaii - Annexation to the United States
2. United States - Foreign Relations 1865-98
3. United States - Territorial Expansion I. Title
DU 627.4.083   996.'028   81-8156
ISBN 0-9633484-1-8   AACR2

Island Style Press
P.O. Box 296
Waimanalo, HI 96795
(808) 259-8666

For My Mother, Dorothy

Contents

100 Years Under the Yoke

This work is the most detailed, objective account available of the arduous attempt to annex Hawaii from 1894 to 1898. According to the author, opposition to the annexation of Hawai'i a century ago "represented, at bottom, a fear that America would abandon her republican tradition and embark upon the dangerous course of empire building." Believing that America would ultimately possess Hawai'i, opponents of annexation argued, in the words of United States House Speaker Thomas Reed, that "empire can wait."

The belief that Hawai'i would inevitably become a part of the United States was also shared by those who believed that it was part of America's "Manifest Destiny." You will learn that "Manifest Destiny" did not lead to the annexation of Hawai'i, however, until Admiral Dewey captured Manila; and even then, only because Congress was concerned that the United States not lose out in carving up the spoils of China by European powers in 1898. It was "imperialism," therefore, a word used for the first time in the Congressional debates of 1898, by those both for and against it, that produced the annexation of Hawai'i. Earlier attempts to incorporate Hawai'i in 1854, 1893-4, and 1897-8 failed.

What we do learn from this book that is relevant in 1998? One reason why attempts to annex Hawai'i so often failed is that Hawai'i was too distant to engage the interest of Washington, except fitfully in connection with other interests. For the same reason, the wishes of the native population of Hawai'i were almost completely ignored. This was likewise true in the case of statehood, and is still true today. It suggests that the main obstacle to a reconsideration of Hawaiian sovereignty may be the difficulty of gaining the attention and support of the United States mainland.

This excellent, comprehensive study deserves your attention and will hold high interest among those on either side of today's history-making sovereignty movement.

Thomas J. Osborne, acclaimed by his colleagues as a distinguished scholar, deals in facts. Happily he has no "enlightened self-interest" ax to grind and no rogue ancestors to defend.

Stephen T. Boggs
Emeritus Professor Of Anthropology   Kaneohe, Hawai'i
University of Hawaii, Manoa   March 1, 1998

Introduction

The United States in the 1890s was faced with a critical foreign policy decision. Was this nation to remain a self-contained continental republic or should she embrace an expansive overseas empire? Not since the 1790s, when the Anglo-French War embroiled Americans and threatened their republican institutions, had there occurred such a searching public debate over foreign affairs. During the last decade of the nineteenth century the United States was confronted with the prospect of abandoning her hallowed tradition of continental expansion and opting for a policy of imperialism.[1] The specific incident that raised this prospect, thereby presaging the dramatic Senate debate of 1898-99 over colonialism, was President Benjamin Harrison's signing and submission to the upper house in February 1893 of the recently drafted Hawaiian annexation treaty.

The importance of the Hawaiian question from the standpoint of establishing a precedent for empire building was recognized by both advocates and opponents of annexation. Captain Alfred T. Mahan, naval historian and vigorous proponent of Hawaiian annexation, stated solemnly in March 1893:

> The United States finds herself compelled to answer a question—to make a decision—not unlike and not less momentous than that required of the Roman senate, when the Mamertine garrison invited it to occupy Messina, and so abandon the hitherto traditional policy which had confined the expansion of Rome to the Italian peninsula.[2]

In a special message to Congress in December 1893, President Grover Cleveland said that the Hawaiian annexation treaty drafted under his predecessor was especially significant "because it contemplated a departure from unbroken American tradition in providing for the addition to our territory of islands of the sea more than two thousand miles removed from our nearest coast."[3] Senator Stephen M. White of California expressed the sentiments of many congressional foes of insular expansion when he told the upper chamber in June 1898: "The annexation of Hawaii will constitute the entering wedge for an imperialistic policy."[4]

In one sense, vigorous opposition to Hawaiian annexation, like Senator White's, seems curious. Of all the areas brought into the Union in the late 1890s, Hawaii had maintained the closest cultural and economic ties with the United States. Beginning in the 1790s New England merchantmen visited Hawaii in order to take on cargoes of sandalwood that were then carried to Canton and exchanged for teas and silks, which commanded a high price in the United States. Often these Pacific-bound trading vessels, upon rounding Cape Horn, headed for points along the northwest coast to acquire fur seal pelts, and then proceeded to Hawaii and the Orient. Shortly after the New Englanders entered the Pacific maritime trade, Yankee whalers sailing out of New Bedford, Nantucket, and Martha's Vineyard began frequenting Honolulu and Lahaina for repairs and supplies. The foothold that these early Yankee visitors established in Hawaii was strengthened by the arrival in 1820 of the pioneer company of New England Congregational missionaries. Some of these missionaries and their coreligionists who later came—most notably Hiram Bingham, William Richards, and Gerrit P. Judd—became leading advisers to the native rulers, whom they urged to adopt Puritan morality and American political institutions. Merchants, whalers, and missionaries, then, extended America's Pacific frontier to Hawaii. To safeguard that Pacific outpost from seizure by another power, President John Tyler issued in 1842 his famous doctrine to the effect that the United States had a special relationship with Hawaii and would not countenance any foreign threat to the independence of the island kingdom. If the Tyler doctrine extended the political arm of Uncle Sam around Hawaii, then the commercial reciprocity treaty of 1875 extended the economic arm. Indeed, that treaty, which remained in effect until the islands were brought into the Union in 1898, tethered Hawaii's economy to that of the United States. In the year 1890, for example, nearly ninety-nine percent of Hawaii's exports were shipped to the American mainland, and seventy-six percent of her imports came from there.[5]

Despite the tendency of these cultural and economic ties to

spur annexation, America did not acquire the Polynesian archipelago until the late nineteenth century. That it took so long to effect this seemingly "natural" union, was due largely, if not exclusively, to the formidable opposition to Hawaiian annexation within the United States. Attempts to incorporate the islands into the Union in 1854, 1893, and 1897 all met with failure. In 1854 King Kamehameha III offered to transfer his kingdom to the United States in order to preclude what he regarded as twin dangers—the threat of internal revolution and the specter of California filibusters seizing his domain. The king's untimely death in December 1854 insured the defeat of the annexation treaty, which he had left unsigned. His successor, Liholiho, refused to resurrect the annexation project. Even if the treaty had been approved by the Hawaiian government, it would not have been ratified by the United States Senate because that document contained provisions for Hawaiian statehood and the payment of a large annuity to the native rulers. In 1893 a revolution was launched in Hawaii by white Americans for the dual purpose of toppling the native monarchy and transferring the islands to the United States. The revolution succeeded; the annexation attempt failed. Shortly after President William McKinley entered office in 1897 he made an abortive attempt to acquire Hawaii by treaty. Not until mid-1898, and then only by the passage over bitter opposition of the Newlands joint resolution, was Hawaii annexed. One might reasonably ask, then, why was there such strong resistance to incorporating the northern Pacific archipelago into the Union? Although historians have paid scant attention to this question,[6] its answer holds important implications for gaining a better understanding of not only the Hawaiian annexation controversy but also the nature of the anti-imperialist movement as well. This is the first study that concentrates on the resistance to the acquisition of Hawaii and which places that movement squarely in the vanguard of the anti-imperialist crusade.

Two auxiliary issues are treated in the present work. First, this account challenges much of what has been written about the anti-imperialists by such New Left-oriented historians as Walter LaFeber, Christopher Lasch, Thomas J. McCormick, and William A. Williams, who have argued variously that the contending sides in the debate over empire differed but slightly, if at all, in their respective outlooks on commercial expansion and race.[7] Second, this study will examine briefly the forces which in 1898 overcame the resistance to the acquisition of the islands. Thomas A. Bailey has explained the breaking of the congressional deadlock over annexation in terms of certain military exigencies arising out of the Spanish-American War.[8] This view, which has gained widespread acceptance among historians, is refuted and a commercial explanation is given as an alternative.

Two dominant themes recur throughout the following pages. First, and of greatest importance, the struggle against the admission of Hawaii into the Union, though multifaceted and complex, represented at the bottom a fear that America would abandon her republican tradition and embark upon the dangerous course of empire. Second, a majority of those who resisted the acquisition of the islands in the 1890s were not unconditionally opposed to it, and sensed the likelihood that Uncle Sam would eventually possess Hawaii. Most of the opponents, whether politicians, publicists, or businessmen, did not want the United States to rush precipitately into the colonial quagmire. For the most part these dissenters seemed to endorse the somewhat circumscribed position of Thomas B. Reed, the House Speaker from Maine, namely, "empire can wait." [9]

With respect to the scope of this study, two points should be noted. Since this is an excursion into the diplomatic history of the United States, the focus, as the subtitle indicates, will be almost entirely upon mainland opposition; resistance elsewhere, including Hawaii, will be treated only as it influenced opposition within the United States. The book will concentrate on the years 1893-98 because they witnessed not only the height of the public debate over the acquisition of Hawaii but also the maturation of the imperialist and anti-imperialist movements.

Before turning to the body of this study, some final comments regarding definitions are appropriate. The term "imperialism," the reader may have noticed, has been introduced. Because this word has taken on so many different meanings since the late nineteenth century, it would seem that a working definition is in order. In the present work "imperialism" is used in the same way that contemporaries in the 1890s utilized the word. The *Oxford English Dictionary* (1901) defined the term as follows: "In the United States, *Imperialism* is...applied to the new policy of extending the rule of the American people over foreign countries, and of acquiring and holding distant dependencies, in the way in which colonies and dependencies are held by European states."[10] It is in this political-administrative sense that the world "imperialism" is used here. Also, the writer employs three terms to refer to the opponents of Hawaiian annexation, each of which relates to the reason(s) for such opposition. The critics of annexation are called "anti-imperialists" when they oppose the acquisition of insular dependencies primarily on the grounds that such a policy is contrary to the American tradition of continental expansion and would endanger republican institutions within the United States. The opponents of Hawaiian annexation are referred to as "anti-expansionists" if their resistance is based on anti-imperialist grounds as just described, or on other ideological grounds, such as moral, constitutional, and racial objections. The first designation, then, is subsumed by the second. Finally, the word "anti-annexationist" is used to refer to a person who is against the admission of Hawaii into the Union for any reason; and, therefore, this is the most inclusive of the three terms. Having defined the key terms used in this study of the resistance to Hawaiian annexation, we can now examine opposition at the close of Harrison's administration.

T.J.O.
Laguna Beach, California
March 16, 1998

1

Opposition at the Close of Harrison's Administration

In late January 1893 accounts of the recent overthrow of the Hawaiian monarchy and the arrival in San Francisco of an annexation commission from the islands made front-page copy in leading newspapers across the country. Upon debarking from the steamer *Claudine* the five-member delegation, comprising Lorrin A. Thurston (chairman), William R. Castle, Charles L. Carter, William C. Wilder, and Joseph Marsden, spent a day in San Francisco talking with reporters and other "Hawaii watchers," including Claus Spreckels and his sons John and Adolph. According to Thurston,[1] the senior Spreckels said he was strongly in favor of annexation and offered the commissioners use of his private railway car for their journey to Washington. They declined the offer but lost no time departing for the capital, arriving there on February 3.

On the following day the commissioners attended the first of what turned out to be seven formal conferences and private interviews on Hawaiian annexation with Secretary of State John W. Foster.[2] The chief purpose of these meetings was to negotiate a treaty of annexation that would prove acceptable to both governments, including of course the United States Senate.

Secretary Foster was an experienced and able diplomat who was to play an important role in the movement to bring Hawaii into the Union. Because he anticipated that there would be opposition to annexation in both houses of the legislature, he tried to frame an accord not likely to antagonize Congress. Therefore, he told the visiting delegates that their requests for a sugar bounty (of two cents per pound payable under the McKinley tariff), an oceanic cable, and permission to retain their own (Chinese) immigration laws and contract system, would be found objectionable to many senators. "By leaving the whole question of the bounty and the tariff out of the Treaty," said the secretary, "the greatest cause for opposition would be eliminated from the

Treaty." He added that the sugar bounty probably would be repealed within a year.[3] According to Foster the inclusion of the bounty clause and a stipulation permitting the importation of Chinese laborers under contract "would have the same effect upon the opposition that a red flag would have upon a bull."[4]

While the convention was still being negotiated, President Harrison, who had already made known to the commissioners his support for annexation,[5] requested the addition of a clause providing for a plebiscite in Hawaii. This request stemmed from the chief executive's desire to give the transaction the "semblance of having been the universal will of the people."[6] Just as Foster had convinced the commissioners that certain items had to be excluded from the treaty, so he dissuaded Harrison from insisting upon a plebiscite.

The secretary of state and the five Hawaiian delegates signed the document on February 14 and it was transmitted to the Senate on the following day, accompanied by Foster's report and President Harrison's message urging prompt and favorable action.[7] Within one month from the outbreak of the Hawaiian Revolution, two weeks of which were spent by the commissioners journeying to Washington, a treaty of annexation had been negotiated, signed, and submitted to the upper house. The Foreign Relations Committee readily approved the compact (Senator George Gray of Delaware was the only committee member who dissented) and transmitted it to the Senate on February 17. Up to that point the prospect for early ratification looked auspicious. The *New York Herald's* poll of the Senate indicated that only three of the eighty-three members of the upper house who responded opposed annexation.[8]

Harrison realized that a two-thirds majority in the Senate could not be obtained without Democratic support. The president, therefore, instructed the secretary of state to confer with Senators John T. Morgan of Alabama and Arthur P. Gorman of Maryland, both Democrats. They informed Foster "that they anticipated no serious opposition to the treaty from their side of the chamber."[9] Democratic Senators Johnson N. Camden of West Virginia, John L. Chipman of Michigan, and Matthew C. Butler of South Carolina had all publicly supported the project.

Scarcely any major newspaper in the country disagreed with the *New York Tribune*'s assertion that two-thirds of the Senate favored ratification.[10] Few of those organs which shortly thereafter were to oppose Hawaiian annexation had as yet taken a position. Also, various state legislatures throughout the nation, including those of California, Colorado, Illinois, Oregon, New Jersey, New York, and Pennsylvania, had either passed resolutions or forwarded memorials to Washington urging Congress to annex Hawaii. Writing from Washington on February 22, 1893, Commissioner Thurston seemed justified in stating to one correspondent that there was "no organized opposition" to the treaty and that it would pass if a vote could be taken in the Senate.[11]

While annexationists had sufficient reason to be jubilant about the chances for Senate passage of the convention in early 1893, signs were not lacking that some formidable obstacles lay in the path of ratification. One such ominous sign appeared on January 30 when Senator William E. Chandler of New Hampshire introduced a resolution asking the president to negotiate a treaty of annexation with Hawaii. Chandler's move was countered by Senator Stephen M. White of California, who caused the measure to lie over until it was referred to the Foreign Relations Committee on February 2. Another warning signal for the annexationists was the appearance in Washington on February 17 of Paul Neumann, Queen Liliuokalani's personal attorney and unofficial envoy.[12] He met immediately with individual senators and presented them with arguments against the treaty. Neumann sought to impress upon American officials and public opinion the view that the natives had not been consulted regarding annexation and that the queen's side of the matter deserved a hearing before any action was taken on the convention. The attorney had with him a remonstrance from the queen addressed to Cleveland. Appended to Liliuokalani's letter of appeal to the president-elect was a *précis* written by Neumann which stated that the queen's surrender had been brought about by the forces from the United States ship U.S.S. *Boston*. As a result of the dethronement of the monarch, testified the queen's attorney, disorder erupted in Honolulu and Minister John L. Stevens used the occasion to proclaim a United States protectorate over the islands. Cleveland received the letter and *précis* at Lakewood, New Jersey, and, doubtless, was influenced by these affidavits when he met with future cabinet members Walter Q. Gresham and John G. Carlisle on February 22 to discuss the Hawaiian problem. Neumann also sent a copy of his statement to the Foreign Relations Committee and was responsible for the *New York World's* publication of his account.[13] The lobbying and propagandizing of Neumann stirred up trouble for the annexationists and probably helped delay an early Senate vote.

Although few members of Congress delivered speeches castigating the treaty before Cleveland assumed office, there were some representatives (mainly Democrats) who at an early date declared themselves against annexation. One of the most vociferous was Joseph H. Outhwaite, an Ohio Democrat and chairman of the Committee on Military Affairs, who described the American role in the Hawaiian Revolution as "an outrage" and "an act of war." He reviled annexation as a "filibustering scheme" launched by the sugar interests on the islands. Thomas E. Watson, the irascible Georgia Populist, charged that annexation was "a job put up by American property owners and sugar planters in Hawaii" who sought only "personal aggrandizement." Other congressmen who ridiculed annexation as a Hawaiian sugar planters' scheme to obtain the American bounty were Populist Jerry Simpson of Kansas, Democrat John M. Clancy of New York, and William E. Haynes and Michael D. Harter, both Democrats from Ohio.[14]

Another major objection, which anti-imperialists in the House were inclined to voice, was that annexation would constitute a dangerous departure from certain traditional policies of the United States, such as continental expansion and noninterference in the affairs of other nations. Bourke Cockran, a volatile Democrat from New York, objected to the United States' acquisition of "colonial possessions" like Hawaii and argued that American supremacy in those islands could and should be maintained without annexing them. "Let the people of Hawaii settle their own affairs" without any "meddling" from the United States, advised Joseph D. Sayers, a Texas Democrat. Other Democratic congressmen subscribing to the above views included Henry W.

Bentley of New York, Charles T. O'Farrell of Virginia, Benton McMillan of Tennessee, and John O. Pendleton of West Virginia.[15]

In the Senate there were few early indications, aside from Senator White's objection to the Chandler resolution, that the pact would encounter stiff resistance. Probably the most outspoken Senate opponent of annexation was Richard F. Pettigrew, a Republican from South Dakota. "This whole matter," he said, "is not much more than an attempt on the part of the great sugar planters of that island [sic] to share in the bounty now paid by this Government on domestic sugars." Generally, members of the upper house who were leaning toward opposition to annexation showed a remarkable disinclination to make public their views during the remaining weeks of Harrison's term. Gray of Delaware said: "My general notion inclines me against annexation, but until the proposition is fully made known I cannot say how I will vote."[16] Republican William B. Allison of Iowa took an even more cautious public stance, saying only that he was opposed to indecent haste in ratifying the treaty.

There was one point upon which both congressional opponents and advocates of annexation were in basic agreement, namely, that regardless of the outcome of the treaty fight Hawaii was to remain within the American sphere of influence. Indeed, in early 1893 many of the anti-annexationists in Congress were not averse to establishing an American protectorate over the islands. There was little exaggeration in Commissioner Thurston's comment that "the entire opposition in the United States to annexation advocates freely the execution of a treaty" establishing an American protectorate over Hawaii.[17]

The early reaction of the American press toward annexation was not unlike that of Congress—initially favorable, subsequently skeptical. In early February most editorial-writers seemed to agree that the absorption of the islands was preferable to allowing them to fall under the domination of some rival foreign power.[18] Already, however, newspapers were evincing a partisan split which was to become increasingly pronounced. As a rule Democratic papers, though somewhat divided, attacked the treaty, whereas most Republican papers favored annexation.

The objections most often raised in the opposition press

included: the involvement of Minister Stevens and American marines in the overthrow of the queen; the belief that the annexation movement was spawned by wealthy island cane planters, like Claus Spreckels, for the purpose of securing the American sugar bounty; the failure of the provisional government to consult the Hawaiian natives regarding the proposed transfer of sovereignty; the belief that the United States, without acquiring the archipelago, could possess whatever commercial and military advantages Hawaii had to offer; the dangers to the American Republic of embarking upon a new policy of colonialism; and the unsuitability of the Hawaiian natives for American citizenship.[19] Of these objections the one posing the greatest threat to early ratification was the growing belief, expressed in many newspapers, that annexation was a sugar planters' scheme. "Our bitterest enemies," wrote William R. Castle in his diary in late February, "are those who charge a job against us—that sugar had done this thing—or Spreckels, or something else. It is not admitted that we can be honest or patriotic."

The opposition press lost little time in propagandizing against the treaty. As early as February 7, 1893, the *New York Herald* queried on its editorial page, "Is Spreckles & Co. the little nigger in the fence of the sugar islands?" This attack by malicious innuendo was continued in the pages of that newspaper until February 24, at which time the *Herald* published a thoughtful editorial attacking Hawaiian annexation. That newspaper effectively summarized the objections of numerous other anti-expansionist organs when it concluded:

> The weightiest objections to the proposed annexation are raised by the extraordinary, not to say, suspicious, circumstances surrounding the matter. The scheme is launched at a time when its success would benefit the sugar ring. Annexation is not asked or desired by a majority of the Hawaiians, but by a minority foreign element which suddenly overthrew the established government.

From late February 1893 until Cleveland left office in 1897, the *New York Herald* remained the nation's leading paper in the journalistic campaign against annexation.[20]

Edwin L. Godkin, editor of *The Nation* and of the *New York Evening Post*, argued wryly in the editorial pages of the latter that annexation could not give the United States any advantage not already possessed "except the privilege of paying the expenses of the Hawaiian government."[21] He favored the establishment of a protectorate over the islands so that the United States could continue to derive all of the advantages while avoiding the draw-backs of annexation. The *New York World* editorially advocated a similar position.

The *Albany* (N.Y.) *Times* expressed the essence of the anti-imperialist case against admitting Hawaii into the Union: "To annex Hawaii would be to enter upon a new policy of foreign acquisition for which the American people are hardly prepared. Once entered upon, where would it end?" The *Seattle Post-Intelligencer*, one of the few large Pacific coast dailies to oppose annexation, also looked with foreboding upon the precedent that Hawaii's incorporation would establish. "We may be asked to take Cuba or Santo Domingo. With this increased responsibility we shall be urged to increase our navy," warned one editorial.[22] As these two newspaper comments suggest, the main objection of the anti-imperialists to Hawaiian annexation was that it would constitute a break with past policy and create a precedent for future insular acquisitions.

While the newspapers opposing annexation quickened their efforts, the president-elect gave serious thought to the Hawaiian matter. On February 22 Cleveland met with his future secretaries of state and of the treasury, Gresham and Carlisle, respectively, at Lakewood to discuss "the case of the Hawaiian Queen."[23] Gresham advised the sending of a commission to Hawaii to determine the validity of Liliuokalani's charges of misconduct on the part of American officials in Honolulu. Cleveland, who doubtless was concerned about the plight of the dethroned monarch, agreed to send an investigator. Shortly after the Lakewood conference Carlisle went to Washington where he contacted leading Democrats in the Senate, and gave them their cue as to the wishes of the incoming president. From that point on the prospects for ratification grew increasingly remote.

In late February there were indications from both houses of

Congress that the treaty would not be ratified during the remaining days of Harrison's administration. The Senate's refusal after February 21 to continue meeting in executive session to discuss annexation was fatal to the document's early passage. In the lower house Bourke Cockran and other Democratic adversaries of the treaty insisted that since the convention contained provisions requiring the appropriation of public funds—both the queen and Kaiulani were to receive federal disbursements in accordance with article VI of the annexation treaty of 1893—ratification could not occur constitutionally without the express approval of both legislative chambers. During the last week of February Congressmen William M. Springer of Illinois and Henry St. George Tucker of Virginia drafted resolutions to that effect. Although neither of these resolutions was called to a vote, they reflected the antagonistic mood of the lower house toward annexation. Sensing that their cause was losing momentum, Charles R. Bishop wrote to Thurston on February 27 stating: "The outlook for Hawaii looks cloudy." On the following day the *New York Herald* exulted: "The Treaty Cannot Be Ratified Now."

The rapid shift in congressional opinion within the span of one month, from seemingly overwhelming support for annexation to stubborn resistance, requires explanation. The Democrats had majorities in both houses of Congress and, therefore, could control the disposition of the treaty. It seems that those Democratic legislators who had declared themselves in favor of annexation in the *New York Herald*'s poll were unwilling to ignore the call of their party chief for delay. So partisanship among the Senate Democrats was one major factor preventing confirmation. Yet that same partisanship could have been enlisted, with perhaps even greater ease, in support of the compact, had that been Cleveland's preference.

The president-elect's view of the matter was the determining factor in the postponement of a Senate vote, which raises the question as to who, if anyone, influenced his thinking. Gresham's influence cannot be discounted entirely.[24] But given Cleveland's known antipathy to colonial ventures as well as his chivalrous and Victorian sense of propriety, it seems doubtful that the president-elect would need much convincing in order to forestall a Senate vote on annexation. The same reasoning applies when one tries to assess the influence of Carl Schurz, the mugwump editorial writer for *Harper's Weekly*, who wrote to Cleveland on February 27 urging that the Polynesian archipelago not be annexed.[25] Besides, this letter was written and received after certain preliminary strategies for handling the Hawaiian problem had been outlined at the Lakewood conference on February 22. The decisions to delay action on the treaty until the new administration assumed office as well as to withdraw it from the Senate shortly thereafter (about which more will be said in the following chapter) were primarily Cleveland's. Certainly he must assume responsibility for these moves. However, it was Gresham's idea to send a commissioner to Hawaii to investigate alleged American wrongdoing.

Notwithstanding the importance of the steps adumbrated at the Lakewood meeting, it is doubtful that Cleveland had made up his mind to oppose annexation in late February. Instead, the incoming president's decisions were more circumscribed and pragmatic; he had resolved to take the Hawaiian matter into his own hands, and out of Harrison's, for future disposition. To do this it was necessary to prevent early Senate confirmation of the annexation agreement.

The Senate's handling of the treaty probably would have been much different had events come to a head earlier in Hawaii or had the Hoosier President been reelected in 1892. Harrison lamented in February 1893: "I am sorry the Hawaiian question did not come six months sooner or sixty days later, as it is embarrassing to begin without the time to finish."[26] Thus, by a combination of choice and circumstance the Hawaiian problem was placed in the custody of the incoming president. At this point it is appropriate to examine the reasons for, as well as the meaning of, Cleveland's withdrawal of the treaty from the Senate.

2

Cleveland's Withdrawal of the Treaty from the Senate

When Grover Cleveland was inaugurated president in March 1893, contemporaries had a difficult time anticipating his response to Harrison's annexation treaty. This difficulty was due in part to a fundamental ambiguity in Cleveland's diplomatic record. In his Inaugural Address in 1885 he had subscribed to the nonentangling, anti-colonial foreign policy of the founding fathers. "Maintaining, as I do," said the newly installed president, "the tenets of a line of precedents from Washington's day, which proscribe entangling alliances with foreign states, I do not favor a policy of acquisition of new and distant territory or the incorporation of remote interests with our own." Though opposed to reciprocity, as well as to the encumbering Frelinghuysen-Zavala isthmian canal treaty, Cleveland, nevertheless, supported the renewal of the entangling 1875 treaty with Hawaii. "I express my unhesitating conviction," he declared in 1886, "that the intimacy of our relations with Hawaii should be emphasized. . . . Those islands, on the highway of Oriental and Australasian traffic, are virtually an outpost of American commerce and a stepping-stone to the growing trade of the Pacific."[1] The chief executive's known aversion to foreign entanglements on the one hand and his warm support for Hawaiian reciprocity (which rendered the islands a virtual economic protectorate) on the other were contradictory. In early 1893 this incongruity in Cleveland's earlier policy, plus his refusal to make a public disclosure of his views regarding the Hawaiian matter, misled many publicists and politicians who were speculating about the new administration's stance on the annexation treaty.

During President Harrison's few remaining months in office the notion was commonly expressed that the incoming Democratic administration would support Hawaiian annexation. In late December 1892 Secretary of State John W. Foster anticipated that Harrison's successor would be "positive and active" in Hawaiian matters and that the next secretary of state (whom he presumed would be Edward J. Phelps) would be "favorable to the acquisition of Hawaii" and willing "to do all he could to push it."[2] Don M. Dickinson, Cleveland's friend and adviser, told members of the press in early February 1893 that the United States needed to annex Hawaii for commercial and strategic reasons. Since this public statement by Dickinson was made just after he had consulted with the president-elect in New York, it was rumored on Capitol Hill that Dickinson spoke for the incoming administration. Leading newspapers on both sides of the annexation dispute reported that Cleveland probably would favor the absorption of the islands.[3]

On March 9 the recently inaugurated president withdrew the Hawaiian annexation treaty from the Senate "for the purpose of reexamination."[4] Two days later Cleveland dispatched special commissioner James H. Blount, a former Georgia congressman, to Honolulu to investigate the Revolution. The recall of the convention raised two closely related questions in the minds of contemporaries. First, to what extent did the president's terse explanation account for the withdrawal? And second, what did this move augur about Cleveland's ultimate handling of the annexation matter?

The first question elicited basically four responses. Some proponents of expansion, like the *New York Tribune*, contended that the Democratic president and his secretary of state halted the treaty's progress because they felt that the Harrison administration was getting too much credit and the former wanted their own names and party more closely identified with the annexation project. John W. Foster blamed Gresham's animosity for Harrison. Thurston and Castle subscribed to Foster's view. Matilda Gresham, the wife of the secretary of state, cited her husband's chivalrous nature. "A woman in trouble," she explained, "my husband would certainly side with her against the power, greed, and lust of man." The anti-expansionist *New York Herald* took the president at his word that more information was needed before the treaty could be considered properly by his administration.[5]

The notion that Cleveland acted for political reasons is

refuted by his subsequent, and politically unpopular, failure to draft a new treaty or to resubmit the old one. The charge that Gresham's opposition to the pact was based upon his inveterate dislike for Harrison was not without substance.[6] But if Gresham were simply trying to injure Harrison, he needed only to reject the latter's treaty and replace it with one negotiated by himself. The fact that Gresham eventually took a far more extreme and unpopular position, that of opposing annexation and advocating the restoration of the monarchy, suggests that his Hawaiian policy, from its inception, was motivated by more than bitterness toward Harrison. Mrs. Gresham's view of her husband's gentlemanly nature was overstated. As a lawyer and judge, Gresham was probably more sensitive to matters of international comity and justice than to the narrower prescriptions governing the conduct of Victorian gentlemen toward ladies. Had the deposed Hawaiian monarch been a male there is no reason to suppose that Gresham's response would have been significantly different.

Like Gresham, Cleveland's opposition to hasty ratification probably was based upon considerations of international morality instead of regard for the national interest as such. Doubtless, his reading of Liliuokalani's declaration that she had been overthrown with the complicity of American forces aroused the chief executive's sensibilities about the importance of ethics in international relations. According to one of Cleveland's biographers the president was inclined to suspect strong nations of international aggression.[7] To allay these doubts the chief executive claimed that he needed more information regarding the United States role in the deposition of the native monarch. The preponderance of the evidence suggests that Cleveland recalled the treaty for the reason he gave, namely, for "reexamination" of the circumstances surrounding the United States involvement in the Hawaiian Revolution. On the day following the retrieval of the pact, Secretary Gresham told Thurston that "with the insufficient knowledge we have of the facts and detail we desire time for consideration of the subject and it has been withdrawn for that purpose."[8] This statement comports with the secret State Department instructions issued to Commissioner Blount, which read in part: "The withdrawal from the Senate of the recently signed treaty of annexation, for reexamination by the President, leaves its subject matter in abeyance. . . ."[9]

For at least four months after the convention had been recovered both the opponents and advocates of annexation remained unsure about the outcome of Cleveland's early action, yet hopeful that their respective side would prevail. The *New York Herald*, leader of the anti-annexationist press, observed on March 10, "There must be further developments . . . before the full significance of the withdrawal of the treaty can be definitely known. . . . Whether another treaty will be the result remains to be seen." The *New York Times*, which also staunchly opposed the acquisition of Hawaii, stated: "Mr. Cleveland has simply taken . . . the step required to make him really the master of the situation, and now that he is so he may be trusted to deal with it in a sensible and broad way." Similarly, the anti-expansionist *Brooklyn Eagle* commented: "In withdrawing the treaty he [Cleveland] has exerted a clear executive right, and has wisely afforded ample time for deliberation upon a difficult and delicate subject."[10]

In the annexationist camp, Representative Samuel G. Hilborn of California averred: "The President's withdrawal of the treaty created a considerable surprise, but that fact is not looked upon as an evidence of any hostility on his part to the annexation of the islands."[11] The *Burlington* (Vt.) *Hawkeye*, which favored the United States acquisition of the Polynesian archipelago, concluded: "It is only fair to assume that the treaty has been withdrawn for more mature consideration and revision."[12] Likewise, the Hawaiian officials at Washington did not regard the chief executive's action as final, and remained optimistic. Thurston wrote to Sanford B. Dole, president of the provisional government of Hawaii, on March 10 describing a recent interview that Gresham had had with Rear Admiral George Brown on March 7 and detailing the conversation that he (Thurston) had had with Admiral Brown on the following day. Brown told Thurston that Gresham was thoroughly in favor of annexation. Based upon information received from Admiral Brown, Thurston reported to Dole that Cleveland was undecided as to whether annexation or a protectorate was the best policy for the United States. On the day following the removal of the convention, Minister J. Mott Smith expressed disbelief that such action meant Cleveland opposed annexation. In early April, Smith wrote to Dole that Gresham "is disposed to annex the islands, unless Mr. Blount's report shows insuperable obstacles."[13]

Even after Blount lowered the American flag at Honolulu on April 1, thereby ending the protectorate established by Minister Stevens, both the opponents and advocates of annexation tended to see their respective causes as being unaffected by the move. Senator George G. Vest of Missouri opposed the treaty but saw nothing in Blount's action that affected the disposition of the annexation issue. Hawaiian Commissioner Charles L. Carter did not regard the termination of the protectorate as an indication that the Cleveland administration was averse to annexation and remained hopeful that a new compact incorporating the islands into the Union would be negotiated.

During the summer both Thurston and Dole were still of the opinion that Cleveland had not yet decided Hawaii's fate. The chairman of the annexation commission stated as much in a letter to his government in mid-June. The following month President Dole wrote to Thurston:

> I am satisfied that Cleveland's plan from the time he sent Blount here, has been not only not to commit himself on the question of annexation, but also not to seek to come to a conclusion in the matter in his own mind, before Blount's complete report is before him; and I believe he has faithfully adhered to such a plan of action, which may be conceded to be a good one.[14]

That Cleveland was not opposed to Hawaiian annexation in principle nor in policy in mid-March 1893 is evidenced in his letter to Schurz: "I do not now say that I hold annexation in all circumstances and at any time unwise, but I am sure we ought to stop and look and think. That is exactly what we are doing now."[15] This remained the president's position until September, when the Blount report was received and scrutinized by the secretary of state. The first explicit indication that the administration had determined not to resubmit the annexation treaty to the Senate appeared in instructions that Gresham sent on October 18 to United States Minister Albert S. Willis at Honolulu. Thus, the evidence strongly suggests that Cleveland and Gresham did not decide to oppose Hawaiian annexation until the fall of 1893.

The administration's eventual decision to pigeonhole the accord led some contemporaries as well as latter-day historians to the erroneous conclusion that Cleveland, from the time he reentered office, pursued a policy of consistent opposition to Hawaiian annexation. At least one well-known journalist of the period, Mary H. Krout, accused the president of withdrawing the treaty in March, under the pretext of needing time for "reexamination," in order to cripple permanently the annexationist movement.[16] Instead of charging Cleveland with deceit for retrieving the pact for reconsideration, the late Allan Nevins argued that from 1885 to 1897 the president consistently and laudably opposed "imperialist tendencies," "Pacific adventures," and "overseas entanglements in general."[17] In *Letters of Grover Cleveland, 1850–1908*, Nevins included a communication sent by the former chief executive to the Associated Press in January 1898. It stated:

> Ever since the question of Hawaiian annexation was presented I have been utterly and constantly opposed to it. The first thing I did after my inauguration in March, 1893, was to recall from the Federal Senate an annexation treaty pending before that body. I regarded, and still regard, the proposed annexation of these islands as not only opposed to our national policy, but as a perversion of our national mission.[18]

Elsewhere in the same letter Cleveland denied Senator John T. Morgan's contention that in 1893 the Democratic president was opposed only to Harrison's treaty and not to Hawaiian annexation as such.

Despite the conflicting appraisals of Cleveland's Hawaiian policy by Krout and Nevins, both of those writers maintained that the former chief executive consistently opposed the acquisition of the islands. Yet evidence has been presented which shows that until the fall of 1893 Cleveland had not taken a stand either for or against the annexation compact. His Hawaiian policy up to that time was characterized by uncertainty and drift. The former president's statement to the Associated Press in early 1898, which Nevins quotes, is hard to reconcile with Cleveland's letter to

Schurz on March 19, wherein the writer failed to give unqualified endorsement to the German emigré's anti-imperialist views. Perhaps the former chief executive's letter to the Associated Press was based upon wishful thinking or a faulty memory. That Cleveland in 1898 was an uncompromising exponent of the anti-imperialist cause, as well as a vigorous critic of Hawaiian annexation, is beyond dispute. Throughout most of 1893, however, he reserved judgment on the issue of Hawaii's possible incorporation into the Union.

At least one historian, Richard D. Weigle, has contended that had the "circumstances surrounding the revolution been different . . . Cleveland would readily have annexed the islands, which would have been a popular policy."[19] Whether or not Weigle is right is difficult to say. More documentation is needed before his contention can be substantiated or dismissed. Given the available evidence, as well as the facts that the former chief executive was an anti-imperialist by inclination and was known to take unpopular and impolitic positions at times, this view of Cleveland as a latent proponent of Hawaiian annexation seems extreme.

What appears certain is that the incoming Democratic president withdrew the treaty in order to gather more information, and until the Blount report was submitted in its entirety and thoroughly analyzed by Secretary Gresham, the Hawaiian matter was held in abeyance by the administration. In the meantime, Cleveland was faced with the problems of buoying up a sinking economy and releasing the federal government from the heavy financial obligations of the Sherman Silver Purchase Act. While the chief executive turned his attention to these domestic difficulties, the campaign to incorporate Hawaii into the Union encountered opposition from American sugar interests.

3

Opposition from American
Sugar Interests

The most damaging charge brought against the annexation movement in the spring of 1893 was that it was simply a scheme to enrich the island sugar planters as well as the mainland refiners and growers. In early March *The Nation* declared that the Hawaiian planters and the Western Sugar Refining Company of San Francisco (which was owned jointly by Claus Spreckels and the American Sugar Refining Company, or the "sugar trust" as the latter was informally called) sought annexation in order to split the lucrative two-cent bounty paid to the producers of sugar. Commissioner Thurston observed that a number of leading opposition organs, including the *New York World, Evening Post*, and *The Nation*, as well as the *Chicago Herald* and *Post* "have made their strongest fight on the ground, as the 'Nation' put it, that the proposed treaty was 'a job, by, of and for sugar.' "[1]

Although the opponents of annexation used the sugar indictment with effect and, probably, sincerity, it was for the most part a false accusation and eventually Thurston was able to persuade the vitriolic editor of the *New York Evening Post* and *The Nation* to drop the charge.[2] The majority of the leading Hawaiian sugar planters were on record as being opposed to annexation both before and immediately after the Revolution of January 1893.[3] Their position was based on the fear that annexation to the United States would interfere with the immigration laws and contract labor system in Hawaii, both of which they deemed necessary for the survival of the sugar cane industry in the islands. While the Hawaiian planters initially opposed and eventually acquiesced in the annexation movement, hoping thereby to stabilize their government, the mainland sugar interests in most instances fought the acquisition of the islands.

Claus Spreckels, the leading refiner of cane and beet sugar west of the Missouri River, was one of the most controversial opponents of Hawaiian annexation. Besides his financial power and aplomb, he engendered controversy also by virtue of the fact that his position on the annexation question changed dramatically during the six months following the dethronement of the Hawaiian queen.

For a brief period during the early months of 1893 Spreckels was an avowed, though conditional, annexationist. Word of the coup d' état in Honolulu reached him in San Francisco on January 28 and that evening he met with Commissioners Castle and Marsden and several local sugar agents in Parlor A of the Palace Hotel to discuss the possible effects of annexation upon American sugar holdings in Hawaii. Castle explained the "reasons for annexation," no doubt emphasizing the need for stable, efficient government in Hawaii (where Spreckels was the largest owner of sugar plantations). Later in the meeting William H. Dimond, a San Francisco sugar factor, spoke of the vital influence that Spreckels could exert on behalf of annexation. As a result of this appeal to Spreckels' interests and vanity, plus assurances from the commissioners that Hawaii's immigration laws and contract labor system would be safeguarded by the prospective treaty, the sugar king was temporarily persuaded to join the ranks of the annexationists. Castle noted jubilantly in his diary: "The mighty Claus is won! He says he will cause annexation to become an accomplished fact."[4] Thurston wrote to President Dole from San Francisco shortly after the commissioner's arrival there, stating that Spreckels was going to Washington to lobby for annexation. On January 29 the *San Francisco Examiner* quoted Spreckels as saying: ". . . I favor annexation of the Hawaiian Islands by the United States and the establishment of a territorial government." Thus, when the opposition press linked Spreckels' name in February 1893 with the annexation movement, it was with some justification.

In late March there were indications that the Spreckels sugar interests had undergone a change of attitude regarding annexation. Claus Adolph (Gus) Spreckels probably spoke for his father when he said in an interview with a New York newspaper that the sugar bounty paid under the McKinley tariff was not likely to be continued much longer. This being the case, "Nothing could be gained by annexation," said Spreckels' son. He then stated the objection which was to be reiterated by his father during the months ahead: "We can do a more profitable business with our contract labor than we could under the laws of the United States, and for that reason we are opposed to a change. We would much prefer that Hawaii remain a kingdom and then we would know that our business would not be interfered with."[5] Claus Spreckels had not yet made up his mind to oppose annexation. These remarks by his son reflected the direction in which the elder sugar baron was moving. To gain more information upon which to take a firm position, Spreckels visited the islands in mid-April.

Several days after his arrival in Honolulu, Spreckels told a reporter that he was still undecided about annexation. A fuller statement of his views was contained in an interview in late April. On that occasion, the sugar magnate said: "I have come down to investigate. . . . The labor question is the all important one and constitutes my only objection to annexation. . . . The contract labor system will not be tolerated by the United States, but that system is essential."[6] Spreckels' concern about the "labor question" led to his calling of a meeting with his business partner William G. Irwin and a prominent Maui planter, Henry P. Baldwin. Irwin drafted a letter that for the most part met with Baldwin's approval and presented it over Spreckels' signature to a group of leading Hawaiian planters. The letter emphasized the importance of the contract labor system to the existence of the Hawaiian cane industry and concluded that annexation would paralyze the islands' sugar economy.[7] Although the letter did not receive the endorsement of the Hawaiian growers, it indicated Spreckels' thinking.

In an interview on May 2 with Charles Nordhoff, the *New York Herald*'s correspondent in Hawaii, Spreckels stated the position he had finally taken. "I am opposed to annexation," he said, "because it would ruin the sugar industry on these islands." Not surprisingly, it was the labor problem that had convinced him to reject annexation. The sugar magnate explained to Nordhoff why Hawaii's alien employment laws were essential to the cane industry:

The importance of the contract system is easily seen, for not only does it secure to the plantation the payment back of heavy advances which are made to transport the laborers from their native country, but it also protects the sugar planters against strikes, which might occur at any time under a free labor system, and which, from the peculiar nature of the sugar business might prove ruinous to the sugar industry here. . . . But this [contract] labor system, necessary to us, is contrary to the laws of the United States, and would be broken up by annexation.[8]

Throughout the duration of Cleveland's second administration Spreckels' only real objection to annexation remained the problem of obtaining Oriental contract labor to operate his Hawaiian sugar plantations. In other words, at this time it was as an island planter more than as a mainland refiner that he opposed the acquisition of Hawaii by the United States.

During the interview Nordhoff asked Spreckels a probing question: "Thinking as you do, why did you not oppose this annexation movement in the beginning?" "Because I knew nothing of it. It was a complete surprise to me," answered Spreckels. Though truthful, this response only partially answered the question. Doubtless, news of the deposition of Liliuokalani did come as a surprise to Spreckels, who was in San Francisco at the time, but why did he not oppose annexation in late January or February after the initial shock subsided? The most plausible answer is that Spreckels believed that the prospective annexation treaty would safeguard Hawaii's immigration laws and contract labor system. The Hawaiian commissioners had assured him of this, he said, and his support for annexation in late January and early February was contingent upon this understanding. Spreckels claimed that those sugar agents (including himself) who were present at the January 28 meeting at the Palace Hotel in San Francisco "were not for annexation unless some provisions were made for imported labor, something we must have in Hawaii." After Thurston and the other commissioners arrived in Washington, complained Spreckels, " they did not carry out their intention in regard to labor. They let everything go in the interest of annexation."[9] When the sugar magnate discovered that the treaty duly signed by Secretary Foster and the Hawaiian commissioners on February 14 did not contain the labor clauses he regarded as indispensable, his support for annexation waned. A visit to the islands, where he consulted with other wealthy planters, probably reinforced his conviction that annexation would be ruinous to Hawaii's sugar economy. At any rate, by early May the sugar king had become, and was to remain, an active opponent of annexation.

Spreckels' hostility toward the annexation movement and the provisional government, from which that movement emanated, is shown in his demand for the repayment of a $95,000 loan which his bank, Claus Spreckels and Company, had previously extended to the monarchy during Liliuokalani's reign. After the Revolution the Dole regime became responsible for the debt. The newly-installed government did not have the funds available for repayment and was forced to solicit money hastily from Honolulu businessmen. Failure to meet the financial obligation would surely have resulted in the erosion of public confidence in the annexation-minded provisional government, which probably is what Spreckels intended despite his later denial. Spreckels' recall of the loan, along with his associations and public utterances, marked him as a royalist and anti-annexationist in the islands.[10]

The fact that Spreckels (a partner in the American sugar trust after 1892) voiced his sentiments so freely to the rabid anti-annexationist, Charles Nordhoff, and that these two gentlemen held nearly identical views regarding Hawaiian matters, led to speculation that Nordhoff and his employer, the *New York Herald*, were being paid by the sugar trust to propagandize against annexation. William De Witt Alexander, historian and annexationist commissioner, wrote to his son in May 1893: "We [the Hawaiian commissioners] believe that the 'Herald' is hired by the Sugar Trust."[11] Former Minister John L. Stevens claimed in July that Nordhoff's son had been an employee of Spreckels in San Francisco. "I hope that you will not fail to expose Spreckles [*sic*] and Nordhoff," Stevens told Alexander.[12] Although both Spreckels and Nordhoff were anti-annexationists as well as royalists, no convincing evidence has been found to show that Nordhoff or the *Herald* were being paid by Spreckels. The fact that the *Herald* began attacking Foster's treaty and Spreckels as well in February, at which time the sugar king supported annexation, demonstrates the newspaper's independence. Nor has evidence been located to show that Spreckels, in opposing annexation, acted in concert with or as a representative of the sugar trust.

After Spreckels decided to oppose annexation the only party or person in Hawaii that he tried to influence (with perhaps the exception of Commissioner Blount) was the major planters, and in this endeavor he ultimately failed. When this lack of success became apparent to him he returned to the United States and resumed his campaign against annexation. Shortly after arriving he expressed preference for an American protectorate over the islands. "By and by, some time, they may be annexed, but not now," he said.[13] Evidently, Spreckels was not irreconcilably opposed to annexation; the labor question, as he said earlier, constituted his only substantive objection to it.

But this objection was important enough to cause him to take his case to the nation's capital in September—a move that led the annexationist *Hawaiian Star* to state satirically on September 19: "As the head and front of the Royalist movement; as the intriguing agent of the sugar trust; as the blatant and egotistical old demagogue his praise would be a bane to any cause and his curses a reward of merit. By all means give him way and room at Washington. We need him there." Indeed, because of Spreckels' reputation as an arrogant monopolist (on at least one occasion he referred to himself as the "sugar emperor") he may have been as much of a liability as an asset to the anti-annexationists.

On September 19 the *Washington Post* published an open letter from Spreckels to Lorrin A. Thurston, who was in Washington lobbying for annexation. In it Spreckels reiterated that Hawaii's sugar plantations could not exist without contract labor and chastised the provisional government for its widespread use of soldiers to maintain its authority. Thurston responded two days later, rebuking the sugar king for his unwillingness to put Hawaii's welfare ahead of his own financial gain. Most of the Hawaiian growers, said Thurston, were unlike Spreckels in that they preferred "annexation, peace, and stability with less money to an increased income and a continuance of the strife and uncertainty of independent government."

Spreckels' main reason for going to Washington, however, was not to engage in newspaper warfare with the Hawaiian annexation commissioners, but instead to persuade the Cleveland administration that annexation should not be consummated. The president, not surprisingly, refused to meet with Spreckels, and the secretary of state agreed to speak with him only briefly. Gresham described to Thurston the nature of his exchange with Spreckels. "He [Spreckels] evidently wanted to talk about the Hawaiian subject, but I did not want to talk to him and turned the subject. With that exception I have not seen or heard anything from him." Gresham added, as regards Spreckels' motives for fighting annexation: "I understand his [Spreckels'] position there [Hawaii] to be simply a dollars and cents one, simply how much he can make out of it."[14] Actually, Spreckels occasionally voiced noneconomic objections to Hawaiian annexation, but he never gave these the same emphasis as the contract labor system.

Although the expansionist press frequently—and for good reason—linked Spreckels with the anti-annexationist movement, it is highly unlikely that he exerted much influence, if any, in the shaping of Cleveland's Hawaiian policy. It will presently be shown that the same conclusion holds true for the other major sugar interests in the United States.

Henry T. Oxnard, president of the American Beet Sugar Producers' Association, was, like Spreckels, associated with the sugar trust and opposed to Hawaiian annexation.[15] In early February 1893, when Oxnard was in Washington, he accused the provisional government of seeking annexation merely to obtain for the Hawaiian planters the two-cent bounty. In assessing the cost of annexation, Oxnard added to the projected bounty disbursements the sum of sugar duties remitted since 1876. He concluded:

> I do not believe, if only from an economic standpoint, that the United States will want to burden itself with a territory which has already cost us over $50,000,000 and would continue to divert $3,000,000 a year from the United States treasury into the pockets of the new Hawaiian government, otherwise known as the Hawaiian sugar planters.[16]

As this statement suggests, Oxnard's objection to Hawaiian annexation was not based upon ethical, legal, or anti-imperialist grounds. But there was more to his opposition than concern for the federal treasury and the American taxpayer. He was, so one newspaper said, "decidedly opposed to annexation on the ground it is opposed to his own interests."[17] No doubt the beet sugar magnate did not want to have to compete with Hawaiian cane growers who, in the event of annexation, would enjoy the twin benefits of the bounty and the duty-free admission of their sugar to the mainland in perpetuity.

Little is known about Oxnard's brief trip to the capital in February 1893. Gresham's correspondence contains no mention of it and it is unlikely that the secretary of state had any contact with him. It is not known whether Oxnard represented the sugar trust, or whether he acted entirely in his own behalf. Although he may have influenced a few members of Congress, it seems unlikely that he had much to do with the formulation of Cleveland's Hawaiian policy.

Throughout President Cleveland's second term the sugar trust maintained a sphinx-like silence regarding annexation. One possible clue to the attitude of the trust would be a five-year contract signed in 1892 between the sugar combine and the island planters which specified that any bounty paid to the latter would be divided equally with the American Sugar Refining Company.[18] This being the case, the trust stood to gain (or at least not to lose) in the event of annexation. Because of this contractual agreement, one historian has interpreted the trust's reticence as indicating "acquiescence in annexation."[19] This notion seems plausible, but more evidence is needed before the sugar trust's position (if it took a position) on Hawaiian annexation during Cleveland's second administration can be ascertained.

The reactions of the Louisiana cane growers and the Nebraska and California sugar beet interests toward annexation remain to be examined. The *Louisiana Planter* served as the leading organ of the sugar cane producers in that state. This publication was not sufficiently concerned about Hawaiian annexation to print anything on the subject in 1893. Nor did the Louisiana Planters' Association even so much as mention the pending treaty in any of its meetings or resolutions. The independent Democratic *New Orleans Times-Democrat* supported the acquisition of Hawaii, which seems surprising in view of the importance of sugar in Louisiana's economy. According to the *New York Times*, both of the Louisiana senators, Edward D. White and Donelson Caffery, had joined the congressional opponents of annexation. Caffery insisted that sugar had nothing to do with his antagonistic view of Foster's treaty. The *New York Times* reported that his opposition was based on the belief that the United States should not acquire territory so distant from its borders.[20] There is no way of knowing to what extent, if any, these two legislators were influenced by the state's sugar industry. According to the poll of Congress published by the *New York Herald* on February 6, two representatives from Louisiana, Newton C. Blanchard and Matthew D. Lagan, were favorable to annexation, while none of that state's representatives were opposed. The evidence suggests that Louisiana's sugar interests were not actively opposed to annexation during the early 1890s.

In Nebraska, one of the nation's leading producers of sugar beets, the major newspapers strongly opposed annexation. The *Omaha World Herald* warned the Cleveland administration to resist the annexation pleas of the unscrupulous sugar barons in Hawaii, who were simply trying to make windfall profits by giving the islands to Uncle Sam despite the native protests. The *Omaha Bee* asserted: "Territorial greed is a dangerous malady, particularly for a republic," and the United States pursuance of an imperial course "must inevitably end in disruption and decadence."[21] No mention was made in either of these newspaper editorials of possible competition from Hawaiian sugar, nor is there any evidence that either organ was influenced by beet sugar interests. Even the *Sugar Beet*, a prominent quarterly that was sensitive to the Nebraska sugar interests, neglected to discuss or take a position on the pending annexation treaty in 1893. In the *New York Herald*'s congressional poll on Hawaiian annexation, Senator Charles F. Manderson of Nebraska was listed as being favorable to annexation. The state's other senator, William V. Allen, spoke in favor of annexation in 1895 and, probably, was not opposed during the preceding two years. One Nebraska representative on Capitol Hill, Omer M. Kem, was reputed to oppose annexation in 1893 for reasons which are not known. It seems that the Nebraska sugar beet interests, which presumably opposed annexation, exerted little influence on either the newspapers or the politicians of that state.

California, a major producer of sugar beets in the Far West, was one of the states that passed a joint resolution directing its members of Congress to vote to annex Hawaii if the islanders were willing. This action was antagonistic to the interests of the two largest beet sugar manufacturers in the state, Claus Spreckels and Henry T. Oxnard, executive officers of the Western Beet Sugar Company and the Chino Valley Beet Sugar Company respectively. The accession of Hawaii would have brought unwelcome competition to the state's beet sugar industry.[22] Although the California beet interests opposed annexation, they lacked the political influence of the San Francisco mercantile establishments, which stood to benefit from closer ties with Hawaii since annexation would result in complete free trade and the construction of a cable.[23] During the remaining weeks of Harrison's administration both of California's senators in Washington, Charles N. Felton and Leland Stanford, were regarded as supporters of annexation. In March 1893 Felton was succeeded in office by Stephen M. White, a vociferous anti-imperialist who was no friend of the state's sugar interests.[24] Stanford died in June 1893 and the remainder of his unexpired term was served by George C. Perkins, whose position on annexation in 1893 is unknown. Six of California's representatives in Congress were considered to be supporters of annexation; none of the representatives from that state were known to be opponents. The *San Francisco Newsletter* was one of the few California newspapers to oppose annexation. Thus, while California's beet sugar producers were against annexation in the early 1890s, they were unable to match the lobbying strength of the San Francisco merchants, bankers, and shippers, whose annexationist views were reflected in the press and who put the state legislature on record in favor of acquiring the islands.

From the foregoing analysis several conclusions seem appropriate. Generally, the sugar refiners and planters throughout the United States were against the acquisition of Hawaii. The opposition mounted by these interests during Cleveland's second administration was not coordinated by any central organization or agency and was largely ineffectual. Although individual affiliates of the sugar trust, like the Spreckels and Oxnard enterprises, lobbied against annexation, the attitude of the trust, as such, is not known. Most significantly, there is no reason to believe that the American sugar interests influenced either Cleveland's decision to withdraw the annexation treaty from the Senate or his subsequent decision to withhold it from further consideration by that chamber. Though sugar was certainly an important element in the annexation debate of the early 1890s, Cleveland's Hawaiian policy (as we have seen in part in the preceding chapter) was shaped primarily by noneconomic considerations, namely, a repugnance to America's role in the recent Revolution and an aversion to colonialism.

Commissioner Thurston perceived clearly the effectiveness, as well as the inaccuracy, of the charge that annexation was merely a scheme initiated by the sugar interests to make windfall profits. He thought that if this argument were refuted, Harrison's treaty would pass. The only other objection, he said, was the claim that annexation was contrary to the United States' traditional policy. He did not think that this contention would impress the American people, however.[25] Thurston was right about the importance of eliminating the sugar argument, but he grossly underestimated the force of the ideological deterrents to Hawaiian annexation.

4

Ideological Deterrents to
Hawaiian Annexation

While the Blount investigation was under way during the spring and summer of 1893, Congress's attention was diverted from Hawaiian affairs to pressing domestic matters, such as the silver and tariff issues. Meanwhile, publicists and newspapers discussed the ethical, historical, constitutional, and racial objections to Hawaiian annexation. Because these ideological considerations constituted the principal deterrent to taking the archipelago, they deserve careful attention.

The most injurious moral charge levied against the annexationist cause was that the United States, in acquiring Hawaii, would be receiving territory which the provisional government had no right to cede. In effect, it was claimed that since the natives supported neither that government nor its aims, annexation would be tantamount to the United States' acceptance of "stolen goods." Probably no one expressed greater moral indignation with as much effect as did Charles Nordhoff, whose lively dispatches to the *New York Herald* were excerpted and commented upon by newspapers throughout the country. In one such dispatch, Nordhoff recounted a statement he had made previously to "two eminently respectable . . . members of the planters' party" in Honolulu. To these gentlemen Nordhoff had said:

> We in America have not the least objection to your revolution if you do it yourselves. What we dislike is that you got the United States troops to help you and made yourselves the rulers of the islands. Then you began to cry for annexation and hastened to Washington to get us to take off your hands what was then your stolen property.[1]

Other aspects of the Hawaiian imbroglio, especially Minister Stevens' conduct during and after the Revolution and Harrison's bid for early treaty ratification, also received moral censure from the opposition press. During the spring months of 1893 such epithets as "conspiracy," "annexation scheme," "annexation job," "annexation plot," "larceny," and "nefarious business," were used routinely by newspapers opposing annexation to express their ethical abhorrence.[2]

The effectiveness of the moral indictment against annexation was due mainly to its visceral appeal; for the public at large it simplified a complex problem in diplomatic relations by offering a clearly defined choice between right and wrong. It will be shown in Chapter 6 that Cleveland's Hawaiian policy was shaped largely in accordance with his and Gresham's moral aversion to the American involvement in the deposition of Liliuokalani as well as to Harrison's attempt to annex the islands without the consent of the natives residing there.

The historical argument against Hawaiian annexation was twofold. First, anti-expansionists held that the acquisition of the islands was contrary to the foreign policy guidelines and precedents established by the founding fathers. Second, they depicted annexation as being inconsistent with the United States' fifty-year-old policy of recognizing and maintaining Hawaii's independence.

The anti-imperialists appealed with effect to the isolationist doctrines laid down by the founding fathers as well as to the American tradition of continental expansion. Colonialism, they argued, contradicted the Declaration's emphasis upon natural rights, and was incompatible with the nonentangling and non-interfering precepts enunciated by former presidents George Washington and James Monroe. Anti-annexationists contended that the acquisition of noncontiguous territory, especially in the tropics, inhabited by people who had no natural affinity for Anglo-Saxon governing principles, would imperil the Republic. Most importantly, anti-imperialists saw in Hawaiian annexation the beginning of a general policy of territorial aggrandizement that would lead in domino-like fashion to the absorption of Cuba and other undesirable tropical islands. The peaceful American Republic, they feared, would be transformed into a militant empire, burdened with the high costs of a large standing army and a powerful navy to defend the colonies and to suppress the natives. The acquisition of the Hawaiian Islands was not, in itself, going to bring about the downfall of the Republic. But anti-imperialists thought such a step would signal the impending decline of basic American principles. Such arguments were difficult to refute, for they were present in numerous writings of the founding fathers and of other revered American statesmen.[3]

References to this particular historical argument against Hawaiian annexation were legion. The *St. Paul Dispatch* averred:

> If we are to set forth on the road to territorial conquest, there is no knowing where we may end. In no other way can we more effectually set at naught the wise teachings of Washington as to our relations with foreign nations. In no other way can we promote the indirect nullification of the Monroe Doctrine.[4]

In a column appearing in the *New York Herald*, Charles Nordhoff declared: "Certainly the annexation of Hawaii, against the will of its people, does not offer us any advantage sufficient to induce sensible Americans to break down a policy advised by Washington and which we have adhered to for a century with benefit to ourselves and without wrong to any one."[5] The annexation of Hawaii would signify, said the *Brooklyn Eagle*, "a new departure from a policy hitherto rejected as inconsistent with the settled principles of the republic." The *San Francisco Argonaut* insisted that "This country, and its traditions [*sic*] of governing with the consent of the governed, can not 'annex' a weak nation which does not want to be annexed." A "widely recognized" and "sagacious" correspondent of the *New York Herald*, writing under the pseudonym of "An American," cautioned: "If we once embark in the annexation business contrary to our traditional policy it will be the dream of unscrupulous demagogues to bring in Cuba and the whole West Indies."[6]

Carl Schurz, the indefatigable editorial writer for *Harper's Weekly*, was probably the most persuasive and consistent publicist of the anti-imperialist cause in the 1890s. From his pen came a steady flow of arguments against the acquisition of Hawaii. In a celebrated article entitled "Manifest Destiny," Schurz presented the classic exposition of the anti-imperialist case against Hawaiian annexation. He maintained that throughout American history only contiguous nontropical territory had been incorporated into the Union. The new "manifest destiny," by contrast, envisaged the acquisition of territory outside the North American continent lying in the tropical climate zones where "so-

called republics . . . constantly vibrate between anarchy and
despotism." History had shown that Anglo-Saxon democratic
institutions could not survive in tropical colonies. "If attached to
the United States," said Schurz, "Hawaii would always retain a
colonial character. . . . No candid American could ever think of
making a state of this Union out of such a group of islands . . "
Schurz wanted the United States to remain a compact, self-
contained, continental republic "bounded by great oceans on the
east and west, and on the north and south by neighbors neither
hostile in spirit nor by themselves formidable in strength."[7]

This article influenced Walter Q. Gresham, who wrote to
Schurz: "I think it will do a great deal of good. . . . It is the best
article of the kind that I have seen, and I sincerely hope to see
something else from your pen upon the same subject." James
Ford Rhodes, the eminent historian, also told Schurz that the
essay would "do a great deal of good." A prominent American
advocate, Frederic R. Coudert, found Schurz's argument "un-
answerable."[8]

The second historical argument against Hawaiian annexation
was more limited in scope and received less press coverage. Anti-
imperialists contended that annexation would be at variance with
the traditional United States foreign policy toward Hawaii first
enunciated by Secretary of State Daniel Webster in 1842. That
policy, which came to be known as the "Tyler Doctrine," aimed at
an independent Hawaii.[9] France and England, claimed the anti-
imperialists, had adhered to this pronouncement by signing a
formal agreement in 1843 renouncing any intention of either
possessing Hawaii or establishing a protectorate over the
archipelago. According to a *New York Herald* correspondent
who called himself "A Disciple of Daniel Webster," the Tyler
Doctrine was "reasserted by Secretary of State William L. Marcy
in 1854, and subsequently by Seward, Fish, Frelinghuysen,
Bayard and Blaine."[10] On May 19 the *Herald* declared: "The past
policy of this country toward the islands must be its future
policy." This meant "no annexation, no protectorate, no foreign
control." The United States, in adhering to its traditional policy,
said that newspaper, should insure the existence of "an independent Hawaiian government."

Closely related to the historical arguments against annexation were the constitutional arguments, set forth in important articles by two noted legal authorities, George T. Curtis and Judge Thomas M. Cooley. Curtis was the well-known plaintiff attorney in the Dred Scott case, whose reputation as a scholar was secured with the publication in 1889 of his *Constitutional History of the United States*. In addition to being an eminent juridical scholar, Cooley was a former justice of the Michigan Supreme Court (1864–85), Chairman of the Interstate Commerce Commission (1887–91), and professor of American history and constitutional law at the University of Michigan (1885–98). His commentary on Hawaiian annexation was widely read and frequently quoted. So formidable were his views on the Hawaiian matter that in 1898, when the annexation issue was again heatedly debated, the Senate imperialists called upon the services of Judge John D. Caton, former Chief Justice of Illinois, to prepare a response to Cooley's earlier arguments.

In "Is It Constitutional?" Curtis claimed that two conditions had to be met before territory could be incorporated into the Union by use of the treaty-making power. First, the territory had to be contiguous or at least situated on the North American continent; and second, there had to be in the opinion of the federal government "a controlling public necessity for its acquisition." These two stipulations were based upon Curtis's study of the Louisiana, Mexican, and Alaskan cessions to the United States, all of which involved the use of the treaty-making power. Because Hawaii was neither contiguous to the United States nor even located on the North American continent, its acquisition would have been inconsistent with the precedents of 1803, 1848, and 1867. In applying his second criterion, that of "a controlling public necessity," Curtis concluded (without offering any reasons therefor) that the annexation of Hawaii was "not necessary to any interest of the United States." Should a precedent be set by annexing these distant islands through a faulty construction of the Constitution, warned Curtis, "there will be no limit to future acquisitions of the same kind."[11]

A more discursive and abstruse case against Hawaiian annexation on constitutional grounds was presented by Judge Cooley in an article entitled "Grave Obstacles to Hawaiian Annexation." His analysis began with the raising of two fundamental questions. First, did the provisional government of Hawaii possess the delegated authority to cede the islands to the United States? Second, did the latter have the constitutional power to accept a cession of the archipelago? With respect to the first question, Cooley maintained that the provisional government was empowered to represent the Hawaiian people only temporarily, until such time as a permanent and legitimate polity was established. Since the natives had not been consulted by this "*pro tempore* government," Cooley concluded that there was no evidence that most of them supported annexation.[12] Legitimacy and consent were constitutional problems that had to be resolved before a valid offer of cession could be made on behalf of the islanders.

Even if the offer of annexation had been bona fide, it would not have been constitutional, according to Cooley, because the federal government lacked the legal power to admit the islands into the Union. The provisional government, he said, was seeking neither statehood nor the conventional territorial status; instead, it was requesting that Hawaii be joined to the United States as an "outlying colony." "Now outlying colonies are not within the contemplation of the Constitution of the United States at all," he declared. The framers of the Constitution intended the Republic's territorial expansion to be restricted to contiguous land which would be settled by Americans of Anglo-Saxon lineage. Such frontier communities, by virtue of their geographical propinquity and the assimilable character of their populations, would eventually enter the Union as coequal states. Anything proposed under the aegis of the power to make treaties, which conflicted with the traditional state-making procedure (in this case, Hawaii's bid for colonial status), was just as forbidden as an act which directly contravened a provision of the Constitution itself. Judge Cooley believed that if Hawaii were annexed in clear violation of this constitutional process governing the formation and entry of states into the Union, a dangerous precedent would be established which would permit the acquisition "of outside colonies hereafter in any part of the world."[13]

The constitutional arguments advanced by Curtis and Cooley do not seem to have had a profound influence upon Cleveland

and Gresham; their influence was far greater upon a few congressmen and a small group of lawyers, judges, and college professors within the eastern intelligentsia. The large daily newspapers opposing annexation tended to give much more extensive coverage to the moral, historical, and racial reasons for denying Hawaii's entry into the Union.

There are no indications that racism played a prominent role in the shaping of Cleveland's Hawaiian policy. Judging by the numerous references in the opposition press to the alleged inferiority of Hawaii's indigenous and Asiatic populations, however, it is evident that racial arguments against annexation carried much weight with the American public, or at least with the newspaper editors who were trying to reach that public. Perhaps this broad appeal can be attributed in part to the popularity of Social Darwinism in late nineteenth century America. Imperialists and anti-imperialists alike used the supposed inferiority of Hawaii's nonwhite population as an argument in support of their respective causes. The opponents of annexation evinced racial objections that varied from genuine regard for the self-governing rights of defenseless and unassimilable Polynesians to diatribes against bringing into the Union a loathsome horde of "Kanakas" [aboriginal Hawaiians], "lepers," and "coolies," who eventually might participate in American electoral politics.[14]

David Turpie of Indiana, one of the leaders of the anti-expansionists in the upper house, showed considerable respect for Hawaii's indigenous people when he averred:

> There is a native population in the islands of about 40,000. They are not illiterate; they are not ignorant. A very large majority can read and write both languages, English and Hawaiian, and they take a very lively and intelligent interest in the affairs of their own country. This is an element which on the proposition of annexation is to be consulted prior to any other; it must accompany any treaty; and any treaty which had been made without consulting this element was properly withdrawn and ought never to have been sanctioned.

Because the Hawaiians were a "feeble folk, neither rich nor numerous" as well as "defenseless," said Turpie, the United States was honor-bound to make certain that no form of coercion was used to bring about a cession of their country. The acquisition of the islands, he feared, "would erase and destroy" the nationality of the natives.[15] The irony here is that Turpie's racial concern regarding annexation was directed more toward the impact of union upon the Hawaiians than upon the Caucasians living in the continental United States.

A slightly less sympathetic view of Hawaii's non-Caucasian population was registered by contemporary historian James Schouler, a vigorous opponent of annexation. He described the *kanakas* as an "interesting and intelligent race." With respect to this ethnic group, Schouler further observed:

> Considerably more than half of them (or seven-tenths in round numbers) can read and write,—a showing with which only England and Germany, perhaps of European countries, can compete: idol worship, equally with cannibalism, they have long since cast aside, and they are now clearly Christian in their religious affinities, besides showing in their own modes of life those distinctive Christian traits, not always predominant among their more civilized teachers, of simple faith, meekness, self-sacrificing hospitality, and forgiveness of their enemies by whom they have suffered. Few thieves or beggars are to be found among them.

Schouler opposed annexation on the ground that Hawaii's heterogeneous population would aggravate America's existing racial problems. He believed that "this Union had enough of the problem of amalgamating races into one brotherhood to last at least for the rest of the century."[16]

Secretary Gresham denied emphatically the annexationists' claim that the Polynesians in the islands were not qualified to be consulted in the matter of who should govern them. To one correspondent he wrote: "It is not true that the people [that is, the natives] entitled to vote under the [Hawaiian] constitution of 1887 are pagans or uncivilized. With few exceptions they have embraced the Christian religion, being Protestants or Roman Catholics, and generally [are] able to read and write." Gresham opposed the acquisition of the archipelago, in part, because "an overwhelming majority of the [Polynesian] people, . . . are dead against annexation." Also, the secretary of state was against admitting Hawaii into the Union because of the political graft that he thought would attend a policy of overseas territorial expansion. "Should we acquire the Hawaiian Islands with their population, we will have a hot bed of corruption," he told Ambassador Bayard.[17]

Charles Nordhoff reported that the Hawaiian natives were not "savages, as in Samoa, but a reading and writing people, for whom at this time several daily papers are printed." He referred to Hawaii's Chinese population as "enterprising" and the half-castes as "charming, well educated and well to do people." Nevertheless, Nordhoff believed that this "mongrel" dark-skinned assemblage of islanders was not suitable for American citizenship. If annexation were to be pursued regardless of the racial objections thereto, he said, the transaction could not legitimately be consummated without the consent of the Hawaiian people, who "have a right to consider whether they shall give their country away."[18]

The plight of the Hawaiian natives was treated sympathetically by the *Boston Daily Globe* which (quoting Nordhoff) affirmed: "The citizens of Hawaii have a right to consider whether they shall give their country away. . . . Even the Kanaka has a claim to be heard when the future of the islands of his ancestors is at stake."[19] The *San Francisco Argonaut* fulminated against incorporating into the United States a multitude of "Chinese, Japanese, Kanakas, and half-breed Portuguese" to whom "we should be loath to grant the franchise." Although these racial elements were not fit for American citizenship, said the *Argonaut*, certainly they were capable of self-government.[20]

Judge Cooley acknowledged in his "Grave Obstacles" article that the American missionaries in Hawaii had converted the natives to Christianity. Still, in his view, the Hawaiians were "for the most part people of colored races with habits and ideas very different from our own." Such "incongruous elements" should not be admitted "into a Union never framed to receive them."

Carl Schurz referred to the Hawaiian aborigines as being "semicivilized" and had nothing complimentary to say about the other nonwhite ethnic groups inhabiting the islands. "If there ever was a population unfit to constitute a State of the American Union, it is this," he exclaimed.[21] George W. Merrill, a former

United States minister to Hawaii (1885–89), warned about "opening the floodgates, and with one fell swoop absorbing into our body politic this heterogeneous population, which must, eventually, be endowed with statehood, and all the resultant rights."[22]

A blatant slur against the native and Oriental inhabitants of Hawaii was made by the anti-annexationist Democratic *Jacksonville Times-Union* which stated:

> The President will find a large portion of the Democratic party almost unalterably opposed to the acquisition of that territory, if only because of the enfranchisement of a great army of ignorant voters which would necessarily accompany it. We are just emerging from a thirty years' struggle with an undesirable class of voters. Let us not 'prolong the war' with the ignorant voters of the Hawaiian islands.[23]

The *Natchez* (Miss.) *Daily Democrat* opposed annexation on the ground that the Polynesians were reputedly "the most leprous people on earth," while the *Wilmington* (N.C.) *Morning Star* argued, "We have a sufficient stock of mongrelism to last us the balance of this century, at least, without taking in the nut brown islanders of the South Pacific."[24] Racial objections to Hawaiian annexation were not limited to any single geographic section of the United States, but the most strident nativist arguments against acquiring the islands, as has been indicated, tended to be voiced in the South.

The foregoing commentary on the racial objections to Hawaiian annexation is pertinent to the ongoing debate among historians over the attitudes of the anti-imperialists toward non-Caucasian peoples inhabiting areas remote from the United States. In writing about the debate over Philippine annexation in 1898–99, historian Christopher Lasch held that the anti-imperialists subscribed to a mode of Social Darwinism "as thoroughgoing as that of the imperialists themselves." Moreover, Lasch stated that there were "no important differences" between the racial views of the Northern and Southern anti-imperialists, or, in other words, he implied that the opponents of empire did not fundamentally differ among themselves concerning the way in which they looked upon nonwhites. Finally, Lasch declared: "The anti-imperialists were in fact no more Jeffersonian in their essential outlook than Theodore Roosevelt or Henry Cabot Lodge or Alfred T. Mahan was, for they did not challenge the central assumption of imperialist thought: the natural inequality of men."[25]

Although Lasch restricted his comments about the racial views of the anti-imperialists to the Philippine controversy of 1898–99, other historians have applied his conclusions to the opponents of empire in general during the late nineteenth century.[26] This being the case, it is appropriate to examine briefly the extent to which Lasch's findings pertain to the critics of Hawaiian annexation in the early 1890s.

It has been shown that during the course of the Hawaiian debate of 1893–94 the anti-imperialists subscribed to a broad range of racial views respecting the mixed population of the islands. The only notion that the opponents of annexation seemed to hold in common was a belief in the supposed superiority of Anglo-Saxon peoples. Anti-imperialists like Turpie, Schouler, Gresham, and Nordhoff, held the Hawaiian natives in much higher regard than did either the expansionists (who rarely admitted that the islanders were capable of self-government) or the Southern opponents of annexation. To claim, as Lasch did, that the anti-imperialists "abandoned the natural rights philosophy of the Declaration of Independence" since they believed in the inequality of man, not only distorts the meaning of that charter but also tarnishes unfairly the Jeffersonian credentials of many who opposed the acquisition of Hawaii. While it is certainly true that the Declaration emphasized equality, it was no less concerned with another principle—that all legitimate governments were "instituted only by the consent of those to be governed."[27] Many of the opponents of Hawaiian annexation, and especially President Cleveland and Secretary of State Gresham,[28] in part objected to the acquisition of those islands because the natives had not given their consent. Although the critics of Hawaiian annexation were vulnerable on the issue of equality as Lasch correctly asserted, many of them were veritable paladins of the Jeffersonian principle of government by consent, an important fact which that historian overlooked. For the most part, Lasch's view of the racial attitudes of the anti-imperialists in the Philippine controversy is too monolithic to be of much help in explaining how the opponents of Hawaiian annexation in the early 1890s regarded the peoples of those islands.

In sum, no evidence has been found to indicate that xeno-phobic considerations significantly influenced the shaping of Cleveland's Hawaiian policy. Among the anti-annexationists there existed a wide spectrum of attitudes toward Hawaii's heterogeneous population. Within that spectrum were found both a large measure of racial intolerance and a high regard for the self-governing capacity and rights of the islands' nonwhite residents. Not only did the opponents of annexation differ among themselves over the way in which they viewed the islanders, but a number of them disagreed sharply with the expansionists regard-ing the characteristics and aptitudes of Hawaii's non-Caucasian population. And many anti-annexationists, unlike their adver-saries, insisted that Hawaii could be acquired justly by the United States only if the inhabitants of that archipelago consented to a transfer of sovereignty.

Although the ideological arguments against Hawaiian annex-ation carried by far the most weight with the Cleveland ad-ministration and the American public in the early 1890s, it should not be supposed that the anti-expansionists failed to plead their case on grounds of the national interest. On the contrary, as we shall now see, those writers and newspapers that opposed the admission of the islands into the Union at times laid considerable stress upon the strategic and economic objections to Hawaiian annexation.

5

Strategic and Economic Objections
to Hawaiian Annexation

In 1893 the critics of Hawaiian annexation framed a number of cogent arguments based upon considerations of the national interest. Although these arguments seldom commanded a great deal of attention at the time, in a somewhat modified form they were to become increasingly important when the issue of Hawaii's admission into the Union was again debated in the late 1890s.

The publication in March 1893 of Captain Alfred T. Mahan's influential article "Hawaii and Our Future Sea Power" touched off a debate over the islands' military value to the United States. The expansionist-minded naval historian argued that the American Republic must abandon her isolationist tradition and emulate England's rise to greatness through the acquisition of an overseas empire. If the United States were to remain secure and prosperous she would have to meet the international competition for the few coaling stations still available in the Pacific. Hawaii's strategic location—situated in line with the prospective isthmian canal route to the Orient, as well as lying off the Pacific coast of the United States—made that archipelago a particularly desirable possession. Mahan deemed the annexation of Hawaii essential to the defense of America's western coastline. "Shut out from the Sandwich Islands as a coal base," he declared, "an enemy is thrown back for supplies of fuel to distances of thirty-five hundred miles,—or between seven thousand and eight thousand, going and coming,—an impediment to sustained maritime operations well-nigh prohibitive."[1]

The anti-annexationists critiqued vigorously and extensively Mahan's argument, beginning with an assault on its underlying premise that the United States should follow Britain's example of acquiring colonies. An anonymous correspondent in the *New York Herald*, "X.Y.Z.," argued that the captain's historical analogy did not apply to the United States. England was an

insular nation situated close to powerful rivals that could wreak
havoc by blockading her ports at home and abroad, and,
therefore, she constantly had to shore up defenses by acquiring
coaling stations and expanding the navy. Moreover, Britain needed colonies to supply natural resources and to absorb her surplus
population. Unfortunately, "the clever young gentlemen"
graduating from Annapolis have "been educated on the needs of
an insular nation like England."[2] "X.Y.Z." believed the United
States, unlike Britain, was relatively isolated geographically and
because of her vast self-sustaining frontier could not easily be
crippled by an enemy's blockade.

The anti-annexationists argued that instead of providing the
United States with a bastion protecting the Pacific coast states,
the possession of the Hawaiian Islands, located 2,100 miles from
San Francisco, would weaken defenses along the western
coastline. Former Minister George W. Merrill observed
somewhat caustically:

> In case of a foreign war, such a possession [as Hawaii] would certainly be a
> source of weakness. . . . It can hardly be contended with reason that an
> outpost or picket guard stationed there, over two thousand miles from the
> main body, would be such a protection of our western coast against sudden
> attack, as would be recommended by a modern military genius.[3]

If Hawaii were annexed by the United States, said Carl Schurz,
instead of a bulwark the islands "would be our Achilles' heel."
Gresham agreed.[4] The *Seattle Telegraph*, a newspaper undoubtedly sensitive to the British presence at Esquimault,
asserted that an American naval station at Hawaii would be
"practically useless while our coasts were undefended."[5] Charles
Nordhoff argued pointedly that one fleet could not protect the
Pacific coastline from Puget Sound to the Mexican border and
simultaneously guard a group of scattered islands situated over
two thousand miles away.

In addition to weakening the west coast's defenses the annexation of Hawaii would result in large federal outlays to protect the
islands from foreign assault, contended the anti-expansionists.
Charles Nordhoff warned readers of the *New York Herald* that
the United States would have to defend four large islands and

four smaller ones, which would require a wartime fleet of twenty-five first-class ships. Furthermore, the United States could count on spending "$20,000,000 or $30,000,000 in erecting forts at Pearl River lagoon and deepening its narrow and tortuous channel to the sea," an expenditure that would be "a very 'fat' thing for contractors and jobbers."[6]

Another strategic argument commonly advanced by expansionists was that if the United States did not annex Hawaii promptly some other nation would take her. Usually Great Britain, but sometimes Japan, was specified. As regards Britain, the contention had no basis in fact. There is no evidence that she had any intention of acquiring Hawaii in the 1890s.[7] Her major concern was the protection of British interests there, and this could be accomplished by means other than annexation. In response to the charge appearing in several annexationist-minded American newspapers that Britain was going to lodge a protest against the recent American actions in Hawaii, the Foreign Office released a firm denial, which was reported in the *New York Times* on February 1, 1893. By that time Great Britain had come to regard the eventual United States annexation of Hawaii as a foregone conclusion. Britain was even willing to recall an offending minister at Honolulu in order to foster cordial Anglo-American relations. During an informal conversation in March between Sir Julian Pauncefote, the British ambassador at Washington, and Secretary of State Gresham, the latter requested unofficially that Major James H. Wodehouse, Her Majesty's minister at Honolulu, be relieved of his duties. Pauncefote promised early compliance if Gresham considered Wodehouse's departure "necessary for the maintenance of harmony and good feeling."[8] The same spirit of cordiality was prevalent in the British press, which betrayed no widespread antagonism toward the United States' possible annexation of Hawaii. Altogether, it seems likely that charges that Britain had designs upon Hawaii were invented in the hope of promoting United States acquisition of the islands. Not for the first time was the Lion's tail twisted for ulterior reasons.

Likewise, there was no basis for the charge that Japan was plotting a takeover of the northern Pacific archipelago.[9] This canard probably was started in Hawaii where some annexationists claimed that Nippon would intervene on behalf of her nationals if the United States did not take prompt and decisive action. The appearance of the Japanese battleship *Naniwa* in Honolulu probably gave the rumor a measure of verisimilitude. But this move was made to protect Japanese interests in the islands. To make certain that no misunderstanding would arise regarding the mission of the *Naniwa*, the ship's officers assured Rear Admiral J. S. Skerrett that "no hostile intentions were entertained." In early April Consul-General Saburo Fujii at Honolulu stated publicly: "I wish to say that the Japanese government has no desire to take possession of the Hawaiian Islands, and from my knowledge of the affairs of state such an idea has never been entertained." The Japanese diplomat referred to the rumor that his government coveted the Polynesian archipelago as "pure fabrication." "It would be nonsense for Japan to assume control so far from home." He also said that the cost of governing Hawaii would greatly outweigh whatever benefits his country might derive.[10] When Commissioner Blount submitted his final report to the Department of State in July 1893, he denied that Japan was threatening to interfere in Hawaii.[11] In point of fact, Japan was seeking the franchise for her people in Hawaii, not annexation, and accordingly, on March 23, Consul-General Fujii requested of President Dole that the suffrage be extended to the Japanese in compliance with the most-favored-nation clause in a Japanese-Hawaiian treaty.[12]

Apparently the opposition press did not take the charges against Japan seriously, for with rare exceptions it limited itself to denials of *British* involvement. Edwin L. Godkin editorialized sarcastically in *The Nation* that Great Britain had shown "a most provoking indifference to the whole [Hawaiian] affair, and as the glory was mostly to be won from vexing and triumphing over her, her calm unconcern had robbed the enterprise of all its glamour." In May that journal concluded from its recent survey of the British press that: "The unanimity with which all the leading English journals of every shade of opinion have refused to treat the Hawaiian question, from the outbreak of the trouble down to the present time, as a matter of special British concern is striking."[13] Also, Godkin's *New York Evening Post* ridiculed the uproar against Britain, which it said had been created by the *Tribune* and the *Sun*. The *Buffalo* (N.Y.) *Express* scoffed that "this cry about forestalling England is a mere bugaboo."[14] "The British lion is not seen to wag his dreadful tail" at Hawaii, commented the *New York Herald*.[15]

Although the opponents of annexation spurned the notions that the United States should imitate Britain's example of colonialism; that Hawaii was essential to the defense of America's western coastline; and that unless the United States acquired the islands some powerful rival would do so—still the anti-annexationists did not deny the contention that Hawaii was located in the midst of the Pacific navigation routes, and thus could serve as a useful coaling station. Since the reciprocity treaty of 1875, as amended in 1884, gave to the United States certain coaling and refitting privileges, anti-annexationists deemed it unnecessary to absorb the islands and most were unwilling even to establish a protectorate over them. In order to prevent international friction over America's exclusive privileges in the islands and to ameliorate the fears of the provisional government that Hawaii would be seized by some other foreign power, some anti-annexationists proposed that the archipelago be neutralized. Under this plan, which was endorsed by Charles Nordhoff, Hawaii would remain independent while the various seafaring nations, in times of both war and peace, would share the benefits of using the islands for fueling and refurbishing. The United States' acceptance of such an arrangement was doubtless precluded by her unwillingness to forfeit the exclusive privileges sanctioned by the existing reciprocity treaty.

Related to the strategic objections were the economic ones. The anti-annexationists held that the admission of Hawaii into the Union was unnecessary for the promotion of American trade in the Pacific; would burden the United States with a very difficult smuggling problem; and would provide little new land for farmers, as well as few opportunities for American laborers and merchants.

The notion that the possession of Hawaii would greatly augment American commerce in the Pacific was one of the most forceful arguments with which the anti-annexationists had to contend in 1893. The acquisition of these islands would help to give the United States the "commercial and military control of the Pacific," affirmed Captain Mahan. Minister John L. Stevens also eulogized the commercial advantages: "The islands will feed the ships composing the commerce of the future [*sic*] Pacific and when the Nicaragua Canal becomes an accomplished fact they will be by far the most valuable possessions in these waters."[16] Senator Joseph N. Dolph of Oregon told the upper house in late January 1893: "It is time we had a well-defined, aggressive foreign policy." He elaborated on this point by stating that the annexation of Hawaii and the construction of an isthmian waterway "will secure to us for all time the supremacy in the trade of the Pacific which our position, our territory, and our products entitle us to."[17]

While accepting the importance of fostering trade in the Pacific, the critics of annexation contended that the possession of Hawaii would not give the United States any commercial advantages which she did not already enjoy under the reciprocity treaty or which could not be secured by a supplemental agreement. According to former Minister George W. Merrill there were only two basic prerequisites to the full utilization of Hawaii's commercial benefits: "a harbor and coaling station, and a cable extending from Hawaii to some point on United States territory." The harbor and coaling facility were legally sanctioned by the reciprocity treaty, as amended in 1884. "There is unanimous sentiment in Hawaii in favor of a cable communication . . . and a large majority favors a terminus on United States territory," he said. From a commercial standpoint, concluded Merrill, annexation was unnecessary since a harbor and cable "will accomplish for us all that is desirable."[18] Charles Nordhoff pointed out that in 1892, according to the annual report of the Collector General of Customs, more than eighty-nine percent of the total value of Hawaii's imports came from the United States. "For the sake of a greater commerce," he said in the *New York Herald* on July 22, 1893, "we certainly need not annex the islands." Variations of these views were expressed in a number of newspapers opposing annexation, including the *Buffalo* (N.Y.) *Express*, the *Morgantown* (N.C.) *Herald*, the *Louisville Courier-Journal*, the *New York Herald*, and the *Annapolis Gazette*.[19]

The way in which the anti-imperialists viewed the matter of

commercial expansion in the 1890s has been the subject of sufficient controversy among diplomatic historians over the past two decades to warrant a brief digression. Developing and refining ideas conceived by William Appleman Williams, certain of the New Left-oriented scholars have argued that during the last decade of the nineteenth century the imperialists and anti-imperialists alike advocated "a militant American expansion into world markets"; the debate over colonialism, so these historians have claimed, represented merely a "secondary" disagreement over the tactics or means to be employed in securing foreign outlets for the surplus products of America's farms and factories.[20] Lloyd C. Gardner, Walter F. LaFeber, and Thomas J. McCormick have declared that the anti-imperialists were actually "anti-imperial expansionists . . . since they took second place to none in affirming the need for overseas markets."[21] LaFeber contended that Walter Q. Gresham and Carl Schurz exemplified the anti-annexationists' commitment to the establishment of a "new empire"; that is, they were "strong advocates of commercial expansion" while, simultaneously, they opposed the acquisition of distant colonies.[22] McCormick included Grover Cleveland and Richard Olney among the anti-imperial trade expansionists.[23]

During the course of the debate over the acquisition of Hawaii in the early 1890s the Cleveland administration and its supporters remained largely unconcerned about using the islands to increase American trade in the Pacific. Cleveland, who in 1886 had expressed interest in the commercial value of Hawaii,[24] made little reference to the subject in either his correspondence or speeches during his second term in office. Significantly, in 1895 he opposed a government cable-building proposal that congressional annexationists had initiated for the purpose, in part, of increasing American-Hawaiian trade. When the administration was formulating its policy toward the islands in the fall of 1893, Gresham and Olney displayed no great interest in using Hawaii as a maritime *entrepôt*. Their correspondence focused on the moral, constitutional, and historical aspects of America's relations with the archipelago; it made little mention of commerce. Schurz valued whatever mercantile benefits the islands offered, but saw no need to bolster the navy for the purpose of helping American trade in the Pacific. He flatly asserted: "We need no large navy for the protection of our commerce. . . . Nor do we need any warships to obtain favorable commercial arrangements with other nations." Schurz disagreed sharply with Senator Dolph about the need for an "aggressive foreign policy," which the legislator equated with militant trade expansion and a powerful two-ocean navy. In an essay attacking Hawaiian annexation Schurz declared:

> When our maritime commerce was most flourishing we had no navy worth speaking of to protect it, and nobody thought that one was needed. The pretense that we need one now for that purpose reminds me of the Texas colonel, who thinks he must arm himself with a revolver when walking on Broadway because he might be insulted by a salesman. . . . And there is no project of territorial acquisition or of 'vigorous foreign policy' ever so extravagant that does not find hot advocates in navy circles. . . . The United States will better fulfill their mission and more exalt their position in the family of nations by indoctrinating their navy officers in the teachings of Washington's farewell address than by flaunting in the face of the world the destructive powers of rams and artillery.[25]

Gresham and other prominent anti-annexationists warmly endorsed this view.[26] In essence, Schurz and most of the other leading opponents of Hawaiian annexation spurned an aggressive governmental policy of trade expansion because they believed it would lead to militarism, which in turn would subvert America's republican institutions.

Each of these four opponents of annexation (Cleveland, Gresham, Olney, and Schurz) doubtless favored the reciprocity treaty with Hawaii and wished to see American commerce flourish in the Pacific. But nowhere in their public or private statements about the Hawaiian controversy in the early 1890s is there clear evidence that they contemplated taking energetic measures (such as building a cable to the islands or strengthening the Pacific fleet) to increase the commercial utility of the archipelago. With perhaps the exception of Senator Stephen M. White and a few others,[27] the major opponents of Hawaiian annexation during Cleveland's second term in office did not make grandiose pronouncements similar to those of Mahan, Stevens, and Dolph, calling for the establishment of American commercial hegemony in the Pacific.

According to McCormick, the Cleveland administration had

no need to be assertive about commercial expansion *vis-à-vis* Hawaii because of the reciprocity treaty.[28] There may be some truth in this point. By the same logic, however, the imperialists should have been satisfied with the benefits accruing to the United States under the auspices of that treaty and should not have insisted, as they frequently did, upon dominating the trade of the Pacific.

In sum, during the course of the Hawaiian annexation controversy in the early 1890s, there was a fundamental difference between the anti-annexationists' desire to see America's Pacific trade prosper, and the commercial chauvinism of those who wanted to absorb the insular nation into the Union. Going much further than an examination of tactics, the debate between the two sides reflected conflicting views of the basic American "mission" both at home and abroad. Generally, the New Left historians have failed to see the difference between the anti-imperialists' desire for commercial prosperity and the imperialists' quest for trade domination. Perhaps because those scholars fail to see this difference, they have tended to minimize the more fundamental philosophical disagreement between the advocates and opponents of empire.

Returning now to the discussion of the economic objections to annexation, we note that in addition to arguing that annexation was unnecessary for America's commercial advantage, the anti-expansionists asserted that if the islands were brought into the Union the federal government would be faced with a virtually insolvable smuggling problem. With a very lengthy jagged coastline to be policed at an exorbitant cost, traffic in such contraband as opium, which was prevalent in Hawaii, would flourish. The additional problem of collecting revenue on dutiable foreign goods entering Hawaiian ports for reshipment to the mainland was alluded to by the *Pittsburgh Chronicle-Telegraph*: "Millions of dollars worth of commodities of all kinds might be surreptitiously entered [into the United States] from Hawaii if once the Custom House inspection were done away with on this continent."[29] In other words, the United States government might be cheated out of large sums of revenue on dutiable goods that, after entering Hawaiian ports and evading a customs inspection, would be shipped duty free to the American mainland.

Another argument maintained that the islands had little to offer white American settlers. Most of Hawaii's fertile farmland was used for sugar; the rest was used for rice. Almost all the land, other than that devoted to these two crops, was mountainous, unsuitable for farming. "It would be the worst kind of a swindle upon American farmers," declared Nordhoff, "to deceive them into going to the Hawaiian Islands to take up lands." Furthermore, the vast influx of Orientals, many of them artisans and mechanics, depressed wages to the lowest level of subsistence. For those American workingmen who were not "fortunate" enough to secure one of the few desirable low-paying jobs, the prospect was even gloomier. Nordhoff stated sardonically: "Now there are numbers of unemployed whites, a good many of whom have been waiting to be enrolled in the 'army of the provisional government,' and I saw three white men sweeping the streets yesterday."[30]

The strategic and economic objections to Hawaiian annexation, much discussed as they were by publicists, must have exerted some influence upon the new Democratic administration. In all probability, however, Gresham's idealistic impulses, namely, his commitment to international morality and aversion to imperialism, were of greater significance. Stirred by Blount's findings, they had much to do with Cleveland's decision to reject the Hawaiian treaty.

6

Cleveland's Decision to Reject the Hawaiian Treaty

Throughout the spring and summer of 1893, administration officials in Washington remained virtually silent regarding the Hawaiian problem. Meanwhile the president's taciturn investigator, who at times was referred to by the islanders as the "Minister Reticent," went about his assignment of gathering facts. When Secretary Gresham received Blount's voluminous report in early August, he promptly began the task of assimilating the myriad details and observations contained in it.

Two of Blount's findings had a profound effect upon the shaping of the administration's Hawaiian policy. First, the commissioner averred that former Minister Stevens and the American forces had aided in the overthrow of Liliuokalani. Second, and of greater importance, the special investigator reported that if the question of annexation were submitted to a popular vote in the islands, it would lose by a margin "of at least two to one."[1]

By mid-August Gresham had acquired a sufficient grasp of Blount's document to debate with Minister Thurston over the circumstances surrounding Minister Stevens' recognition of the provisional government and Liliuokalani's surrender of her authority. That Gresham had mastered the report and framed a policy based thereon by mid-September is evidenced in his letter to Schurz, which stated:

I can say to you in confidence that if anything can be established by proof, Mr. Blount's reports show that the action of the American Minister and the presence of the United States troops in Honolulu overawed the Queen,—put her in fear—and induced her to abdicate and surrender to the so-called Provisional Government, with the understanding however, that her case would be fairly considered by the President of the United States. Should not this great wrong be undone? 'Yes,' I say decidedly. Aside from the President and Cabinet, this is more than I have said or written to any one, and you will understand the importance of not allowing this letter to fall into other hands.[2]

So by early fall Gresham had decided to reinstate the deposed queen. Although this epistle made no explicit mention of the fate awaiting Harrison's treaty, the rejection of annexation was implicit in the policy of restoration, for unless Hawaii was prevented from entering the Union, there would be no monarchy to restore. Significantly, until Hawaii became a nominal republic in July 1894, the issue of annexation as such was sometimes eclipsed by the related controversy over the reestablishment of the monarchy. In addition to delineating the administration's Hawaiian policy, Gresham's letter to Schurz indicates that the latter was a confidant of the secretary of state in Hawaiian matters.

During the fall of 1893 at least one representative of the provisional government seemed to sense that the administration was not going to revive the moribund annexation project. When Frank P. Hastings, the Hawaiian secretary of legation at Washington, learned in September of Albert S. Willis's appointment as United States minister at Honolulu and of the replacement of Rear Admiral J. S. Skerrett, the highest ranking naval officer at Hawaii and a reputed annexationist, by Rear Admiral John Irwin, he remarked presciently, "the jig is up as far as annexation is concerned."[3] The *New York Herald* reported on November 8 that the replacement of the highest-ranking American diplomatic representatives and naval commanders at the islands "has been accepted in many instances as an inkling of the administration's policy toward Hawaii."

While the interested parties in the annexation dispute conjectured about the contents of Blount's report and the policy to be pursued by the administration, the secretary of state began the preparation of a formal statement on Hawaii for the president. Meanwhile, at a cabinet meeting on October 6, Gresham raised the Hawaiian problem, and this seems to have prompted Attorney General Richard Olney to draft a very important position paper which was to influence the secretary of state and, more so, the president. Olney, who up to that time had played virtually no role in Hawaiian matters, was able to lend a sorely needed modicum of practicality to Gresham's plans. The head of the

Justice Department began his paper, dated October 9 and addressed to the secretary of state, by acknowledging that "a great wrong" had been done to the Hawaiian queen and commending "the good sense, the statesmanship and sound morality" of Gresham's proposal to restore Liliuokalani to her throne. But since the Dole regime, which was duly recognized by the United States, had been "generally exercising all the functions of a legitimate Government" the task of restoring the deposed monarch was not going to be simple. There was the possibility, though not the likelihood, admitted Olney, that military force would have to be used to dislodge the provisional government. A resort to arms would constitute an act of war, which required congressional sanction. Even if such authorization were forthcoming, the ensuing devastation and alienation would preclude a return to the status quo that had existed before the United States troops intervened in Hawaii the previous January.

In the event that force was not required, there remained "certain considerations of vital importance" that ought to govern any attempt to reinstate the queen. Because the oligarchy headed by Dole was recognized by the United States and other nations, the acts of the provisional government ought to be regarded as legal "unless shown to be *mala fide*" and the officers of the new regime should be exempt from any loss or punishment. Then Olney came to the key point of equity, for which he had been laying the groundwork. "In my opinion," he said, "the honor of the United States is hardly less concerned in securing justice and fair play for the Stevens Government and its members and adherents, than in the restoring to power of the Queen's constitutional Government."[4] To Olney this meant that full amnesty should be granted to the usurpers by Liliuokalani if she were to expect President Cleveland to negotiate for her reinstatement. As long as the members of the provisional government were assured that no vindictive action would be taken against them by the queen, they would readily comply with the chief executive's recommendations. Even though the attorney general was more pragmatic than the secretary of state, and had a superior grasp of the competing equities involved in the Hawaiian case, still, as events were to disclose, Olney grossly underestimated the provisional government's resolve to stay in power.

Approximately one week after Gresham received Olney's letter, the secretary of state submitted his official recommendations on the Hawaiian problem to the president. The nine-page missive recapitulated the major findings of Commissioner Blount, quoted several documents to show that Minister Stevens' recognition of the provisional government had been premature and that the queen had surrendered to the United States forces with the expectation that her case would be decided in Washington, and recommended that the annexation treaty not be resubmitted to the Senate and that Liliuokalani be restored to the throne. The head of the State Department did not say how restoration was to take place, that is, whether or not force would be employed if necessary.

The positioning of two key passages contained in Gresham's epistle to Cleveland is illustrative of the connection between the secretary's opposition to annexation and his insistence upon the restoration of the monarchy. The two passages, which were not separated by intervening textual material, appeared in the following order and stated:

> A careful consideration of the facts will, I think, convince you that the treaty which was withdrawn from the Senate for further consideration should not be resubmitted for its action thereon.

> Should not the great wrong done to a feeble but independent state by an abuse of the authority of the United States be undone by restoring the legitimate government? Anything short of that will not, I respectfully submit, satisfy the demands of justice.[5]

It is significant that Gresham's call for reinstatement of the queen came after his recommendation that the treaty not be returned to the Senate. This suggests that in the thinking of the secretary of state the policy of restoration was predicated upon the assumption that annexation would not occur. If this is true, then Gresham's letter of October 18 supports this writer's earlier contention that the secretary probably had decided against the resubmission of Harrison's treaty, and, therefore, to oppose annexation, as early as September 14 when he wrote to Schurz about the United States' obligation to restore the queen. No evidence has been found to suggest that either Gresham or Cleveland opposed the acquisition of Hawaii before mid-September 1893.

A cabinet meeting was held on October 18, the same day that Gresham submitted his official recommendations to the president. Olney and Carlisle emphasized that regardless of how badly the Hawaiian monarch had been treated by John L. Stevens and the naval officers attached to the U.S.S. *Boston*, protection had to be given to those islanders of American citizenship who, after having received assurances of support from the United States minister, participated in the overthrow of the Hawaiian monarchy.[6] Within a few hours after the cabinet meeting ended, Secretary Gresham prepared instructions for Minister Willis. The secretary of state informed him that the president would not return the annexation treaty to the Senate, and directed him to communicate the president's decision to the Hawaiian monarch. Then Gresham came to that portion of the instructions which seemed to show most clearly the moderating influence of Olney, and perhaps of Carlisle as well. He wrote:

> You will, however, at the same time inform the Queen that, when reinstated, the President expects that she will pursue a magnanimous course by granting full amnesty to all who participated in the movement against her, including persons who are, or have been, officially or otherwise, connected with the Provisional Government, depriving them of no right or privilege which they enjoyed before the so-called revolution. All obligations created by the Provisional Government in due course of administration should be assumed.[7]

Ironically, Olney's seemingly reasonable modification of Gresham's restoration policy served as a major stumbling block to its implementation because the queen found the provisions relating to amnesty and financial obligations highly objectionable. Willis must have gasped in disbelief when she gave her reply to the stipulation that full amnesty must be granted to the revolutionists. In words both measured and solemn the queen responded: "My decision would be, as the law directs, that such persons should be beheaded and their property confiscated to the government."[8] The fanciful scheme of restoration would have failed regardless of Olney's conditions and the queen's vindictiveness, however, because Liliuokalani could be returned to power only by the employment of military force and neither the president nor Congress was willing to go to that extreme. It is possible that, before Olney counseled Gresham, the secretary of state may have considered the use of arms to reinstate the Hawaiian monarch, but there is no evidence indicating that Cleveland ever did so. The chief executive's scrupulous observance of the constitutional limits of his authority may have been due in part to Olney's salutary influence.

Who conceived of the restoration plan and upon what reasoning was it based? These are pertinent questions whose answers will illuminate more fully the administration's Hawaiian policy.

The wife of Secretary Gresham believed that her husband devised the policy of restoration. "From the records it appears that Mr. Gresham originated it in his report of October 18, 1893, to the President," she stated.[9] Matilda Gresham could have gone back further to her husband's letter to Schurz, dated September 14, wherein the secretary of state affirmed the need to rectify the great wrong committed against Liliuokalani. Journalist Mary H. Krout, who went to the islands in 1893 to investigate the annexation movement (with which she was in sympathy), concluded, without offering any evidence, that the "Quixotic scheme" of restoration was conceived by President Cleveland.[10] In the absence of any statement by the chief executive on the subject prior to his annual message to Congress on December 4, 1893, the letters written by Gresham establish the secretary of state as the most likely originator of the plan to return the queen to her throne.

The reasoning upon which the plan was based unfolded during the course of several discussions held in November 1893 between Gresham and Thurston. These conversations were instigated by Thurston soon after he read in the November 7 edition of the *Chicago Evening Post* a news item about Gresham's instructions to Minister Willis, dated October 18, ordering the reinstatement of the Hawaiian monarch. Thurston met with Gresham at the State Department on November 14, hoping to learn whether or not the administration intended to restore Liliuokalani by force and, if so, the grounds upon which such action would be taken.

When Gresham admitted to Thurston that the administration intended to place the deposed monarch back upon her throne, the Hawaiian minister responded that such a policy could be carried out only by the use of superior force. Even if the United States were willing to take such hostile action against a friendly government to which she had accorded diplomatic recognition, said Thurston, the policy of reinstatement would fail unless American troops not only restored the queen but maintained her in power. The Hawaiian minister assured the secretary of state, "unless you are prepared to maintain a force on shore and hold her in position, she will be overthrown as soon as your troops leave."[11] A second overthrow of the monarchy undoubtedly would be occasioned by violence, warned Thurston. The secretary of state rejoined, rather evasively, that the United States would take no action that would endanger the lives or property of Thurston and his friends. Furthermore, Gresham declared that restoring the queen to power and supporting her afterward were two different matters. Although Thurston was not entirely sure of what Gresham meant, he drew two inferences from these statements: first, that the United States probably did not intend to use force to reinstate the queen; and second, that even if Uncle Sam used force to restore Liliuokalani, that same force would not maintain her regime.[12]

Displaying more persistence than tact the zealous minister proceeded to dispute with the secretary the right of the United States to interfere in the internal affairs of a sovereign nation. In what must have been a tense exchange, Gresham defended the logic underlying his plan of restoration. The secretary of state's argument derived from two premises. First, in accordance with the wording of the revolutionists' proclamation of January 17, 1893, the provisional government was "to exist until terms of union with the United States of America have been negotiated and agreed upon."[13] Second, the Hawaiian monarch surrendered to the American forces from the U.S.S. *Boston* with the understanding, shared by the provisional government, that her case would be investigated and decided by President Cleveland. From these premises Gresham reasoned that the provisional government's right to exist was only temporary; that is, it could rule only until the annexation issue was resolved. By the terms of the queen's capitulation, which were "endorsed by President Dole,"[14] the question as to whether or not annexation would take place was to be left for President Cleveland's disposition. In effect, the secretary of state argued that both parties were looking to the president of the United States to determine who should rule the islands.[15] Gresham concluded that, since after careful inquiry the Cleveland administration had decided against annexation, the provisional government should in accordance with its proclamation relinquish its temporary power and permit the queen to be reinstated.

The secretary of state's letter of October 18 to the president, recommending that the queen be returned to power, was released to the press on November 12, thereby rekindling a public debate over Hawaii. Gresham, distressed that some people gained a mistaken impression from the letter, wrote to a correspondent:

> You seem to think my letter to the President implies that, while I am opposed to the treaty annexing the Islands which the President withdrew from the Senate for further consideration, I am not opposed to annexation. I am opposed to annexation, especially of territory not a part of our continent. If I were in favor of annexation, however, I should oppose taking the Islands by force and fraud.[16]

This letter and others like it establish the fact that, contrary to what some historians claim, Gresham was an anti-imperialist.[17] For the most part, however, the secretary's stand against the acquisition of Hawaii did not become a highly publicized issue following the release to the press of his letter of October 18. Instead, the question of annexation as such receded temporarily into the background as the contending sides in the debate focused on the advisability of resurrecting the monarchy.

Gresham's proposed course received considerable approval from anti-annexationists. Ambassador Thomas F. Bayard wrote to the secretary from the Court of St. James, stating: "I am greatly pleased with the dignity and justice of your treatment of the Sandwich Island matter—This Country is too great and aspires to too high a place in civilization to stoop [to] the small arts of trickery or bullying a scanty and feeble set of Islanders out of their rights—whatever these rights may be—"[18] Not surprisingly, Schurz expressed high regard for the secretary's letter. Likewise, Henry Watterson, the outspoken editor of the *Louisville Courier-Journal*, who was noted for being critical of the Cleveland administration, warmly praised Gresham's epistle. Recognizing that the secretary's proposal would encounter strong opposition, Watterson pledged to do whatever he could to help further Gresham's plan. At least one important letter was addressed to President Cleveland himself; A. B. Farquhar, president of the executive committee of the National Democratic organization, assured him: "You are entirely right. The people may not see it that way now, but they will later on."[19]

The Democratic press generally responded favorably to Gresham's restoration plan. Of course, the *New York Herald*, the newspaper having the closest ties to the administration in Hawaiian matters, warmly praised the decision to reestablish the monarchy, a decision for which it claimed part of the credit because of its publication of Nordhoff's anti-annexation dispatches. *The Nation* endorsed the administration's proclaimed course as "the only just one possible."[20] This same view was voiced in the editorial pages of the *New York Times* and *Post*. The Republican press, on the other hand, generally opposed the reestablishment of the monarchy. Among the most frequently cited reasons were the following: placing the deposed monarch back upon her throne against the expressed wishes of the provisional government would constitute an act of war for which congressional approval would be necessary; the restoration of the fallen queen was futile in that she would be overthrown as soon as the American forces were withdrawn; the establishment of a monarchy by the United States was inconsistent with her republican tradition; and the logic implicit in such an act would call into question the legitimacy of America's previous territorial acquisitions.[21]

At times the Republican opposition to restoration was accentuated by mocking invective aimed at Cleveland and Gresham. Murat Halstead, the acerbic independent Republican journalist whose columns were syndicated throughout the East, castigated the administration's plan as futile and misguided. It was bad enough, said Halstead, that the president and secretary of state treated the annexation question as a "miserable little law case," thereby throwing away the opportunity to acquire Hawaii. But to compound the administration's "implacable stupidity" by trying to restore the "wretched royal imposter" was more than he could fathom. Halstead excoriated the "frost-bitten lawyerism of the Gresham brief" of October 18 and concluded that Cleveland "must be not merely mugwumped but hypnotized" by its arguments.[22]

The announcement of Gresham's restoration policy injured the anti-expansionist cause by alienating those newspaper editors who, though opposed to the acquisition of Hawaii, were unwilling to see Liliuokalani reinstated by United States intervention. Both the Democratic and Republican parties were represented by these papers. The Democratic *New York World* scoffed:

> Now comes a Platonic era of negotiation, in which our Government, after having fully recognized the revolution, grows suddenly conscientious and chivalric, and proposes to restore the dusky-faced and, perhaps, otherwise dusky Queen to her throne. . . . The Monarchy which it is proposed to reestablish . . . has shown itself unable to muster a battalion of armed and determined men for its support. The farce grows tedious. Ring down the curtain.[23]

The *Philadelphia Record* asserted that Cleveland's reputation in history would be tarnished permanently if he restored the Hawaiian monarch. After scoring annexation as "utterly impracticable," the Republican *San Francisco Argonaut* advised that the United States let the Hawaiians decide whether or not the queen should be restored. Similarly, the Republican *Chicago Record* rejected annexation except "as a last resort." "But the grotesque barbarism of the United States beating down an established Government of honorable men," said the *Record*, "is a suggestion in every way unworthy of the Secretary of State."[24] The Republican *St. Paul Pioneer Press* also rejected both annexation and restoration.

For nearly five weeks after the publication of Gresham's letter to Cleveland, Washington officials and the press waited anxiously for some indication from Minister Willis as to whether or not Liliuokalani had been placed back upon her throne. Meanwhile, on November 20 several of Blount's dispatches were published in the eastern papers, thereby provoking additional controversy over the Hawaiian issue. Writing to Gresham on December 9,

Nordhoff affirmed: "Mr. Blount's report can't be successfully attacked, for the points are all so far as I can see, Established on Provisional Government people's testimony. It is a very able piece of work."[25] The *New York Herald* boasted that every line of Blount's report confirmed the dispatches of Nordhoff. On the other hand, noting the similarities between some of Nordhoff's communications to the *Herald* and Blount's findings, the annexation-minded *New York Sun* charged that there was collusion between the correspondent and the commissioner. Both Minister Thurston and John L. Stevens took exception to the Blount revelations and published emphatic rebuttals.[26]

On December 4, 1893, Cleveland delivered his first annual message to Congress. Only a small segment of the address dealt with the Hawaiian problem, partly because the chief executive was awaiting fresh news from Honolulu about Willis's attempt to reinstate the queen. The president alluded to the "serious embarrassment" which he had faced upon entering office as a result of having to deal with his predecessor's annexation treaty. He had withdrawn that convention from the upper house "for examination," said Cleveland, and had sent James H. Blount to the islands to conduct "an impartial investigation" into the Revolution and the annexation movement. Blount's findings showed "beyond all question" that the constitutional government of Hawaii was overthrown with the complicity of Minister Stevens and the American forces from the U.S.S. *Boston*. The only "honorable course" was to restore as far as possible the state of affairs existing at the time of Stevens' intervention. Pursuant to this goal the president reported that he was attempting, "within the constitutional limits of executive power," to place the queen back upon her throne. He said that he had no definite results to report, but when he had more information he would send a special message to Congress.[27]

The chief executive's message touched off a debate in Congress over Hawaii that continued intermittently until late May of the following year. Immediately after the address the Senate heard speeches for and against both annexation and restoration. Most important, as far as the preparation and timing of Cleveland's forthcoming Hawaiian message was concerned, was the introduction of George F. Hoar's resolution requesting the president to submit to the Senate copies of all instructions given to United States diplomatic representatives and naval officers assigned to Honolulu since March 4, 1893. Although there was doubtless some truth in the *New York Herald*'s charge that Hoar was attempting to gain partisan advantage by creating the false impression that the Republicans had to force Cleveland to disclose the facts, the resolution passed. The Senate debate then widened into a full-scale partisan conflict over the moral, historical, constitutional, racial, strategic, and commercial aspects of the Hawaiian question.[28]

The House passed its own resolution of inquiry, drafted by Robert R. Hitt of Illinois. The measure asked the chief executive for copies of all the diplomatic correspondence to and from Honolulu since March 4, 1889.[29] Cleveland complied with this request in mid-December 1893 and a lengthy House debate on Hawaii followed.

While Congress sought more information on Cleveland's policy toward the islands, the president gave close attention to his forthcoming Hawaiian message. He still did not know whether Willis's mission had succeeded. The most recent dispatches from the islands showed that an impasse had been reached. Liliuokalani still refused to grant full amnesty to the revolutionists; the provisional government had fortified the public buildings with sandbags and artillery, and had organized a thousand-man militia and a five hundred-man reserve, in preparation for any attempt to reestablish the monarchy.[30] Cleveland had first asked Gresham to prepare the message, but disliking Gresham's draft, he had turned to Olney. The latter's draft proved satisfactory; it formed the largest part of the special message.[31]

Cleveland's six thousand-word communication, sent to Congress on December 18, emphasized at the outset that "right and justice should determine the path to be followed in treating this subject." The message reviewed at length the major findings of Commissioner Blount and in a forceful and logical manner defended the administration's stand against the annexation treaty and in favor of the reestablishment of the monarchy. The president offered primarily moral, but also historical, reasons for his decision not to return the treaty to the Senate. He claimed that the American diplomatic representatives and naval forces had assisted in the overthrow of the Hawaiian queen and had established the provisional government "for the purpose of acquiring through that agency territory which we had wrongfully put in its possession." After questioning the right of the provisional government to transfer the sovereignty of Hawaii to another nation without the consent of the Polynesians, Cleveland announced his decision with respect to the treaty: "Believing, therefore, that the United States could not, under the circumstances disclosed, annex the islands without justly incurring the imputation of acquiring them by unjustifiable methods, I shall not again submit the treaty of annexation to the Senate for its consideration . . ." The president mentioned that he opposed the convention also because "it contemplated a departure from unbroken American tradition in providing for the addition to our territory of islands of the sea more than two thousand miles removed from our nearest coast." However, Cleveland said that by itself, the latter objection might not justify the rejection of Harrison's accord.

Immediately after Cleveland gave his reasons for rejecting the compact, he discussed the ethical considerations that had prompted him to attempt to restore the queen. There was such a thing as "international morality" he insisted, and because "a substantial wrong" had been done to a weaker nation by the representatives of the United States, the latter incurred the obligation to repair the injury. In order to remedy the injustice committed against the Hawaiian monarch, the president said he had tried unsuccessfully to restore the status quo that existed before the "lawless landing" of the United States troops in Honolulu on January 16, 1893. He attributed the failure of his restoration policy to the queen's unwillingness to accept the conditions, especially the granting of full amnesty to the revolutionists, upon which his aid depended. Without making any recommendations for further action, the chief executive commended the entire Hawaiian matter to Congress.[32] Altogether, Cleveland's Hawaiian message presented in a compelling manner the moral and anti-imperialist grounds for his opposition to annexation.

Significantly, the president had stated in this message that he declined the proffer of annexation "under the circumstances disclosed." Although Cleveland was an anti-imperialist by inclination, the above statement suggests that his moral repugnance to the particular circumstances surrounding the annexation movement of 1893 probably carried the most weight in his decision to reject Harrison's treaty. What the Democratic chief executive would have done respecting annexation had a different set of conditions prevailed is largely conjectural. However, the present writer believes that the president, for anti-imperialist reasons, probably would have opposed the acquisition of the islands even if the natives had given their consent to a transfer of sovereignty.

The newspaper reaction to the president's special Hawaiian message generally followed the same partisan lines witnessed in the earlier press response to the publication of Gresham's letter of October 18. As on that previous occasion, the chief executive could count on editorial support from many leading Democratic papers. "Mr. Cleveland has never sent to Congress a stronger message," exclaimed the *New York Herald* on December 19. According to the *New York Times* of the same date, the "clear and forcible" message indicated that "the President has performed his own duty in a straightforward and upright fashion." Similarly, the *Chicago Herald* declared: "The paper is one that will raise Mr. Cleveland greatly in the esteem of the country."[33] However, several more newspapers were now added to the growing ranks of Democratic and independent publications unfriendly to the administration's Hawaiian policy. Thus the Democratic *New York World*, although anti-annexationist, commented trenchantly on Cleveland's attempt to restore Liliuokalani: "Carried to its logical extreme, the President's contention would restore this continent to the Indians and surrender to the English, the Spaniards and the Mexicans a large part of our territory. It is not possible to conduct governments or to advance civilization on the refinements of ideal justice."[34] The independent *St. Louis Post-Dispatch*, which also opposed annexation, was equally critical of the administration's attempt to resurrect the monarchy. The Democratic *Cincinnati Enquirer* complained that the president's policy had exhausted the public's patience and had tarnished the reputation of the administration. Especially vitriolic was the annexation-minded Democratic *New York Sun*, which remarked:

> Five-sixths of the Message is a restatement in Mr. Cleveland's own language of the argument for the policy of infamy [restoration?] rendered familiar to everybody through the previous efforts of Blount, Gresham, and the various hirelings of Claus Spreckels. . . . Mr. Cleveland's presentation is no stronger than was Secretary Gresham's; Mr. Gresham's carried no more weight than Blount's; what Blount's is worth, the whole country, including Congress, now perfectly understands.[35]

The *Chicago Tribune*'s response to Cleveland's special Hawaiian message was characteristic of that of many other Republican papers:

> In this emergency the President leaves the entire question with Congress, where he should have left it at the beginning, instead of usurping the functions of that body. The story as told by the President will not add to his reputation as a statesman. It records the failure of the most bungling piece of diplomacy ever attempted by representatives of this government.[36]

The *Omaha Bee* was one of the few Republican newspapers to endorse the president's message.

The rather mixed newspaper response may have been offset somewhat by letters of commendation received at the White House. Democratic Senator Daniel W. Voorhees of Indiana doubtless spoke for many other party regulars in the upper house when he wrote to Cleveland: "There is but one opinion on our side of the Chamber and that was most Complimentary, in every respect to you. I am most mistaken if this splendid State paper does not Control the public Sentiment of this Country and of the world as but few official documents have ever done on a given subject."[37] Oscar S. Straus, a prominent Democrat and diplomat, expressed his "sincere Congratulations upon your admirable Message on Hawaii. . . . Of your many great public Acts I regard this last the greatest."[38] Ambassador Thomas F. Bayard wrote to Gresham: "I fully agree with you—that our great Republic will perish if we embark upon an Imperial system of acquisition of outlying dependencies—and that the methods employed under the late administration in the Hawaiian Kingdom were disgraceful to our Country, and will not be sustained by the American people when they are fairly comprehended." Former secretary of the treasury Benjamin H. Bristow, who like the secretary of state was politically independent and high-minded, sent a letter to Gresham praising the president's message. Senator Stephen M. White of California, who by 1898 was to become one of the leading anti-imperialists in the nation, also expressed approval.[39]

However gratifying the president may have found such letters, the unpleasant fact remained that his Hawaiian policy had been only partially successful. Cleveland's main objective, after studying Blount's full report, was to prevent the annexation of Hawaii by the United States or any other nation. This the president accomplished. But his second goal—to reinstate Liliuokalani—was absurdly impractical and could not have been realized without transforming Hawaii into a garrison state.

Scholars have taken different views of Cleveland's actions. Recognizing the futility of the restoration policy, historian Allan Nevins concluded, nevertheless, that the chief executive's "final policy deserves not blame but praise. . . . In an era of international land-grabbing Cleveland, despite angry sneers, had insisted that the United States should meet the loftiest obligations of honesty and unselfishness; in an era when the rights of small nations were almost universally trampled on, he had displayed a sensitive consideration for one of the weakest of them all."[40] Historian William A. Russ, Jr., censured Cleveland and Gresham "for their impractical endeavor to undo what could not be undone without involvement in questionable international proceedings and complications." Russ suggested that Cleveland could have satisfied his desire to redress the wrong done to Liliuokalani, and could also have pursued a viable Hawaiian policy, by abandoning the plan of restoration immediately after the queen's refusal to "follow a humane policy towards those who had deposed her." In this way America's honor would have been vindicated while the willful monarch would have received much of the blame for the failure of the restoration attempt. A wiser course still, said Russ, would have been for Cleveland to have withdrawn the annexation treaty from the Senate as he did, but to have refrained from pursuing the Hawaiian matter further; thereby he would have permitted "history to deal with Harrison and Stevens." When Cleveland commended the problem to the discretion of Congress he "was asking for what he got; interparty and intraparty strife."[41]

In some ways Russ's view is quite sensible. Those aspects of Cleveland's Hawaiian policy which impressed Nevins the most, namely, the president's high regard for international morality and the courage to fight for it, would still have been present even if he had abandoned the queen after her refusal to grant amnesty. And the chief executive made a mistake by submitting the Hawaiian question to Congress, in that this action needlessly fanned interparty and intraparty discord. But there is a striking internal inconsistency in Russ's notion that Cleveland should have pigeonholed the treaty upon entering office and left to history the final verdict regarding the United States' role in the Hawaiian Revolution. For without the Blount investigation, which led to the gathering of valuable first-hand testimony, modern historians would have far less information upon which to base a thorough and judicious assessment of America's involvement in the overthrow of the Hawaiian monarchy.

Unlike Russ, the present writer thinks that the most statesmanlike course for Cleveland would have been to withdraw the treaty and to conduct the investigation as he did and then to have notified the Senate as soon as possible of his decision not to resubmit the treaty to that body. In this way he would have acted on the basis of investigative findings, however biased, rather than simply on the vague suspicion that Harrison's annexation compact was tainted with impropriety. Had Cleveland confined his policy to the rejection of the annexation treaty in this manner, there would have been far less risk of embroiling Congress and his party over the Hawaiian issue.

The president evidently did not think through the manifold difficulties involved in carrying out the recommendations of his visionary secretary of state. Olney's advice was helpful in pointing out the broad range of equities involved in the restoration plan. But he, like Gresham, failed to take into account the intransigence of the queen and the determination of the provisional government to remain in power. The attorney general's recommendation that the Hawaiian problem be submitted to Congress led the president into committing an additional blunder.[42] On balance, Cleveland did not receive very prudent advice in Hawaiian matters, though he must assume the ultimate responsibility for not implementing a more workable policy.

At any rate, in late 1893 the chief executive had rejected the treaty. Afterwards he could do little but encourage congressional resistance to Hawaiian annexation.

7

Congressional Resistance
to Hawaiian Annexation

At the time that Cleveland delivered his special message on Hawaii the Democratic-controlled Congress seemed to support the administration's stand against annexation, though not the plan for restoration. Writing to President Dole in mid-December from the Hawaiian Legation in Washington, Commissioner Alexander observed:

> It is hard to find any supporters of the Gresham doctrine [restoration] just now. The annexation question has dropped into the background, where it is wisest to keep it for a while at least. . . . Many people while wishing us success, are deeply impressed with the objections to annexation. It is not certain that a joint resolution for it would pass both houses at present.[1]

Alexander's view presaged the outcome of the stormy and protracted debate over Hawaii that ensued on Capitol Hill.

The House began to consider the Hawaiian matter in earnest on December 18, 1893, at which time the president transmitted to the lower chamber his special message plus the documents requested by Representative Robert R. Hitt of Illinois and an accompanying *précis*. After the message and *précis* were read the annexation-minded Republicans, led by Charles A. Boutelle of Maine, proceeded to nettle the anti-expansionist Democrats with a barrage of obstructionist maneuvers which doubtless were intended to discredit the administration's Hawaiian policy. Boutelle started the turmoil and partisan bickering, which lasted throughout the entire course of the House debates, by asking that certain of Gresham's instructions to Willis be read in open session rather than sent to committee. The Democratic Speaker, Charles F. Crisp of Georgia, rejected Boutelle's claim that such a request was privileged, and the House then became entangled over rules. Without conceding in principle, Crisp granted Boutelle's request, and Gresham's communications of October 18, November 24, and December 3 were read before the House.[2] Later that same day the Maine congressman attempted to offer another of what were to be his numerous resolutions denouncing the president's handling of the Hawaiian problem. In the meantime the chair had recognized another speaker, but Boutelle insisted that his resolution was privileged and refused to take his seat until the sergeant at arms was called.

On the following day similar disruptive tactics were employed by William B. Cockran of New York, who offered what he considered to be a privileged resolution deriding Cleveland's Hawaiian policy. Boutelle again entered the fray by attaching as an amendment to Cockran's proposal a statement condemning the administration for invading the rights and dignity of the House by secretly instructing Minister Willis to conspire against the government of Hawaii. When James B. McCreary of Kentucky denied that the Cockran-Boutelle resolution should be treated as privileged, the peppery congressman from Maine created a commotion with his verbal pyrotechnics. Encouraged by applause from the Republican side, Boutelle evaded the question of privilege, which he was supposed to be addressing, and instead reviled the "shameful policy . . . originated by [either] a renegade Republican [Gresham] or a Democratic usurper."[3]

On December 21, after a good deal more strife between Republicans and Democrats over resolutions seeking additional information from the president, the anti-expansionists succeeded in getting one of their own proposals read before the House. McCreary authored a measure which, after being accepted by the Foreign Affairs Committee as its majority report, was eventually passed by the lower chamber. The resolution contained two clauses, the first of which condemned former Minister Stevens for "illegally aiding" in the overthrow of the Hawaiian monarchy and establishing a regime which lacked popular support. The second clause is especially pertinent and, therefore, is quoted in its entirety as follows:

Second: That we heartily approve the principle announced by the President of the United States that interference with the domestic affairs of an independent nation is contrary to the spirit of American institutions. And it is further the sense of this House that the annexation of the Hawaiian Islands to our country, or the assumption of a protectorate over them by our Government, is uncalled for and inexpedient; that the people of that country should have absolute freedom and independence in pursuing their own line of policy, and that foreign intervention in the political affairs of the islands will not be regarded with indifference by the Government of the United States.[4]

Thus the resolution was unequivocal in its rejection of Hawaiian annexation and in its insistence that the islands remain independent. Conspicuously absent was any support for the administration's abortive restoration policy.

Later that same day the Republican minority reported out a resolution introduced by Hitt. The measure denounced Cleveland's attempt to bring about the resignation of the Dole government and stipulated that the United States should not interfere further in Hawaii's domestic affairs. The proposal also stated that the United States would regard foreign intervention in the islands as an unfriendly act.[5]

During the holiday recess the beleaguered House Democrats, hoping to gain the upper hand over such Republican firebrands as Boutelle, Cockran, and Hitt, appealed to the administration for help. On January 1, 1894, Congressman Isidor Rayner of Maryland wrote to Gresham about the importance of seizing the offensive from the Republicans. When Congress reassembled, said the Maryland legislator, McCreary was to open the debate and Speaker Crisp "promised to recognize me [Rayner] next." "*I wish you would remind him of this so that it is done*," the congressman told the secretary of state.[6] On the same day Rayner sent a telegram to Gresham asking for a meeting to discuss the Hawaiian debate.

After the holiday interlude the Hawaiian problem came up again for discussion in mid-January, at which time Hitt sponsored a resolution requesting all the information which the president had on the matter.[7] Additional documents arrived forthwith, setting off a new round of verbal sparring between the supporters and adversaries of Cleveland's policy. With little to show for all the wrangling that had occurred over Hawaii in late January, the House turned briefly to another pressing issue, the Wilson tariff.

On February 2 the Democratic majority was ready to press for the passage of the McCreary resolution. Deliberations got under way with an exchange between Thomas C. Catchings of Mississippi and Boutelle, when the former requested permission to present a report from the Committee on Rules. Boutelle objected, saying that he had introduced a privileged resolution six weeks earlier (accusing Cleveland, in effect, of levying war on Hawaii without consulting Congress) which was due for consideration. Catchings, who, probably like many other Democratic supporters of the president, had grown weary of Boutelle's parliamentary gymnastics, resorted to a personal attack: "I would like to turn him [Boutelle] over to a lunatic asylum if I had charge of him."[8]

After the preliminary skirmish between Catchings and Boutelle, McCreary delivered a lengthy speech in support of his resolution. He began by chiding the Republicans for not taking an affirmative stand on Hawaiian annexation in the Hitt resolution. The failure to do so, said McCreary, was tantamount to a disavowal of President Harrison's annexation project. The Kentucky congressman praised Cleveland for his "courageous and patriotic" efforts to rectify the injustice done to the Polynesians by representatives of the United States. McCreary found nothing wrong with any aspect of the president's Hawaiian policy, including the unconfirmed appointment of Blount for which, he said, numerous precedents existed. The congressman rebuked Stevens for aiding in the overthrow of the constitutional regime in Hawaii and for helping the annexationists through his precipitant recognition of the provisional government. McCreary said that if Stevens had not misled Harrison on Hawaiian matters, the former chief executive would not have supported annexation. Both the so-called Revolution (which was nothing "but a conspiracy") and the annexation movement were opposed by the Hawaiian people, said the congressman. These "facts," he averred, had been established by Blount and Nordhoff.

McCreary offered the standard anti-imperialist reasons for his opposition to Hawaiian annexation. Special emphasis was given to the historical, constitutional, and racial objections to acquiring the islands. He quoted Judge Cooley's views to show that the American constitutional system was not designed to govern distant colonies inhabited by unassimilable races. In short, said McCreary:

> The principle involved in the annexation of the Hawaiian Islands is far-reaching and of the greatest importance. If it is proper to annex the Hawaiian

Islands, it may soon be proper to annex Santo Domingo, or any other country that may send commissioners to propose annexation. This has not been the policy taught by the framers of our Constitution, or the statesman who have guided and guarded our country in the past.[9]

This was the central argument of the anti-imperialists in 1893 and it remained the most formidable obstacle in the path of Hawaiian annexation right up to the moment the islands were acquired by the United States in mid-1898.

On February 3 Rayner delivered a speech supporting Mc-Creary's resolution. The first half of his address was devoted to censuring Stevens for leading the "conspiracy" which brought about Liliuokalani's dethronement. Republican John Van Voorhis of New York buffeted the speaker with embarrassing questions, asking Rayner, for example, how many people were engaged in the so-called conspiracy. The Maryland congressman stammered a bit before admitting that he did not know. Having satisfied himself, at least, that Stevens was guilty of conspiring to bring about the deposition of the Hawaiian queen, Rayner upheld Cleveland's rejection of the treaty and attempt to reestablish the monarchy. Unlike most of the other leading anti-expansionists, he opposed annexation unconditionally, stating: "So far as I am concerned, I am opposed to the whole policy of annexation, either of these islands or of any other island or place. . . . If we once enter upon schemes of annexation there will be no end to them."[10] Rayner then came to the question of what course should be pursued toward Hawaii. He said that no additional attempts should be made to reinstate the queen since she had proved uncooperative—a remark applauded by the Republicans. In support of McCreary's resolution, he concluded that the United States should neither annex the Hawaiian Islands nor establish a protectorate over them.

Hitt spoke for the Republicans by defending the minority report (authored by himself) of the Foreign Affairs Committee. In a lengthy discourse, which began on February 2 and continued the following day, he challenged the accuracy of Blount's findings; maligned the character of Liliuokalani, whom he cast as "the tiger protégé of Mr. Cleveland"; criticized the president for attempting to restore the queen; and derided Willis for violating international law.[11]

The speeches of McCreary, Rayner, and Hitt typified the remaining addresses delivered in the lower chamber prior to the February 7 vote on the McCreary resolution. During the last week before the vote numerous speeches, all by Democrats, were heard on behalf of that resolution. The first was delivered by Fernando Money of Mississippi on February 3. He devoted nearly all of his frequently interrupted presentation to showing how Stevens conspired with a handful of American usurpers in Honolulu for the purpose of toppling the monarchy and bringing about the annexation of the islands. Money concluded that Stevens had violated international law and that Cleveland was justified in opposing annexation as well as in trying peacefully to reinstate the queen. In an address delivered on February 5 Josiah Patterson of Tennessee, like Money before him, rebuked the conduct of Stevens as described in Blount's report and supported Cleveland's bid to place the queen back upon her throne. Basing his opposition to annexation primarily upon racial grounds, Patterson said that the president rightfully rejected those "leprous islands 2,000 miles from our western shores."[12] Before the day ended, the anti-expansionists gave three more speeches. On February 6, the final day of the forensic marathon, Henry G. Turner of Georgia voiced the central argument of the opponents of Hawaiian annexation: "Some gentlemen on the other side have advocated on this floor the adoption of a great colonial policy. I denounce it. I believe that an entrance upon that system of imperialism is inconsistent with the spirit of our institutions."[13] Several other speeches on that final day supported the Cleveland-Gresham policy, all of them covering the same familiar ground without adding substantially to the administration's case.

The Republicans made several desperate though unavailing attempts to avoid a vote on the McCreary resolution. On February 6 Henry W. Blair of New Hampshire offered an amendment to Hitt's resolution; calling for the recognition and eventual annexation of Hawaii, it was defeated handily. The House then rejected Hitt's resolution, which censured Cleveland for his restoration attempt and recommended strict noninterference in Hawaiian affairs, by a vote of 103 yeas to 159 nays, with 89 abstentions.[14]

Unable to secure passage of their own measure, the

Republican expansionists, led by Thomas B. Reed of Maine (who was to be a stalwart opponent of Hawaiian annexation in 1897–98), tried to obstruct the efforts of the Democratic majority to get a vote on McCreary's resolution. But Reed's motion to recommit the resolution was resoundingly defeated. Nevertheless, the path was still not clear for the adoption of McCreary's resolution, and a vote on it failed of a quorum due to Republican absences. The frustrated Democratic majority was only able to pass a resolution empowering the sergeant at arms to request the presence of all House members, except the sick, at the session the following day.

On February 7 Reed embroiled the House in an extended debate over what constituted a quorum. After seemingly endless parliamentary scuffling, Rayner called for what he hoped would be the final vote. This time a quorum was obtained and the McCreary resolution passed by a count of 177 yeas to 78 nays, with 96 abstentions.[15] Before turning to other pressing issues, the House decisively defeated Boutelle's proposal, which accused the president of invading the rights and dignity of the lower chamber by his attempts to restore the queen.

Thus the House formally condemned Stevens for his Hawaiian role, declared against annexation as well as a protectorate, and abjured any further attempts to reinstate the fallen monarch. This was a victory, albeit a qualified one, for the administration. It is to be noted that the McCreary resolution did not explicitly condone Cleveland's efforts to reestablish the Hawaiian monarchy; on that point the measure was silent. The triumph was somewhat less than complete in another sense; that is, only 177 out of 215 Democrats voted to sustain the chief executive—a result that to some extent reflected the dissension within party ranks after the president's fight for partial repeal of the Sherman Silver Purchase Act.

Not surprisingly, the newspaper reactions to the adoption of the McCreary resolution tended to reflect the customary partisan alignment on the Hawaiian issue. With a few exceptions, the Democratic papers were inclined to give the House verdict a rather bland endorsement. "We trust that a similar declaration will be made by the Senate," stated the *New York Herald*.[16] The *New York Times* observed that the vote "probably represents very fairly the sentiment of the country."[17] One of the more enthusiastic supporters of the House decision was the *Philadelphia Times,* which exulted: "The declaration is sound, just, and right, and fairly expresses the deliberate judgment of the American people."[18] Generally, the Republican papers criticized the lower house. The *Boston Journal* exclaimed bitterly: "The Bourbon victory is complete. The 'cookoos,' as one of our Massachusetts Congressmen [Elijah A. Morse] aptly if inelegantly called them, have won by brute force of numbers." Less venomous objections to the passage of the McCreary resolution were registered by such Republican organs as the *New York Tribune,* the *Pittsburg* (Kans.) *Commercial Gazette,* the *Denver Republican,* and the *Columbus* (Ohio) *Dispatch.* The independent newspapers were about evenly divided in their views of the House's decision.[19]

In the Senate, where the Democrats held only a slight (44–40) majority, the president's Hawaiian policy received a great deal of scrutiny and criticism. Cleveland began transmitting the previously requested Hawaiian documents to the upper chamber on December 18. Two days later that body passed a resolution, introduced by John T. Morgan of Alabama, which authorized the Foreign Relations Committee to investigate the conduct of the United States officials in Honolulu during and after the *émeute* of January 1893.[20]

After a brief holiday recess the Senate resumed deliberations on the Hawaiian question in January 1894. The focal point of the prolonged clash that ensued was a resolution introduced by David Turpie of Indiana on January 8. It stated:

> *Resolved,* That from the facts and papers laid before us by the Executive and other sources it is unwise, inexpedient, and not in accordance with the character and dignity of the United States to consider further at this time either the treaty or project of annexation of the Hawaiian Territory to this country; that the Provisional Government therein having been duly recognized, the highest international interests require that it shall pursue its own line of polity. Foreign intervention in the political affairs of these islands will be regarded as an act unfriendly to the Government of the United States.[21]

This was the original Turpie resolution; a significantly modified version of this proposal was to pass the Senate in late May, after nearly five months of heated argument.

Turpie spoke on behalf of his resolution on January 11. He condemned Stevens for unlawfully waging war against the government of Hawaii and for establishing a United States protectorate over the archipelago. According to the Indiana senator, Stevens tried to bring Hawaii into the Union through disreputable means. Moreover, Turpie said that before annexation should be consummated, a plebiscite ought to be held in the islands to determine the wishes of the 40,000 native inhabitants. If Hawaii were to be acquired in the future, the transaction must be "clean, pure, [and] untainted," he insisted. Significantly, it does not appear from Turpie's address that he was irreconcilably opposed to the absorption of the islands. "Granting that the acquisition of the Hawaiian Islands may be ever so desirable," he said, "it must be attained in a different manner."[22] In this statement, as throughout his entire speech, he seemed to quarrel more with the means of annexation than with the policy as such, and instead of categorically renouncing the proposition for all time, he concluded merely that annexation was inexpedient at the present time.

On January 23 the Turpie resolution was reported favorably by the Committee on Foreign Relations. Although the committee had made several minor alterations in the wording of the measure, none of these had changed its substance.[23] Joseph N. Dolph of Oregon, an ardent annexationist, was the only member of that committee to cast a dissenting vote.

On the following day Senator George G. Vest of Missouri offered a resolution that disavowed forever any intention of acquiring Hawaii.[24] Noting that Turpie's proposal seemed to condone annexation at a later date, the Missouri senator said that a resolution was needed that did not anticipate the future incorporation of the islands into the Union.

Gray of Delaware, who strongly opposed annexation, objected to Vest's substitute resolution on the ground that it did not conform as well as did Turpie's measure to the wording of Cleveland's special message rejecting the Hawaiian treaty. The senator from Delaware told his colleague from Missouri that the Senate should adopt a resolution that followed closely the chief executive's circumscribed phraseology. According to Gray, the president had said in essence on December 18, 1893, that "it was not wise or expedient . . . to resubmit, under present conditions, that treaty to the Senate."[25] Since none of the anti-expansionists in the upper house came to Vest's defense, with the result that his rather sweeping resolution was laid aside, it seems evident that the Senate critics of Hawaiian annexation preferred taking a qualified stand, similar to that of the administration, against the acquisition of the islands.

Henry M. Teller of Colorado ushered in the next round of debate on January 29 by delivering a spread-eagle speech calling for the creation of an American empire of which Hawaii was to be an integral part. After reminding the president's supporters that territorial expansion was a time-honored Democratic policy, the Colorado senator exclaimed:

> I am in favor of the annexation of the [Hawaiian] islands. I am in favor of the annexation of Cuba; I am in favor of the annexation of the great country lying north of us. I expect in a few years to see the American flag floating from the extreme north to the line of our sister Republics on the south. I expect to see it floating over the isles of the sea—not only these, but in the Great Gulf and in the West India seas.[26]

Hawaii was especially needed, said Teller, because it was situated in the midst of the Pacific trade routes. He concluded by asserting that the acquisition of Hawaii was not incompatible with America's venerable republican institutions nor with the Monroe Doctrine.

On February 12 and 13 Gray responded to Teller's plea for wholesale territorial expansion. He recounted in detail each stage of the Hawaiian Revolution as well as the testimony linking Stevens with the scheme to abolish the monarchy and bring about annexation. Further, he censured Harrison for trying to rush through the Senate a treaty that would embark the United States "on a career of empire and colonization never before attempted." But, rather than rejecting annexation outright, Gray advised circumspection and hoped that if Hawaii were ever acquired it would be under circumstances that would not smack of conspiracy. "If we are . . . ever to step from the shores of this continent out upon a career of empire and colonization, let it be with head erect and above even the suspicion of dishonor, intrigue, or low dealing."[27]

John W. Daniel of Virginia, a supporter of the administration, delivered a lengthy address on February 19 and 20 criticizing Stevens for involving the United States in the Hawaiian Revolution, for deceiving Harrison into thinking that the American naval forces had played no role, and for establishing a protectorate over the islands. But he defended Cleveland's withdrawal of the treaty, appointment of Blount, and attempt to restore Liliuokalani. Although Daniel opposed annexation under the existing circumstances, he did not seem to object to the future acquisition of the archipelago, which he regarded as inevitable. In language both convoluted and euphuistic, the senator declared:

> When American civilization had planted itself on the Pacific shore of California, civilization had belted the globe. . . . What may be its [American civilization's] career in that broad ocean beyond we can not yet define, but we know from the signs and omens that, as our lands are filled up with a teeming population, destiny points its finger to the farther shores. . . . This little colony in Honolulu answers the prophetic finger of that extended hand.[28]

Senator Stephen M. White of California spoke at considerable length on Hawaiian affairs on February 21. While being questioned repeatedly by Teller, White dealt with Stevens' conduct throughout January and February 1893; Stevens' diplomatic accreditation after the fall of the monarchy; Cleveland's appointment of a special commissioner; Blount's authority to abolish the United States protectorate; the president's restoration policy; and, most importantly, the matter of annexation. White gave three reasons why he opposed the admission of Hawaii into the Union, any one of which, he said, had force enough to determine his vote. First, the provisional government had not been in office long enough to execute a transfer of sovereignty. Second, annexation should not occur because, as Blount had demonstrated, the Hawaiian people were opposed to it. The senator appealed to the Declaration of Independence to show that American tradition ordained that there could be no just government without the "consent of the governed." Third, the absorption of Hawaii would be contrary to the United States' interests. By this he meant that the islands were so far-removed from the American mainland that they would be difficult and expensive to defend, and that the inhabitants were not fit for American citizenship. In short, the senator's aversion to the acquisition of the islands, like that of Gray and others, derived primarily from anti-imperialist assumptions.

Although White vigorously denounced Hawaiian annexation, he, like many of the other leading anti-imperialists in the upper house,[29] was not categorically opposed to it. "I am not prepared at this moment to lay down absolute doctrine, from which I shall never deviate in any contingency, against the acquisition of foreign lands, provided the people desire such annexation; but I see at this time no reason to qualify or doubt the correctness of the principle [that distant territory should not be brought into the Union] maintained from Jefferson to Cleveland."[30]

On February 26 the prolix debate in the upper house was enlivened by the issuance of the findings of the Committee on Foreign Relations.[31] The voluminous document, commonly known as the Morgan report (because Committee Chairman John T. Morgan of Alabama authored it), was primarily a rebuttal to Blount's earlier report. The report vindicated everyone involved in the Hawaiian affair, excepting the queen and her cabinet. It upheld Stevens' view that Liliuokalani triggered the Revolution by attempting to promulgate a new constitution on January 14, 1893. Because of the disorder ensuing from the queen's act, the report condoned Stevens' landing of United States troops and his recognition of the provisional government. But the document did not approve the minister's establishment of a protectorate. It exonerated both the Harrison and Cleveland administrations of wrongdoing in their actions on the annexation treaty. Also, the report cleared Blount of any malfeasance, although it declared that his conclusions were mistaken. Finally, the report disapproved Cleveland's restoration plan; however, to the extent that the president did not intend to use force, it declared the plan justified. It made no recommendations as to future policy. Only Morgan endorsed all of the report's conclusions. The remaining eight committee members, consisting of four Democrats and four

Republicans, approved only those findings which coincided with the stance of their respective parties.[32]

With few exceptions, the anti-expansionist press was critical of Morgan's findings. The *New York Times* of February 27 referred to the Alabama senator as "that antique Southern Whig" and dismissed his document as a "rather picturesque bit of patchwork, . . . not of the least consequence." "Senator Morgan's report," scoffed the *Philadelphia Record*, "is a mere incoherent yawp of jingoism." The *New York Evening Post* admitted that it was perplexed by the fact that Morgan could issue a report condoning the actions of Harrison and Stevens while simultaneously pronouncing the opposite course of Cleveland and Blount as "wise and patriotic and constitutional." One of the few anti-annexationist papers to editorialize favorably about the committee findings was the *Detroit Free Press*, which stated: "The course of the President, so carefully reviewed by the Committee, reflects the highest credit upon himself and the Nation."[33]

The Senate discussed Morgan's document intermittently for several weeks following its submission in late February. Meanwhile, Turpie's resolution languished because the Republicans were dissatisfied with its rejection of annexation. When Turpie attempted to bring it to a vote on March 20, Dolph objected. Later that day James Z. George of Mississippi delivered an extended discourse supporting Cleveland's Hawaiian policy, but added nothing that had not been said repeatedly during the preceding months. While the Senate remained bogged down in what seemed a fruitless quarrel over Hawaii, the provisional government, acting through Legation Secretary Frank P. Hastings in Washington, urged the Republican annexationists to permit the passage of Turpie's resolution in order to obliterate the hopes of the queen's supporters in Honolulu for United States intervention on their behalf. But before the Senate could act, the tariff issue intervened again.

In late May several proannexationist senators offered resolutions upholding Hawaii's independence and declaring that the United States would not interfere further in the affairs of that insular nation. The Senate anti-imperialists, however, were insistent upon enacting Turpie's proposal. In order for that measure to pass, it was necessary to delete the first part of it, which explicitly repudiated annexation. This Turpie did. He then submitted the amended resolution, which stated:

> Resolved, That of right it belongs wholly to the people of the Hawaiian Islands to establish and maintain their own form of government and domestic polity; that the United States ought in nowise to interfere therewith, and that any intervention in the political affairs of these islands by any other government will be regarded as an act unfriendly to the United States.[34]

On May 31 the Senate passed the resolution by a count of 55 to 0, with 30 abstentions.[35]

The Senate's action unequivocally ruled out any further attempts by the United States to restore the deposed queen. By implication, it also rejected annexation, at least for the time being, since the incorporation of Hawaii into the Union would have interfered with the right of the islanders "to establish and maintain their own form of government and domestic polity."[36] Therefore, at most, the passage of the Turpie resolution constituted only a partial victory for Cleveland and Gresham,[37] although some of the leading anti-expansionist newspapers interpreted the Senate's move as a complete vindication of the administration's Hawaiian policy.[38]

Notwithstanding the fact that the Senate and House passed different resolutions (with that of the latter more fully representing the views of the Cleveland administration), the upper and lower chambers were in complete agreement on two issues: first, that no attempt should be made to undo the Hawaiian Revolution; and second, that no foreign government should be allowed to intervene in the islands. Since Cleveland previously had asked Congress for guidance in the Hawaiian matter, he had no choice but to accept this verdict. Under the new "hands off" policy the commercial reciprocity treaty was to continue, but in August 1894 the U.S.S. *Philadelphia* was recalled from Honolulu, which left the islands without a protective American warship for the first time since 1889.

Despite the decisions reached on Capitol Hill in 1894, the Fifty-third Congress (March 4, 1893 to March 3, 1895) had not entirely disposed of the Hawaiian problem. Two events in January 1895—a royalist uprising in Honolulu and a request by Cleveland to Congress regarding Necker Island (a small uninhabited rock approximately 400 miles from Honolulu)—revived the Senate debate over annexation.

After having received assurances from Secretary Gresham that the United States would not interfere in any struggle between the royalists and the provisional government in Hawaii,[39] the queen's supporters planned a coup d'état for January 7, 1895. The natives and half-castes behind the movement were probably encouraged by the absence of an American warship in Hawaiian waters. Rumors of the royalist scheme leaked out several days in advance of the scheduled revolt, and the provisional government, after a few skirmishes with the queen's followers, crushed the insurrection.[40]

When the news of the ill-conceived *putsch* reached Capitol Hill, a new round of debate over Hawaii took place in the Senate. The Republicans capitalized on the foresight of Henry Cabot Lodge of Massachusetts, who, before the uprising occurred, had offered a resolution urging the sending of an American war vessel to Honolulu to prevent civil disorder. Doubtless to the satisfaction of Lodge and the other Senate annexationists the U.S.S. *Philadelphia* was promptly reassigned to the islands, but this did not end the debate.

The tempo of the discussion quickened on January 9 when Cleveland issued a special message to Congress asking that the reciprocity treaty of 1884 be modified so as to permit Hawaii to lease Necker Island to Great Britain for use as a cable station linking Canada and Australia.[41] The request fell like a bombshell upon the Senate expansionists, who for some time had been suspicious of the president's allegedly pro-British views, especially his advocacy of the gold standard and low tariffs. Also, it did not go unnoticed that on December 3, 1894, the chief executive had proposed a complete withdrawal from a tripartite arrangement over the Samoan Islands, which would have left Britain and Germany in charge of those islands. It seemed to some annexationists, like Lodge, that Cleveland was willing to let Britain encroach upon United States interests not only in Hawaii but also throughout the Pacific Ocean. On January 21, 1895, the Massachusetts senator offered a resolution calling for the annexation of the Polynesian archipelago, opposition to any measure that would permit another government to secure a lease of Hawaiian territory, and construction of an American cable to Honolulu.[42] Three days later James Z. George of Mississippi assailed Lodge's proposal, but William V. Allen of Nebraska called for annexation on the ground that the provisional government could now make a valid cession, having demonstrated its stability by quashing the royalist insurrection. None of these proposals came to a vote.

The anti-expansionists in the Senate rose to the challenge. Caffery of Louisiana objected to absorbing into the Union the heterogeneous population of the northern Pacific archipelago. Gray of Delaware reiterated the familiar anti-imperialist objection to Hawaiian annexation:

> I believe [he said] that our policy is a continental one, and that we are not called upon by anything in our past history or by anything in the necessities of our situation to step off this continent in a career of colonial aggrandizement. That belongs to a past age; it belongs to other forms of government.[43]

The Senate then resumed the discussion of the cable. Although it rejected Cleveland's request that Britain be permitted to lease Necker Island, annexationists in the upper house maneuvered for the building of a cable linking Hawaii with the American mainland.[44] They must have been surprised when on February 8 White of California spoke in favor of laying a cable from the west coast of the United States via Hawaii all the way to the Orient. After declaring his opposition to the acquisition of the islands, he stated: "I do not consider . . . that the cable and annexation plans are at all interdependent." White concluded that the commercial advantages to be derived from the construction of a cable to Honolulu, which hopefully would be extended to Asia, would be very great.

On February 9 the Senate attached an amendment to the Diplomatic and Consular Appropriation Bill providing $500,000 toward the expense of constructing a submarine cable between the United States and Hawaii.[45] The House refused to concur in the amendment and the upper chamber, upon receiving word from Joseph C. S. Blackburn of Kentucky that the president would veto the amended bill if it reached his desk, yielded in the matter. Blackburn was right. The president saw embedded in the cable amendment the veiled threat of annexation. In a letter written on February 13 to Ambassador Bayard in London, Cleveland said: "I do not see how I can make myself responsible for such a departure from our traditions as is involved in an appropriation in the Diplomatic bill, for building a cable by the Government to Hawaii. . . . I do not believe we should in present circumstances boom the annexation craze by entering upon Government cable building."[46]

Interestingly, whereas Senator White thought that the annexation and cable issues were independent of one another, President Cleveland saw them as closely related. This difference of opinion between two leading anti-expansionists suggests that the opponents of annexation, even when they happened to be members of the same political party, at times had to contend with conflicting perceptions of what collateral moves would further, or perhaps endanger, their cause.

Thus Congress not only refused to allow Britain to build a cable facility on Hawaiian soil, but also defeated plans for a cable connecting the United States with the islands. These decisions virtually brought to a close the anticlimactic Hawaiian debate of 1895.

Throughout the remainder of Cleveland's second term the Hawaiian issue was eclipsed by other matters: the outbreak of rebellion in Cuba; the dispute with Britain over the Venezuelan boundary; the need to bring about economic recovery; and the stirring election of 1896. Until William McKinley entered the White House in 1897, the anti-annexationists had little to fear regarding the fate of Hawaii. The Republican president was in office less than four months when the expansionists in his party persuaded him to submit to the Senate a treaty providing for the acquisition of Hawaii. Quickly the opponents of annexation mobilized for the campaign against the treaty of 1897.

8

The Campaign against
the Treaty of 1897

The Republican party platform of 1896 stated that Hawaii should be "controlled" by the United States. Although this did not amount to an explicit endorsement of annexation, William McKinley's election to the presidency revived the hopes and energies of the expansionists. While the new chief executive, on assuming office in early 1897, expressed interest in Hawaii,[1] his main concern was the tariff. Realizing this, the annexation commission (comprising Alfred S. Hartwell, Francis M. Hatch, William A. Kinney, William O. Smith, and Lorrin A. Thurston) sent to Washington by the Republic of Hawaii unobtrusively pursued its cause. The commissioners eschewed newspaper publicity as they planned their strategy with key supporters in Congress. Although the president seemed receptive to the idea of union, the delegates from the islands soon learned to their dismay that the new secretary of state, John Sherman, was opposed to the acquisition of Hawaii on anti-imperialist grounds, and that he even denounced the reciprocity treaty.[2]

While the commissioners and their allies in Congress were not able to overcome entirely the twin obstacles of the tariff and the secretary of state, the annexationists were able to work around these impediments. Amid some inadvertent though timely agitation from Japan, the administration submitted to the upper house on June 16 a new treaty providing for the annexation of the Polynesian archipelago to the United States.[3]

Resistance was immediately forthcoming. The hastily formed opposition bloc consisted primarily of Senators White of California, Caffery and McEnery of Louisiana, Bacon and Clay of Georgia, Gray of Delaware, Mills of Texas, Pasco of Florida, and Pettigrew of South Dakota. Recognizing that there was little chance of getting sufficient votes for ratification, the friends of the treaty decided on June 18 to have it reported from committee but to postpone the Senate debate until the winter session of

1897-98. Accordingly, the treaty was reported favorably by the Foreign Relations Committee on July 14 and ten days later Congress adjourned without having acted on it. During the recess and the legislative session that followed, the sugar interests, organized labor, and, most importantly, the anti-imperialists, mounted a vigorous opposition.

The United States sugar interests, which in mid-1897 opposed unsuccessfully the continuance of the Hawaiian reciprocity treaty,[4] were primed for a campaign against McKinley's annexation pact. However, until Congress reassembled in December they put up only sporadic resistance. Thus Senator Stephen M. White, that inveterate foe of annexation, told one constituent in June 1897 that the admission of Hawaii into the Union would "involve the beet sugar industry in ruin,"[5] and John D. Spreckels and Henry T. Oxnard jointly lobbied against annexation in Washington during the summer. On October 14 President Edward P. Ripley of the Atchison, Topeka, and Santa Fe Railway warned Secretary of the Treasury Lyman J. Gage that the prospect of annexation was harming the nation's beet sugar enterprise. Several weeks later the Alameda Sugar Company in California, writing to Secretary of Agriculture James Wilson, decried the fact that "a product three times the consumption of the Pacific Coast is by the generosity of our government, permitted to enter there free at one-half the cost of the local production." In late November the Association of Beet Sugar Manufacturers passed at its annual meeting in San Francisco a unanimous resolution protesting against the incorporation of Hawaii into the Union and urging the abrogation of the reciprocity treaty.[6]

When the Senate commenced debate on the annexation treaty in January 1898, the sugar forces launched an all-out drive against union. Claus Spreckels had recently purchased the *San Francisco Call* in the name of his son John for the purpose of combating annexation and reciprocity, and beginning with the edition of December 1, 1897, members of Congress regularly received complimentary copies of the paper. The reason for Spreckels' hostility to Hawaiian annexation was not the same in 1897-98 as it had been in 1893. On the earlier occasion the sugar king had thought that the application of United States immigration laws to

Hawaii would destroy the islands' contract labor system. In 1897-98 it was as a California beet sugar refiner, rather than as a Hawaiian cane grower, that Spreckels opposed annexation.

The Hawaiian minister at Washington, Francis M. Hatch, in a memorandum of late December 1897, explained the sugar king's attitude. First, Spreckels, who had recently lost control over the importation of Hawaiian sugar through the expiration in late 1897 of a five-year contract with the island planters, was fearful of competition from raw yellow sugar which would undersell his refined product. To insure that there was no competition with this "grocery grade" variety as it was called, Spreckels had stipulated in the five-year contract that the Hawaiian planters could sell this particular product only to the Western Sugar Refinery of San Francisco. Annexation would result in the duty-free admission of the relatively less expensive "grocery grade" sugar, which, in the absence of a contract with the island planters, would be marketed up and down the Pacific seaboard. Second, Hatch claimed that Spreckels feared that annexation might lead to the establishment of refineries in the islands, thereby breaking the monopoly of the Western Sugar Refinery Company.[7]

However, Spreckels did not wield much influence over California's politicians, business groups, or its newspapers.[8] Senator White, it has been shown, viewed annexation as threatening the state's beet sugar industry, but his stand was dictated mainly by ideological considerations. Because Senator George C. Perkins vacillated on the treaty, historian Richard D. Weigle suggests that the legislator was influenced by the California beet sugar interests.[9] While this is probably true to some degree, it is nevertheless doubtful that Perkins would have voted against the treaty in early 1898, when in fact he voted for the Newlands joint resolution that brought Hawaii into the Union. What seems most likely is that Perkins was influenced by sugar interests to the extent that he withheld his endorsement of the treaty but that party loyalty ultimately dictated his vote in favor of the joint resolution. The Los Angeles Chamber of Commerce passed a resolution opposing annexation on the ground that it would be "decidedly detrimental to the beet sugar interests of Southern California." On the other hand, the Los Angeles Board of Trade voted against annexation without mentioning sugar. The *Los Angeles Times* was one of the few major California newspapers to denounce McKinley's treaty, but its stand was based upon anti-imperialist sentiment.[10]

While Claus Spreckels was trying to marshal opinion in California against the accord, Henry T. Oxnard was doing likewise in the midwest. Working through the American Sugar Growers Society in Chicago, Oxnard circulated in Nebraska a letter warning of the danger posed by Hawaiian sugar to the promising beet industry in that state. Each recipient was asked to write his members of Congress urging the defeat of the annexation treaty. In order to insure that the Nebraska beet sugar farmers opposed treaty ratification, the Oxnards (that is, Henry and Robert, who were brothers and business partners) inserted into their contracts with the growers in that state the stipulation that if Hawaii were acquired they were to be penalized by a price reduction of fifty cents per ton.[11] The Beet Growers Association of Nebraska protested against the penalty clause and some farmers refused to grow any beets until it was repealed. When the defeat of the annexation pact seemed assured in April 1898, the clause was deleted. Notwithstanding the conflict with the Oxnards, the Beet Growers Association sent circulars throughout the country urging people to oppose the admission of the islands and to advise their spokesmen in Congress accordingly. Additional evidence of the pressure exerted by the Oxnards and the midwestern beet sugar interests is seen in various petitions sent to Capitol Hill entreating that Hawaii be kept out of the Union.[12]

Among the leading newspapers in Nebraska, both the Republican *Omaha Bee* and the Democratic *Omaha World-Herald* opposed annexation. However, neither based its stand upon sugar considerations. The *Bee* denied being influenced by the Oxnards, claimed that it had resisted the acquisition of Hawaii long before those brothers had become involved in the state's beet sugar enterprise, and declared that its position was predicated upon the belief that annexation would constitute an unwise departure from America's traditional foreign policy. As a secondary argument the *Bee* claimed that annexation would endanger the domestic beet sugar industry.[13]

It is difficult to assess the extent to which the Oxnards and the

Nebraska beet sugar interests influenced the two senators from that state—Populist William V. Allen and Republican John M. Thurston. Allen's brief Senate speech on January 12, 1898, against the treaty made no mention of sugar. Thurston did not speak on the Hawaiian matter in the Senate but the annexationists regarded him as an antagonist.[14] Thurston, under great pressure from the Oxnards, was probably influenced more than was Allen by the Nebraska sugar interests. It is reasonable to assume that neither of these legislators disregarded that industry when they formulated their respective positions on the treaty.

Not surprisingly, there was strong sentiment against Hawaiian annexation in Louisiana, too, the center of the nation's cane sugar enterprise. The *Louisiana Planter* complained about the unfair competition resulting from the Hawaiian growers' use of contract labor. The *New Orleans Daily Picayune* urged the state's cane producers to unite with the beet farmers throughout the country in voicing disapproval of both annexation and reciprocity. Minister Hatch correctly regarded both of the senators from Louisiana—Donelson Caffery and Samuel D. McEnery—as opponents of the pending treaty. Caffery had emphasized anti-imperialism in 1893. It is not known to what extent, if any, the basis for his opposition to Hawaiian annexation shifted by early 1898. During the summer of that year McEnery expressed apprehension about the effect annexation would have upon Louisiana's sugar industry.[15] Presumably, he had held the same position several months earlier when the Senate debate was taking place.

Secretary of Agriculture James Wilson dealt a sharp blow to the domestic sugar interests when he sent a letter to the upper house on January 17, 1898, asserting that the accession of Hawaii would not injure America's growers and refiners. The reasons for this, he said, were twofold: first, Hawaii's soil was nearing exhaustion, which would require planters to use expensive fertilizers; and second, annexation would end contract labor in the islands. But Henry T. Oxnard rebutted these arguments; the *Omaha Bee* disputed them and reiterated the dangers posed by annexation to Nebraska's beet sugar interests; and the *Louisiana Planter* charged Wilson with having sold out to the Republican Party leaders.[16]

While the skirmish continued over the potential dangers to beet sugar, a veritable propaganda war was shaping up over the role of the sugar trust. As was the case in the early 1890s the trust, as such, did not seem to take a clearly defined position on annexation.[17] It seems that the primary role of the American Sugar Refining Company during the treaty debate was that of a bogey. Both sides claimed to be opposing the giant sugar cartel. For example, anti-imperialist Stephen M. White asserted that the trust favored the acquisition of Hawaii, while expansionist-minded newspapers such as the *Washington Evening Star* insisted that it did not.[18] The confusion was compounded when Henry T. Oxnard denied that he and the American Sugar Refining Company took similar positions on the Hawaiian question. In a statement issued on January 27, 1898, he maintained that through annexation the trust hoped to obtain large quantities of cheap brown sugar to refine. "The talk of the opposition of the American trust," he affirmed, "is pure fabrication." Although some historians believe that the trust was against McKinley's treaty, the evidence needed to establish this point is lacking. What does appear certain is that during the winter of 1897–98 the American beet and cane producers, as distinct from the giant trust, launched their strongest campaign thus far against Hawaiian annexation. "The hardest fight against Hawaii is being made by the beet sugar interests headed by Claus Spreckels," Senator Lodge observed.[19]

In the late 1890s the proponents of Hawaiian annexation encountered a new enemy—organized labor. Although not all America's workers protested against annexation, such groups as the Sailors' Union of the Pacific, the San Francisco Central Labor Union, the San Francisco Labor Council, the Sacramento Federated Trades Council, the American Federation of Labor, the Knights of Labor, and many other workingmen's organizations certainly did so. Not until the signing of McKinley's Hawaiian treaty did the labor movement come to grips with the issue of American imperialism. Why the movement was not involved in the annexation dispute of 1893 remains an unanswered question. One may conjecture that by the late 1890s, but not earlier, the prolonged unemployment crisis made American workers increasingly apprehensive about competing for jobs with Hawaiian Asiatics migrating to the mainland, as they would be able to do after annexation. Moreover, at the beginning of the decade blue collar employees were probably extending their organizations and, like most other segments of American society, "looking inward," without perceiving that their interests might be affected by foreign affairs.[20]

The relatively nondoctrinaire American trade unions objected to McKinley's treaty principally because they believed that the annexation of Hawaii not only would bring contract labor to the United States but also would undermine the policy of Chinese exclusion, for which wage earners had fought since the end of the Civil War. On the west coast, where labor opposition to the treaty seems to have been the strongest, the *Coast Seamen's Journal* (the official organ of the Sailors' Union of the Pacific) claimed that if Hawaii were acquired it would be as "a slave State." As such the islands would have their full complement of senators and representatives in Washington defending a mode of labor abhorrent to American trade unions. But this intolerable situation could not last indefinitely, for as Lincoln had once said (and as the *Coast Seamen's Journal* frequently repeated): "No nation can exist part slave and part free." To show that the federal government apparently was not averse to sanctioning the contract system of labor, the periodical noted that President McKinley stated publicly that special laws might be enacted by Congress to accommodate the peculiar conditions existing in Hawaii.[21] The San Francisco Central Labor Union had similar apprehensions; on June 18, 1897, it drafted a petition attacking annexation on the basis of the contract labor issue and sent copies to California's senators in Washington.[22]

In the *American Federationist*, the official organ of the American Federation of Labor, Samuel Gompers warned that the acquisition of Hawaii would threaten American wage earners with servile contracts. The titular leader of the A.F. of L. alluded to the decision handed down by the Supreme Court on January 25, 1897 (*Robertson* v. *Baldwin*), upholding seamen's contracts even in instances where involuntary servitude was the palpable result of so doing. The admission of Hawaii, he said, would involve the Supreme Court in similar litigations concerning labor contracts in the islands and the verdicts reached would be even more disastrous for workers than the recent decision pertaining to seamen. Gompers admonished that those decisions which "will be applicable to the laborers of Hawaii will be equally enforcible [sic] upon the workers of the United States."[23] This warning was not without effect. At the annual convention of the A.F. of L. in December 1897, a resolution was passed which stated, in part, that America's acquisition of Hawaii would result in "the enslavement of labor in general." The San Francisco Call voiced its support for this action. Annexation Commissioner Lorrin A. Thurston, greatly concerned about the resolution, wrote to President Dole stressing the need to abolish contract labor in the islands.[24]

Even more menacing to labor than the detested contract system was the prospect of having to compete for jobs with Hawaiian Orientals. Furthermore, the Asiatic workers did not seem disposed to cooperate with unions; collective bargaining was utterly foreign to this class of labor. The Sailors' Union of the Pacific felt especially vulnerable to competition from Hawaiian Orientals and complained that passage of the treaty would practically nullify the policy of Chinese exclusion.[25] Of course, there was a strong element of racism implicit in such a view, which was consistent with the Kearneyism of the preceding generation in California. This is not to deny that anti-Chinese sentiment was nationwide; however, the California unions seemed to give special stress to the "yellow peril" argument.

Perhaps in anticipation of the charge that wage earners were seeking only their selfish economic interests, American labor organizations utilized a range of subsidiary arguments. Gompers insisted that Hawaii need not be acquired in order to protect the west coast. He argued that the possession of the archipelago would require the trebling of America's naval forces, "entailing expenditures and taxation, which . . . will be forced upon the shoulders of workers." Besides, America's laborers could be suppressed by a greatly strengthened military establishment. Without denying that United States trade in the Pacific might be increased by the annexation of Hawaii, the Coast Seamen's Journal doubted that the commercial benefits would outweigh the disadvantages. The American Federationist maintained that the United States would always have a safe market for her surplus manufactures in Hawaii, regardless of the outcome of the treaty fight. Annexation was merely a plot to safeguard the $30 million invested in the Polynesian archipelago by American capitalists, charged the *Journal of the Knights of Labor*—a portrayal of the expansionists that may have carried some weight with farmers in the South and West.[26]

When one looks at organized labor's objections to the Hawaiian treaty in a broad sense, it becomes evident that the trade unions subscribed to the basic assumptions of the anti-imperialists, with slight modifications, rather than to those of any radical group outside the mainstream of American society such as the socialists.[27] Perhaps because workingmen's organizations were striving for respectability and acceptance in the late nineteenth century, unions opposing Hawaiian annexation sanctified their protests by appealing to America's republican tradition. Some labor journals invoked the warnings of George Washington against the evils of foreign entanglements, and depicted imperialism as inimical to the welfare of the Republic and its democratic institutions. However, the terms "republic" and "democracy" were frequently given a nineteenth-century proletarian twist. Instead of idealizing the nonmonarchical, yeoman commonwealth of the preceding century, workingmen in the late 1890s envisioned Chinese exclusion laws, protective tariffs, and the recognition of labor's right to organize and resist capitalist exploitation. The *Coast Seamen's Journal* did not view democracy as resting upon the rule of a pluralistic Madisonian majority composed of competing classes and factions; instead, it declared: "Democracy rests upon the political power of the producing classes."[28] Because Hawaii's "producing classes," that is, the nonwhite field workers, had no "political power," they were regarded as unfit for American democracy. The prospect of incorporating into the Union a population of Oriental vassals with no conception of the democratic processes of government, combined with the threat of reviving the contract labor system, led some trade unionist journals to conclude that annexation would constitute a dangerous departure from America's republican tradition. In short, these journals warned that the passage of McKinley's treaty would mark America's first step down a foreboding path of empire.[29]

Although the labor opponents of Hawaiian annexation embraced the free enterprise system, with protective safeguards for the working classes, the evidence does not suggest that they were militant trade expansionists.[30] It has already been shown that the Sailors' Union of the Pacific was willing to forgo any commercial benefits of annexation. However, historian Ronald Radosh suggests that beginning in 1898 at least one very prominent labor leader who opposed annexation, namely, Samuel Gompers, favored the establishment of an "informal economic empire abroad" and thus was a vigorous trade expansionist at that time.[31] In virtually ignoring the Hawaiian treaty debate, however, that scholar presents no evidence showing that Gompers was an economic imperialist prior to the fall of 1898. If the A.F. of L. president was an ardent commercial expansionist at the time that the annexation pact was being discussed in the Senate, some evidence of this should be found in his writings. An examination of Gompers's correspondence does not indicate that he favored a policy of commercial imperialism. The labor leader's well-known article, "Should Hawaii Be Annexed?", which appeared in the *American Federationist*, made little mention of the commercial side of the issue. He commented briefly: "We hold our own in commerce and industry in these islands as against any country on the face of the globe. . . . Hence, for a safe market in the Hawaiian Islands for any surplus products which we may have, none can enter into successful competition with our people."[32]

Compare Gompers's statement with that of Senator William P. Frye of Maine, an undoubted expansionist but no labor leader, who in late January 1898 advocated Hawaiian annexation in the following words:

> If I were a dictator with absolute power in this Republic, I would build the Nicaragua Canal, I would annex the Hawaiian Islands, I would aid in the construction of a railroad from our Southern border down to Terra del Fuego [*sic*], I would establish swift steamship lines to China, Japan, Australia, and to every commercial port in South America, and then, by reciprocity treaty or in any other lawful way in which it can be done, I would participate largely in the trade of the Orient, and I would take entirely the trade of Mexico, of South America, and of the Central American states by the free admission of all our goods into them.[33]

This pronouncement, together with that of Gompers, suggests

major differences not only between Gompers and Frye, but also between the imperialists and anti-imperialists, over America's trade in the Pacific.[34] In terms of scope of vision, the A.F. of L. president mentioned only the American-Hawaiian traffic and was pleased that the United States was holding her own. Frye, on the other hand, envisioned a much larger potential market embracing practically every continent bordering the Pacific. The Maine senator was not content for the United States to hold her own or to compete favorably with other countries in this ocean-wide market; he wanted undisputed commercial hegemony. Furthermore, Gompers made no mention of the specific steps to be taken for the purpose of increasing trade, whereas Frye had a grandiose plan which included an isthmian canal, a hemispheric railroad, steamship lines traversing the entire Pacific, and reciprocity treaties with practically every nation using that ocean. The only items the senator neglected to mention were an enlarged navy and a submarine cable connecting the United States mainland with Hawaii—and his failure to urge these was doubtless a mere oversight, for he had been a consistent champion of such undertakings. Lloyd C. Gardner, Walter F. LaFeber, and Thomas J. McCormick have declared, as noted earlier, that the opponents of empire "took second place to none in affirming the need for overseas markets." Clearly, in the Hawaiian treaty controversy of 1897–98 the trade union critics of annexation took a distant second place to the imperialists when it came to advocating commercial expansion.

The most vigilant and effective adversaries of McKinley's annexation pact were the ideological foes of empire.[35] Even before it was submitted to the Senate, Carl Schurz had sought from the recently inducted president some assurance that Hawaii would not be acquired. On the day that the treaty went to the upper chamber, Stephen M. White said he was prepared to stay in Washington all summer in order to prevent ratification.[36] Also, the anti-imperialist press (spearheaded by the *New York Times*, the *Evening Post*, and *The Nation*) lost no time in voicing disapproval of the convention.

The arguments of the anti-imperialists in 1897–98 were basically the same as those used in 1893–94. Once again special emphasis was given to the ideological (that is, to the republican, historical, constitutional, and racial) objections to annexation. Senator White was one of the first anti-imperialists to publish a major article attacking McKinley's treaty. His thesis, which was the most powerful argument against the treaty, was that the United States should adhere to her republican tradition and not embark upon a new policy of imperialism. In addition to quoting the writings of past American statesmen in this regard, the California senator excerpted a paragraph from John Sherman's autobiography, *Recollections of Forty Years* (1895), which warned that the Republic would be imperiled by the acquisition of distant dependencies. The possession of Hawaii by the United States, said White, would mark the beginning of a dangerous departure from America's traditional foreign policy. If Hawaii were taken, Samoa would be acquired next, he warned.[37]

Speaker of the House Thomas B. Reed denounced imperialism in a highly publicized article entitled "Empire Can Wait." The *American Monthly Review of Reviews* predicted that the title of this piece would "become the rallying cry for the opponents of Hawaiian annexation."[38] Reed's essay was essentially an apologia of Baron de Montesquieu's small republic theory. Vast geographical distances and separate regions within the United States, said the House Speaker, presented serious obstacles to the attainment of national unity. He argued that in order for the common interest to be promoted the American people had to "be in touch with each other."[39] The acquisition of overseas dependencies would imperil the already fragile union of states, and modern America, like ancient Rome, would destroy herself as a result. Although this might be the fate of all great civilizations, concluded Reed, there was no compelling reason why the United States should rush the process.

In an editorial entitled "The Momentous Decision," presumably written by E. L. Godkin, *The Nation* agreed with Captain Alfred T. Mahan that the absorption of Hawaii would launch the United States upon a new career of empire. Such a course, said Godkin, constituted a perversion of America's mission to extend her republican institutions, including "law and liberty, and brotherly kindness," by example instead of by "guns and trumpets."[40]

One of the most influential publicists of the anti-imperialist cause in 1897 was the Englishman James Bryce. His essay, "The Policy of Annexation for America," was widely quoted in the leading American journals and newspapers. It argued cogently that Britain's tropical possessions in Africa and India had proved to be burdensome liabilities rather than orderly, self-governing commonwealths. Since Great Britain, with centuries of colonizing experience, had so much difficulty governing her tropical dependencies, it did not seem likely that the more democratic United States, which lacked an imperial tradition, would serve her own best interests by annexing Hawaii. Imperialism would lead to militarism, and both were incompatible with the republican maxims of the founders, he affirmed.[41] It was as though the venerable British sage were using two optical instruments to teach the lessons of statecraft to Americans: the first being a mirror to reflect the enviable image of their past and present Republic; and the second being a telescope to gaze across oceans and time into the abyss of empire.

Opposition to Hawaiian annexation was also forthcoming from two elder American statesmen who were to become prominent in the affairs of the Anti-Imperialist League: Grover Cleveland and George S. Boutwell. On January 24, 1898, the former Democratic president denounced the proposed acquisition of Hawaii as "a perversion of our national mission."[42] Boutwell, a Republican who formerly represented Massachusetts in both houses of Congress, delivered a lengthy address before the Boot and Shoe Club of Boston on December 22, 1897, criticizing Hawaiian annexation mainly on the ground that it would jeopardize America's republican institutions. The United States federal system was not intended to embrace overseas colonies, averred Boutwell.[43]

Addressing the national Democratic convention in September 1897, Moorfield Storey, a mugwump Republican, admonished that the passage of McKinley's treaty would constitute "the first step in an absolutely new departure from the settled policy of this country." If Hawaii were annexed, he feared that a dangerous precedent would be established for the eventual admission of Cuba into the Union.[44]

Constitutional historian Hermann E. Von Holst, in a speech to the Commercial Club of Chicago on January 29, 1898, warned that the annexation of Hawaii would lead to further acquisitions of insular territory. The ratification of the pending treaty, he cautioned, would repudiate the teachings of Washington's Farewell Address and would mark the beginning of a new and unsafe imperialistic policy for the United States. So momentous was this contemplated departure, said Von Holst, that throughout the whole span of American history the Hawaiian issue was out-ranked in importance only by the struggle for independence from Britain, the adoption of the Constitution, and the war to preserve the Union.[45]

In 1897, as in 1893, some anti-imperialists argued that annexa-tion would be inconsistent with America's traditional "hands off" policy toward Hawaii. Disagreeing sharply with President McKinley's declaration that annexation would be a fitting sequel to America's long history of close relations with the Pacific archipelago, Senator White said in "The Proposed Annexation" article that the history of those relations showed only that the United States favored Hawaiian autonomy coupled with strong commercial ties between the two nations. Schurz expressed a similar view, as did the *New York Times*.[46]

The constitutional argument against the passage of McKin-ley's treaty received extended, though unconvincing, treatment by Daniel Agnew, a Republican and former justice of the Penn-sylvania Supreme Court. Agnew built his case upon two prem-ises, the first of which was that the Constitution contained no provision explicitly allowing for the annexation of foreign territory by treaty or otherwise, and that such a power could not be implied. Precedents did not amend the Constitution, he in-sisted. His second premise was that acquisitions of foreign territory could be "justified" (Agnew's term) only if they could be regarded as an "imperative necessity" by the federal government.

The former justice recited briefly the earlier cases of annexa-tion involving Louisiana, Florida, Texas, and Alaska; and, without attesting to their constitutionality, asserted that each was justified because it met some "imperative necessity." According to him the same could not be said for Hawaii, which offered only commer-cial advantages that were offset by the undesirable population of the islands. Moreover, he warned, the admission of Hawaii into the Union would surely lead to further acquisitions such as Cuba, Santo Domingo, and other islands in the Caribbean. Agnew asserted that, given the above reasons, the ratification of McKinley's treaty would be "unconstitutional, unwise, and dangerous."[47]

This argument was, of course, flagrantly inconsistent. While declaring all accessions of foreign territory (which presumably would include Louisiana, Florida, Texas, and Alaska) to be unconstitutional, he disapproved only of Hawaii's incorporation. In effect, he was inadvertently arguing against Hawaiian annexation on grounds other than constitutional ones, namely, on those of "imperative necessity" and race. This being the case, the title of his article, "Unconstitutionality of the Hawaiian Treaty," was misleading to say the least.

A stronger and more concise constitutional argument against the treaty appeared in *The Nation* under the title, "How Are We to Govern Hawaii?" In that article Godkin asseverated that before reaching a decision on annexation, the Senate should consider the problem of how the archipelago would be governed if brought into the Union. He then proceeded to raise such thorny questions about the manner of government as to prove, at least to his own satisfaction, the folly of granting statehood. Consequently, only a territorial status remained. In every case involving the acquisition of territory since the Ordinance of 1787 local governments were established by universal suffrage. But if universal suffrage prevailed in Hawaii, annexation itself would be rejected. Furthermore, Godkin depicted restricted suffrage in the islands as inconsistent with Section 1859 of the *Revised Statutes of the United States Respecting Territories*, which declared that all male citizens above the age of twenty-one are entitled to vote and hold office in the Territories.[48] Yet, if this law were implemented in Hawaii, the Americans would be voted out of office, and Godkin did not wish that to happen. Until these difficulties connected with governing the Pacific archipelago were resolved in a manner compatible with the United States code of laws, the question of annexation should be held in abeyance, he declared.

Although most anti-imperialists seemed to take for granted

the racial superiority of Anglo-Saxons, the opponents of the treaty exhibited an array of attitudes concerning Hawaii's nonwhite population. Senator White regarded the Polynesians as both civilized and literate, but he was not so complimentary about the Orientals inhabiting the archipelago. Former Senator Fred T. Dubois of Idaho, who with Senator Richard F. Pettigrew of South Dakota visited Hawaii during the fall of 1897 for the purpose of discovering how the islanders felt about annexation, found them "a kind and gentle and humane people." And American physician Prince A. Morrow, while believing that the susceptibility of the Polynesians to leprosy was sufficient reason to reject annexation, noted their "fine physical qualities and superior intelligence."[49]

Of course, there was within the anti-imperialists' camp a large degree of hostility toward Hawaii's nonwhite residents. One publicist warned in the pages of a leading journal that if annexation occurred, the "detested and dangerous Asiatic" would be a baneful influence in American elections. The *Los Angeles Times* inveighed against incorporating the "semi-savage" inhabitants of the Pacific archipelago. J. D. Spreckels' *San Francisco Call* shrilled in banner headlines: "Hordes of Coolies in Hawaii Waiting to Come." Organized labor, especially on the Pacific coast, evinced a great deal of bigotry toward Hawaii's Orientals, who were referred to as "leprous Asiatics" by the *Coast Seamen's Journal*.[50] Doubtless, the southern anti-imperialists and their newspapers vented their share of racial vendetta and hyperbole upon Hawaii's dark-skinned people.

Notwithstanding this range of opinion, the critics of empire were nearly unanimous in their belief that no transfer of sovereignty should take place without the consent of the natives of Hawaii. The expansionists showed no such regard for the Polynesians.

The commercial and strategic arguments for annexing Hawaii were given special emphasis in the treaty dispute of 1897–98 as a result of the partitioning of China and the continuing strife in Cuba.[51] The anti-imperialists rose to the challenge. Carl Schurz argued in a *Harper's Weekly* editorial that the dismemberment of the Celestial Empire was more likely to serve than to injure America's commercial interests in the Far East.[52] He reminded readers that before the recent intervention very few Chinese ports were open to Yankee merchantmen. The editor believed that as a result of the European presence in China more harbors than ever before would be opened to American trade; he cited Britain's establishment of free ports as a precedent. America was the most powerful nation in the world, he contended, and, therefore, would have no difficulty in securing her fair share of commerce in Asia. The annexation of Hawaii, a distant unguarded outpost in the Pacific, would only compromise her chances.

In another *Harper's Weekly* editorial Schurz responded to a recent address by Senator Frye to the National Association of Manufacturers in New York. Frye had told businessmen that the United States, through her citizens, owned $30 million worth of property in Hawaii and controlled nearly ninety-three percent of the commerce of the islands, which amounted to $23 million in 1897. If the annexation accord were rejected, warned the Maine senator, this considerable market would be lost. Schurz countered by stating that the Hawaiian property and trade had been acquired by the United States or her citizens while the islands remained independent, and that the archipelago need not be annexed in order to retain these commercial benefits.[53]

Senator White concurred, declaring in "The Proposed Annexation" that acquisition was unnecessary to preserve American trade with the islands. A properly framed reciprocity treaty would bring "all desirable Hawaiian commerce to the United States." George S. Boutwell was in basic agreement except that he thought that the existing reciprocity treaty furnished the United States with sufficient commercial benefits.[54]

Fred T. Dubois, back from his recent trip to Hawaii, believed that the administration wanted to annex the islands primarily to expand the China trade. In a series of public lectures, he argued that the United States already had a tremendous home market that could absorb her surplus manufactures and therefore, "We do not need any other market." Japan and China, in his opinion, would dominate the trade of Asia. Senator Pettigrew had Dubois's statements printed as official Senate documents.[55]

The *New York Times*, which was in the vanguard of the newspaper opposition to the treaty, suggested editorially on

January 25, 1898 that instead of annexing the islands the United States should follow Britain's example in Asia and make Hawaii a free port. Then all the commercial powers could compete on equal terms in the trade of the Pacific.

Seldom did any of the leading anti-imperialists advert to any pressing need to construct an isthmian waterway or lay a cable between the west coast and Hawaii in order to increase American commerce in the Pacific. They were practically unanimous in their aversion to building a larger navy to protect trade. This author's examination of the public statements and private correspondence of nearly all the anti-imperialists mentioned thus far in this chapter revealed that during the treaty fight of 1897–98 these gentlemen did not come close to envisioning the extensive commercial empire conceived of by Cushman K. Davis, William P. Frye, Henry Cabot Lodge, Alfred T. Mahan, John T. Morgan, and Henry M. Teller. The opponents of McKinley's annexation treaty favored commercial prosperity; but few, if any, were militant trade expansionists.[56]

The critics of empire marshaled an array of arguments against the notion that the United States must absorb Hawaii for strategic or military reasons. Senator White prepared a comprehensive rebuttal to the defense argument, which appeared in the *Forum* article in August 1897. He began by noting that Hawaii was unfortified and that a large navy would have to be built to protect the islands in case of war. A naval fleet of this magnitude would require years to build (he mentioned that it took nearly eighteen months to turn out one twelve-inch gun) at a cost of at least $100 million per year. Consequently, he said, the inadequate coastal defenses would continue to be neglected.

In the event of a war in the Pacific, White thought that the most likely targets of an enemy attack would be such seaports as San Francisco. If the assailant were Britain, then the threat would come from Esquimault, and America's defenses in Hawaii would be useless in protecting the west coast. If the enemy were Japan, which seemed improbable to the legislator, the Mikado's fleet would have to sail 3,600 miles just to reach Honolulu. In White's opinion, the Japanese did not regard Hawaii as sufficiently valuable to attempt her conquest. In the unlikely event that Japan did seize Hawaii, the senator believed that America's weakly guarded Pacific seaboard would be in no greater danger. "If we are to defend ourselves, we must do so at home," said White.[57]

Next, the California senator denied the contention that it was necessary to annex Hawaii in order to guard the western terminus of the prospective Nicaraguan Canal. Because of the distances involved, that future waterway could be defended much more effectively from California than from Hawaii, he argued.[58] Nor did White believe that the isthmus would be imperiled if Hawaii were occupied by an enemy.

In response to the assertion that the United States needed Hawaii as a coaling station, the senator averred that Pearl Harbor could be used without possessing the islands. An even better choice, said White, would be to use the Aleutian Islands, which were much closer to the usual steamship route between Asia and North America.

Although most of the discussion over the Hawaiian treaty of 1897 took place in the press, the annexation issue was given sporadic consideration in the Senate from December 1897 through early March 1898. When Congress reconvened in late 1897, Senator George F. Hoar of Massachusetts, who at that time probably opposed annexation, presented a remonstrance against the pending treaty from the Hawaiian Patriotic League, signed by 21,269 citizens of the island republic.[59] White of California presented a protest from the Federated Trades Council of Sacramento,[60] and similar petitions were offered by other senators. Liliuokalani's presence in Washington doubtless gave an added fillip to the anti-imperialist cause. Although the opponents of the treaty failed to get the House Democrats and Populists to declare against annexation in caucus, opposition to ratification remained strong as the year drew to a close.

When the Senate reassembled in early January 1898, the Hawaiian matter came up for debate. An intermittent nine-week discussion was held in executive session at the insistence of the expansionists and, therefore, no transcript of the speeches was made. However, a fairly clear idea of what the anti-imperialists said and did can be gained by using other sources of information.[61]

While the treaty was under consideration in the upper house

most of the speech-making was done by the annexationists. However, the anti-imperialists were not entirely inactive. On January 12 Senator William V. Allen, a Nebraska Populist, briefly assailed the military argument for annexation and denied the suitability of Hawaii's mixed population for American citizenship. One week later Augustus O. Bacon of Georgia offered an amendment providing that the treaty could not become operative until approved by a majority of the voters in Hawaii; it was sent to committee and eventually tabled.[62]

During the latter half of January the silver question intruded, causing a temporary rift among the expansionists, and the upper chamber did not resume discussion of the treaty until February 1, when White and Pettigrew raised the familiar anti-imperialist arguments. The Senate had pending before it a resolution offered by Pettigrew on January 28 declaring it to be American policy not to acquire territory that required a navy to defend it. The measure, derived from a Jeffersonian maxim, was buried in committee. On February 3 White proposed a resolution stating that the people of Hawaii had a right to govern themselves and that foreign intervention in the islands would be regarded as unfriendly to the United States. This was essentially a restatement of the Turpie resolution adopted by the Senate in May 1894. White's measure lay over until February 7 when Morgan crippled it by submitting an amendment (in the form of a joint resolution) providing for the annexation of Hawaii. White then abandoned his resolution, which was subsequently tabled in committee. The anti-imperialists, for good reason, regarded the introduction of Morgan's amendment as an admission by the expansionists that the treaty was in serious trouble. The opponents of annexation reasoned that if the friends of the treaty were confident of its ratification, they would not have proposed a joint resolution, which required only a simple majority in both houses for its passage. Significantly, on the same day that Morgan offered his amendment Henry M. Teller of Colorado, a leading annexationist, expressed openly before the Senate his doubt that the treaty would be ratified.[63]

Because the annexationists were uncertain about whether or not they had the two-thirds majority needed in the Senate, they

decided at first to maneuver for a test vote on an amendment by
Bacon which provided that a plebiscite be taken in the islands
before the treaty could become effective. Naturally, they opposed Bacon's amendment, but they wanted to see whether two-
thirds of the senators would vote against it. If not, then the treaty
probably would not pass, in which case the expansionists planned
to resort to a joint resolution.[64] But the test vote was never taken.
With appropriation bills yet to be considered, and facing
demands for prompt adjournment when that business was completed, the expansionists on the Foreign Relations Committee
then decided on March 5 to proceed at once by way of a joint
resolution. At least one prominent historian has mistakenly
claimed that this decision was followed by McKinley's withdrawal of the treaty from the Senate.[65] The evidence clearly
shows, however, that the pact remained pending in the upper
chamber as a warning to other nations that might have designs
upon Hawaii.[66]

Meanwhile, the House deliberated briefly—but openly—on
the Hawaiian matter. On January 15 James H. Lewis of Washington offered a resolution requesting from the president a copy of
the treaty as well as an explanation of the authority by which the
chief executive could contract for the payment of the Hawaiian
debt without the approval of Congress. When the proposal was
tabled, Lewis modified its language and submitted it as a new
resolution. But it, too, was laid on the table.[67]

At least one major speech against the treaty was heard in the
lower house when Henry U. Johnson of Indiana spoke on
February 22. Johnson scored Hawaiian annexation mainly on
anti-imperialist grounds. He viewed the Hawaiian question as one
of the most far-reaching, in terms of its consequences, with which
the Senate had had to deal in the past quarter of a century and
blamed the secrecy of the proceedings in the upper chamber for
the public apathy. The Indiana congressman recalled the
shameful role of the United States in the Hawaiian Revolution of
1893 and the subsequent suppression of the natives by the
provisional government. The Polynesians were opposed to
annexation, he insisted, and forcing union upon them without
their consent was un-American. After critiquing the strategic and

commercial arguments for acquiring the islands, Johnson came to "the most lamentable feature of this entire transgression"—the dangerous precedent that would be established by ratification of the treaty. Hawaii would feed America's growing appetite for empire, he feared. Next, imperialists would clamor for Cuba, and then Samoa. Such a betrayal of America's republican tradition would usher in decay and disintegration. Thus, we see in Johnson's speech a restatement of the main argument that had been used by the anti-annexationists since 1893 to keep Hawaii out of the Union. Anticipating that a joint resolution would soon be before the House, Johnson urged his fellow congressmen not to rush with "indecent haste" into a momentous decision. So warm was the applause given this speech that Charles H. Grosvenor of Ohio, an ardent expansionist, felt impelled to deliver a point by point rebuttal nearly four months later when the House was deliberating on the Newlands joint resolution.[68]

Why did the attempt to ratify the treaty of 1897 end in defeat? John W. Foster, the treaty's drafter, suggested that during the winter of 1897–98 the Cuban situation diverted the attention of senators away from the Hawaiian treaty.[69] However, even if the Cuban situation had not existed, it is unlikely that the treaty would have passed at that time. According to newspaper polls and other estimates, the annexationists were between three and ten votes short of the necessary two-thirds majority in the Senate in mid-June 1897, and the evidence indicates that this deficit had not been made up by the following December, at which time Cuban affairs had just begun to preoccupy the government.[70] Although the Cuban problem did divert the attention of Washington away from Hawaii, it was not the main reason for the defeat of the treaty.

Foster also alluded to the partisanship of the Democratic senators as an important reason for the defeat of the accord. While this was a factor, it was of relatively little importance. The Democratic Party platform of 1896 made no mention of the Hawaiian issue. William Jennings Bryan, the titular head of that party, seemed to favor (or at the very least not to oppose) Hawaiian annexation in July 1897. Senator White was urged by the California Democratic organization to support the acquisition of the islands and his refusal to do so led to a bitter attack on him by the Democratic *San Francisco Examiner*. Moreover, the treaty of 1897 was supported by such major Democratic newspapers as the *New York Evening Journal* and *Herald*. Senator John T. Morgan of Alabama was one of the leading supporters of annexation and at least six of his fellow Democrats in the upper house sided with him. In short, the Democratic Party, as such, took no stand on the Hawaiian issue.[71] Cushman K. Davis, a staunch Republican, blamed four members of his own party—Senators Morrill, Thurston, Spooner, and Gear—for the failure of the treaty.[72] Senator Pettigrew was another active Republican opponent.

Outside the Senate chambers, the beet sugar and labor interests mounted a campaign against annexation. As between these two interests, the diplomatic dispatches of the Hawaiian officials in Washington, as well as the correspondence of Senate expansionists such as Lodge, indicate that beet sugar exerted much more pressure on Capitol Hill than did all of the labor organizations combined.[73]

If there was one bond which more than any other united such disparate elements as Republicans, Democrats, Populists, silverites, labor leaders, and sugar spokesmen, it was anti-imperialism, the notion that Hawaii's admission would mark an abandonment of America's time-tested anti-colonial tradition and would embark the Republic upon the perilous course of empire. Indeed, most of what Senator White wrote in "The Proposed Annexation of Hawaii" could just as easily have been ascribed to Morrill of Vermont, Bacon of Georgia, Allen of Nebraska, Pettigrew of South Dakota, Gompers of the A. F. of L., or the editor of the pro-sugar newspaper, the *Omaha Bee*. Another way of analyzing the defeat of the treaty is to raise the question: why did the anti-imperialists triumph? This certainly was not due to their superior organization, nor to any disparity in the abilities of the two sides to articulate their viewpoints. And neither side was more resolute than the other. The basic fact is simply that the anti-imperialists carried the day by appealing to hallowed American doctrines decrying territorial expansion overseas.

During the spring of 1898, however, an intensified scramble

among the powers for spheres of influence in China raised fears around the world of a major war. This dangerous turn of events spotlighted the importance of Hawaii as a base in the volatile Pacific. The sudden alarm over the Far East, as will be shown presently, augured the defeat of the anti-annexationists.

9

The Defeat of the
Anti-Annexationists

After a brief hiatus in the Hawaiian controversy the Foreign Relations Committee on March 16, 1898, reported favorably an annexation resolution presented by Senator John T. Morgan. Ominous developments in China, where the great European powers were presenting demands that threatened to lead to the imminent partitioning of the old empire and even to a general European war, may have helped stimulate the committee's move. Accompanying the resolution was a lengthy document setting forth the commercial and strategic reasons why the islands should be acquired, and rebutting twenty arguments of the anti-imperialists.[1] The committee action elicited very little response from the opposition press. Cuban matters, especially the anticipated report on the *Maine* explosion, seemed to occupy the attention of Washington and the rest of the nation. In mid-April Hawaiian Minister Francis M. Hatch observed a "lukewarmness" toward annexation on Capitol Hill,[2] and after the United States decision to intervene in Cuba the Senate became bogged down with a war revenue bill.

Since the annexation movement seemed checked in the Senate, the administration turned to the House, where a joint resolution was introduced on May 4 by Francis G. Newlands of Nevada. But Hatch told his government that the opposition had "great strength, and . . . will fight us to the very utmost;" he depicted Speaker Thomas B. Reed of Maine as the major obstacle to the passage of Newlands's resolution.[3] Nevertheless, the anti-imperialists feared that the war with Spain might give an impetus to the annexation movement, and some of them felt called upon to make their views known. Carl Schurz advised McKinley in early May that annexation was not only unnecessary to prosecute the war but would confirm European suspicions that the United States was fighting for territory rather than humanity. Annexation could "safely wait." John Sherman, recently replaced by William

R. Day as secretary of state, expressed the same views. At a commencement address at the Lawrenceville School in New Jersey on June 21 former President Cleveland gave warning that the United States must not be lured into a policy of imperialism by the conflict with Spain.[4]

The Newlands annexation resolution was reported favorably by the Foreign Affairs Committee on May 17. Chairman Robert R. Hitt of Illinois cited strategic and commercial reasons in support of the committee action. The minority report, authored by Hugh A. Dinsmore of Arkansas, advanced eight objections to annexation and offered a substitute resolution pledging the United States to guarantee the independence of the islands. Dinsmore emphasized that the people of Hawaii had a right to be consulted about the proposed transfer of sovereignty, that Congress lacked the constitutional power to admit by joint resolution territory not destined for statehood, and that Hawaii's mixed population was not assimilable with that of the American Republic. The report mentioned the remoteness of the islands, as well as the difficulty of defending them, and held that they were needed neither to protect the Pacific coast nor to promote commerce. In general, the minority report stressed that the acquisition of Hawaii would constitute "a new departure from our historical course."[5]

Expansionist sentiment was quite strong in the House and there was little doubt that that body would pass the Newlands measure when it was brought to a vote. However, Speaker Reed used his powerful influence as chairman of the Committee on Rules to prevent the fixing of a voting date. In late May Senator Henry Cabot Lodge of Massachusetts complained to Theodore Roosevelt that "the opposition now comes exclusively from Reed, who is straining every nerve to beat Hawaii."[6] Senator Morgan made a similar observation and warned that the Speaker was trying to defeat the Newlands proposal by working for an early adjournment of Congress. For three weeks the Maine congressman nearly single-handedly obstructed the passage of the joint resolution. House expansionists, led by Charles H. Grosvenor of Ohio, applied strong pressure to bring the Hawaiian matter up for consideration in the lower chamber. Reed eventually felt compelled to consent, and it was arranged to begin the House debate on June 11 and vote four days later.

Tyler Dennett declared that the Hawaiian debate which ensued in the House and then in the Senate (June 20–July 6) was "one of the greatest in . . . American congressional history."[7] Many of the critics of expansion said that the Hawaiian issue was the most important controversy in the nation's history since the Civil War. Anti-imperialists in both houses of Congress assailed the Newlands joint resolution on ideological, strategic, and economic grounds. The most frequently cited objection (as had been the case since 1893) was that the acquisition of Hawaii would constitute a dangerous departure from America's republican tradition and augur the beginning of imperialism.[8] The anti-annexationists feared that passage of the Newlands proposal would lead to large standing armies and an expanded navy—in short, militarism, which they regarded as inimical to democracy. The Hawaiian issue involved far more than the accession of eight or so islands in the North Pacific. Anti-expansionists in Congress observed that the same reasoning that was being employed to bring Hawaii into the Union could be used to justify additional territorial acquisitions. They made numerous references to the general policy of imperialism that would be inaugurated by the passage of the Newlands joint resolution. Senator Donelson Caffery of Louisiana spoke for dozens of like-minded colleagues on Capitol Hill when he admonished: "The Hawaiian scheme is but the entering wedge that cleaves a way open for empire." Samoa and Spain's insular possessions would be acquired next, warned the anti-imperialists.[9]

The anti-expansionists argued that annexation was contrary to the United States' historical policy toward Hawaii. Senator Justin S. Morrill of Vermont, for example, asserted that ever since the enunciation of the Tyler Doctrine in 1842, America had consistently proclaimed Hawaii's independence. He concluded that the acquisition of those islands would be regarded by the European powers as a breach of "our recorded word."[10]

Constitutional objections to the proposed acquisition of Hawaii were given more emphasis in mid-1898 than ever before.

Doubtless this was due to the fact that annexationists resorted to the use of a joint resolution. Whereas during the earlier debates over Hawaii's admission into the Union anti-imperialists questioned the constitutionality of annexing the islands by treaty, in the summer of 1898 few such objections were heard. This was probably due not only to the annexationists' recourse to a joint resolution but also to the confidence of the anti-expansionists that a treaty could be beaten decisively if a vote were taken.

However, if there was little talk about the constitutionality of annexation by treaty, there was a great deal of debate over the constitutionality of a joint resolution. Senator Augustus O. Bacon of Georgia and other anti-imperialists argued that the accession of territory by the United States was legally permissible only under the treaty-making power of the Constitution.[11] To attempt the acquisition of Hawaii by a joint resolution, they maintained, would infringe upon the exclusive prerogatives of the Senate and chief executive to act in matters relating to the incorporation of foreign territory.[12] Interestingly, several key opponents of annexation in the House concurred in this view. The opponents of empire argued that if the treaty-ratifying powers of the Senate were usurped by resorting to a legislative act, a dangerous precedent would be established. Also, they declared that a joint resolution could have no binding effect upon people residing outside the jurisdiction within which such a measure was passed; hence, the Newlands proposal could not become operative in Hawaii.

The anti-imperialists denied that the acquisition of Texas by joint resolution in 1845 offered a precedent for admitting Hawaii. Most anti-annexationists in mid-1898 believed that Texas had been brought into the Union legally under the congressional power to admit new states. But since statehood was not proposed for Hawaii, they insisted that those islands could be annexed only by the exercise of the treaty-making power.

Senator William B. Bate of Tennessee averred that the use of a precedent had to be sustained by analogous facts. From this premise he argued that Texas was contiguous territory which, prior to 1845, had been settled by white Americans. Furthermore, Bate noted that the joint resolution utilized in the Texas case was approved by a plebiscite held in the Lone Star Republic. Hawaii, by contrast, was a distant archipelago, not destined for statehood, and populated mainly by nonwhites who were to be given no vote in the matter of annexation.[13]

Also, the anti-imperialists rejected the expansionists' claims that the islands could be annexed under various other constitutional provisions and related political doctrines. Senator William V. Allen of Nebraska disputed the notion that Hawaii could be acquired under the aegis of the general-welfare clause. That provision had to be construed in terms of the founders' intentions as evidenced in the Constitution itself and in other documents of that earlier period. Stephen M. White of California, the leader of the Senate anti-imperialists, declared that Hawaii could not be annexed legitimately by use of the president's war power as commander in chief since the constitutional provision pertaining thereto applied only to the seizure of property belonging to an enemy. In response to Senator Henry M. Teller's assertion that the authority to annex territory was derived from the sovereignty belonging to every national ruling body, Senator Thomas B. Turley of Tennessee retorted that the federal government was not fully sovereign and possessed only delegated powers.[14]

Not surprisingly the anti-imperialists objected to passage of the Newlands joint resolution on racial grounds. Mainly they held that the non-Caucasian people of the Pacific archipelago were not capable of handling the responsibilities of United States citizenship and that if Hawaii were annexed she would constitute a pernicious influence in American electoral politics.[15]

As on earlier occasions the congressional opponents of Hawaiian annexation exhibited an array of attitudes toward the mixed population of the islands. Senator Richard F. Pettigrew of South Dakota observed that a higher rate of literacy existed among the native islanders than could be found among the people of the United States. Senator Bate described the Polynesians as "a docile, unsuspecting, and honest race of people." The Japanese were portrayed as being "industrious" and "great manufacturers" by another congressional anti-expansionist. At the other end of the spectrum could be found a considerable degree of racial hostility toward Hawaii's nonwhite elements. One opponent of the Newlands measure, whose sentiments were echoed by others, depicted the Hawaiians as "ignorant and brutal" and balked at the prospect of absorbing into the Union "this variegated agglomeration of the fag-ends of humanity."[16]

Seldom, however, did the anti-expansionists claim that the inhabitants of Hawaii were not capable of self-government, and the assailants of the joint resolution were practically unanimous in their conviction that annexation should not occur without holding a plebiscite in the islands open to all adult males. Senator Bacon offered an amendment to the Newlands measure to this effect, but it was defeated by the annexationists.[17]

Because of the martial spirit, or the "jingo bacillus" as one congressman termed it, that infused the American people in mid-1898, the anti-imperialists went to great lengths to demonstrate that Hawaii was of little strategic value to the United States. The primary military argument with which the opponents of the Newlands joint resolution had to contend was that, allegedly, it was necessary to annex Hawaii in order to prosecute the war against Spain. After Commodore George Dewey's resounding victory over Rear Admiral Patricio Montojo y Paserón at Manila Bay on May 1, many expansionists insisted that the United States had to possess Hawaii in order to send supplies and reinforcements to the imperiled American forces in the Philippines.[18] Senators White and Pettigrew arranged for the printing in the *Congressional Record* of detailed charts and maps showing that the United States harbor at Kiska in the Aleutian Islands was situated along the shortest route from the west coast to Manila. They asserted that over 400 miles and at least three days' sailing time could be saved by steaming from San Francisco to the Philippine capital by way of the northern course rather than over the Hawaiian route. The lack of coal at Kiska could be remedied easily by sending a fleet of colliers there. Moreover, Pettigrew noted that most ships could not carry sufficient coal to get from Honolulu to Manila, whereas virtually all American naval vessels could carry enough fuel to steam from Kiska to the Philippines. In response to the claim that the harbor at Kiska was shrouded in fog and beset with dangerous shoals, currents, and icebergs, the anti-imperialists replied that the Canadian Pacific Line (which had the record time for crossing the Pacific) utilized that Alaskan port regularly during winter and summer.

The opponents of the Newlands measure said that if a coaling station were needed at Hawaii, which they did not concede, it could be had without annexation. Senator White quoted a recent statement by former Secretary of State John Sherman to that effect. In answer to the contention that United States rights at Pearl Harbor could be abrogated with the reciprocity agreement, White affirmed that if that were true, suitable treaty arrangements for a permanent naval facility at that harbor would not be difficult to obtain. If a military installation were needed at Pearl Harbor, stated the California senator, that circumstance did not necessitate the annexation of the entire Hawaiian archipelago. Reasoning by analogy, he remarked satirically: "If we need a coaling station in China, it does not follow that we need China."

In response to the expansionists' claim that the United States should approve the Newlands resolution in order to prevent further violations of Hawaii's neutrality by American troops, the critics of annexation replied that no untoward consequences were likely to follow from these breaches of international law. Aside from Spain, the European powers had not protested against the preferential treatment accorded the United States by the island Republic. Senator White declared that Madrid did not have the capacity to retaliate against Hawaii for aiding the American forces. Moreover, the anti-imperialists averred that Uncle Sam was in a position to assume any claim for damages brought against Hawaii or to compel prostrate Spain to release the insular nation from liability. On the other hand, Senators Morrill and Bacon suggested that if the United States would use lighters and small craft, coal could be stored at Pearl Harbor and boarded on warships anchored offshore, thereby preserving Hawaii's undeclared neutrality.[19]

Some annexationists argued that it was necessary for the United States to acquire Hawaii in order to protect the west coast from a possible Spanish attack. The opponents of the Newlands measure did not believe that the western coastline was in imminent danger of such an assault, especially after Dewey's victory at Manila Bay. Representative Richard P. Bland of Missouri observed that practically all of the United States warships previously stationed along that shoreline were en route to the Philippines to assist Dewey because the Pacific seaboard was safe.[20]

In short, the anti-expansionists rejected all of the various claims to the effect that it was necessary for the United States to acquire Hawaii in order to carry on the conflict with Spain. Representative Johnson spoke for many others when he exclaimed that the war prosecution plea furnished "simply a pretext for annexation, not a reason for it."[21]

The anti-imperialists also rebutted several strategic arguments for annexation that went beyond the exigencies of the pending war. They denied the contention that Hawaii was the "Gibraltar of the Pacific"—a veritable mid-ocean fortress that if annexed could afford the United States great military advantages, such as the protection of her commerce on the high seas. Generally, the foes of empire viewed the islands, not as a military asset, but as a strategic weak spot due to their lengthy coastline and distance from the American mainland.

With regard to the claim that Hawaii would be useful in protecting the west coast from future enemies, Senator White replied that it was not practicable to defend the Pacific seaboard from a naval station located 2,100 miles away. He claimed that even if the islands were held by a hostile power, an enemy fleet composed of vessels of the class of the *Oregon* would barely have sufficient fuel, sailing at the most economical speed, to reach the west coast before having to return to Honolulu. Furthermore, the senator said that colliers could be used by an invasion force intent upon attacking the Pacific coast regardless of United States occupancy of Hawaii.

In response to the notion that the prospective isthmian canal could be defended from Hawaii, the anti-expansionists argued tellingly that the future waterway could be protected more effectively from California. Senator White demonstrated that San Diego was 2,000 miles closer to the western terminus of the proposed Nicaraguan canal than was Honolulu.

The final military argument advanced by the annexationists was that Hawaii had to be acquired by the United States in order to prevent some other foreign power (usually Japan was mentioned in this regard) from seizing the archipelago. Senator Pettigrew correctly pointed out that Nippon had repeatedly disclaimed any designs upon Hawaiian sovereignty. He quoted an interview with President Dole reported in the *New York Journal* on January 24, 1898, in which the Hawaiian chief executive denied that the Mikado's government was menacing the islands. Representative Johnson had printed in the *Congressional Record* a long excerpt from a recent journal article by the Japanese minister at Washington, Toru Hoshi, in which the latter stated emphatically that Tokyo had no desire to possess the northern Pacific archipelago. Senator White arranged for a reading in the upper house of Minister Hoshi's detailed response to Senator Cushman K. Davis's unfounded charge of Japanese aggression in Hawaii. In that response Hoshi explained that his government sought only the same rights for Japanese nationals as were enjoyed by the citizens of other countries domiciled in Hawaii. Also, the minister quoted former Secretary Sherman's statement to the effect that the United States government did not take seriously the talk about an imminent Japanese takeover of the islands.[22]

Representative Johnson and Senator White called attention to the fact that Britain and France had by formal agreement mutually renounced any intention of acquiring the Polynesian archipelago. It was noted that Britain already had an impregnable Pacific fortress at Esquimault and, therefore, had no need to annex Hawaii. Had the anti-imperialists known that a British diplomat, Sir Cecil Spring Rice, was unofficially urging Washington to take Hawaii, they could have had more ammunition, even if not conclusive, to combat the groundless charge that London was eager to seize the islands if the United States did not do so first.[23]

One of the chief economic objections to passage of the Newlands joint resolution was that sugar interests were purportedly behind the measure. Referring to the annexation project, Senator John L. Mitchell of Wisconsin exhorted: "Saccharine trickles out all around it; the trail of sugar is over it all." Legislators from the cane and beet producing states of the South and West, especially Representative Broussard and Senators Caffery and McEnery (all of Louisiana) as well as Allen of Nebraska and

White of California, expressed concern about the effect of annexation upon the domestic sugar industry. At Senator Allen's request, a letter was read to the upper chamber written by Herbert Myrick, the editor of several agricultural journals who claimed to represent nearly a million farmers, predicting the demise of America's cane and beet sugar enterprises if Hawaii were brought into the Union. Also, Allen attempted—unsuccessfully—to amend the Newlands joint resolution so as to impose an excise tax of one percent on all Hawaiian sugar entering the United States mainland for ten years after the passage of the annexation measure.

Both sides in the debate claimed to be opposing the sugar trust. However, no evidence supporting these contentions was offered and historians have still been unable to show convincingly where the trust stood (if it indeed took a position) on the issue of Hawaiian annexation. Senator White asserted that the sugar combine would be "in clover" if the Newlands joint resolution passed, since the business of the trust was to refine cheap raw sugar. Also, he affirmed that the friends of the trust in Congress were supporters of annexation. Meanwhile, White himself was accused of representing the giant combine.[24] At least one anti-imperialist in the upper house, William Lindsay of Kentucky, was forthright enough to confess that he did not know whether the cartel favored or opposed the acquisition of Hawaii. Nobody doubted that certain associates of the trust, such as the Spreckels and Oxnard interests, were hostile to annexation.

The anti-expansionists in Congress expressed concern about the damaging effects the passage of the Newlands measure would have upon American workingmen. "I am not prepared to put the American father and son, in the field or shop, in deadly competition with Chinese who live on a bowl of rice and a rat a day," exclaimed Senator Allen. Representative Champ Clark of Missouri expressed a similar view and concluded that organized labor was against the acquisition of Hawaii. Senator Alexander S. Clay of Georgia arranged for the printing in the *Congressional Record* of a letter (dated June 11, 1898) from Samuel Gompers to Speaker Reed cautioning that annexation would flood the American labor market with Chinese coolies and threaten the reestablishment of slavery in the United States. To reduce the likelihood of such an eventuality Senator Pettigrew vainly offered an amendment to the Newlands measure that would have abolished the contract labor laws in Hawaii if annexation occurred.[25]

The anti-imperialists responded in a variety of ways to the argument that America's commercial interests would suffer if Hawaii were not annexed. Congressman John S. Rhea of Kentucky was not alone in maintaining that the reciprocity treaty provided the United States with sufficient mercantile benefits to render annexation unnecessary, while others, like Senators Morrill and Pettigrew, attached practically no value to American-Hawaiian commerce and were willing to terminate the reciprocity agreement. Senator White argued that the Polynesian archipelago was not located along the prospective canal route to the Orient. He claimed that merchantmen entering the future isthmian waterway from the Caribbean would sail north to San Francisco and then take the Aleutian track to the Far East. Some anti-expansionists responded to the commercial plea for annexation by declaring that foreign trade should not be expanded until the home market was effectively developed. Senator McEnery maintained that the South had no interest in overseas commerce. If Hawaii were acquired, he said, New England merchants would use their considerable profits from the China trade to penetrate the market in the western part of the United States and "drive out the goods that are manufactured in North Carolina, South Carolina, and Georgia." More importantly, he feared that a policy of overseas colonization would divert northeastern capital away from the South, thereby retarding its industrial growth. Senator Bate concluded that whatever commercial gains the United States might realize from possessing Hawaii would be far outweighed by the resulting injury to America's republican institutions.[26]

Although the anti-annexationists responded in various ways to the commercial argument for possessing Hawaii, these gentlemen were similar in outlook in one sense—they were not trade chauvinists. Most wanted nothing more for the United States than a continuation of the existing American-Hawaiian mercantile relations, and some would have been pleased to forgo even that. Few, if any, of them shared the heady plans of some expansionists for American commercial domination of the Pacific and the Far East.[27]

There were a number of miscellaneous arguments against the Newlands proposal which deserve mention. Some anti-expansionists declared that annexation would jeopardize the Monroe Doctrine, in that the United States could hardly forbid the European colonization of the western hemisphere while acquiring overseas possessions of her own. Senator Morrill and others inveighed against the acquisition of territory outside the North American continent. More than a few anti-imperialists decried the cost of providing for Hawaii's defense. Some warned that if annexation were approved the United States would be acquiring a colony of lepers. Senator White claimed that passage of the Newlands annexation resolution would violate Article Thirty-two of the Hawaiian Constitution which provided only for the negotiation of a treaty to bring about a union with the United States. Finally, because the anti-expansionists saw in the Newlands proposal the beginning of a dangerous imperialistic policy, they held that Congress should postpone its decision at least until the termination of the pending war, when the public mood would be less bellicose.[28]

On June 15 the House, after defeating Dinsmore's substitute measure, approved the Newlands joint resolution by a vote of 209 to 91.[29] Representative John Dalzell of Pennsylvania announced that Speaker Reed, who was absent due to illness, would have voted against annexation. Over three-fourths of the southern representatives and nearly a third of the western congressmen voted "nay." Aside from the anti-imperialist considerations that seemed to carry the most weight with these legislators, there were practical reasons that help to explain their vote. In the South these included racism; hostility toward what was probably regarded as a Republican measure; concern about the domestic cane sugar industry; and fear that northeastern capital might be withdrawn from the area as a result of businessmen seeking overseas investments. Western opponents of the Newlands joint resolution were worried that hordes of Oriental laborers would descend upon the Pacific coast in the event of annexation, and that the domestic beet sugar industry would be destroyed by competition from Hawaii's "grocery grade" product.

In the Senate on July 6 the Newlands measure passed 42 to 21, with 26 abstentions.[30] Although a two-thirds majority was obtained by the expansionists, it does not necessarily follow that the treaty would have passed, since many of the twenty-six senators not voting might have cast dissenting ballots had McKinley's compact been up for consideration. In other words, the relative ease of gaining a simple majority on the joint resolution may have discouraged some anti-expansionists from voting. Politically and geographically the Senate balloting reflected the same pattern as that of the House vote, and for the same reasons. On the following day President McKinley signed the annexation measure, and on August 12 Hawaii was formally incorporated into the Union. Grover Cleveland's response to these developments was characteristic of that of most other anti-imperialists. To Richard Olney he wrote disgustedly: "Hawaii is ours. As I look back upon the first step in this miserable business and as I contemplate the means used to complete this outrage, I am ashamed of the whole affair."[31] And so in the summer of 1898, after more than five years of unwavering opposition, the efforts of the foes of annexation ended in utter failure.

The anti-annexationists were dedicated to their cause, capably led, and had strong arguments. Why, then, were they defeated? To answer this question fully would necessitate a lengthy study in itself. However, a brief answer, by way of postscript, seems in order.

It is especially important to examine the connection that many historians have seen between the Spanish-American War and the annexation of Hawaii. The view of Thomas A. Bailey in particular—a view that has gained wide acceptance—needs attention. Bailey and the scholars who have followed his lead have claimed that the Spanish-American War was mainly responsible for annexation.[32] According to these historians the United States annexed Hawaii primarily for two reasons, each of which was connected with that war. First, Commodore George Dewey, having triumphed at the battle of Manila Bay, was in need of troop reinforcements and supplies that annexationists insisted could only come from an American-owned Hawaii. Second, there was a belief in Washington and throughout the nation that the west coast could not be defended during the pending war with Spain, or afterward, unless Hawaii were brought into the Union.

Significantly, historians have not questioned the military interpretation of Hawaiian annexation. The present writer believes that the conflict with Spain was of secondary importance in overcoming the opposition to Hawaiian annexation; of primary importance in that regard was the drive to expand American trade, particularly with the Orient.

With respect to the first reason offered by historians adhering to the military interpretation, Bailey acknowledges that the war measure argument of the annexationists was fallacious; he nevertheless maintains that it carried "great weight both in Congress and out," and that "largely as a war measure" the Senate approved and the President signed the Newlands annexation resolution.[33] The present writer, on the other hand, believes that Bailey et al. grossly exaggerated the influence of the war measure argument in bringing about annexation.

It is doubtful that President William McKinley believed, as did apparently some members of Congress and many newspaper editors, that the United States needed to annex Hawaii in order to send troops and supplies to Dewey at Manila. Evidence of this is seen in the way he used the war measure argument as a political ruse to call attention to Hawaii's military role and simultaneously to accuse the anti-annexationists in the Senate of interfering with the war effort. On the morning of May 31 Lodge had one of his frequent meetings with the president, who urged him to impress upon the Senate the military urgency of acquiring Hawaii, and to fight against the adjournment of the upper house until it had acted on annexation. Later that same morning Lodge spoke before the Senate. After he made his plea to postpone adjournment he referred to Hawaii's role in the pending war, at which point he was interrupted[34] and the Senate went into a secret legislative session. Writing to William M. Laffan that evening Lodge said he was "very glad" about the interruption and the move into a secret session because "it will call more attention to the opposition to the President's policy of [Hawaiian] annexation than any dozen speeches I could make." By this Lodge meant that he had publicized effectively the president's call for Hawaiian annexation as a war measure by provoking the anti-annexationists in the Senate to cut off his speech and move into a secret session— actions which, in his opinion, made the anti-annexationists look like they were hindering the administration's prosecution of the war. This clever strategy, though carried out by Lodge, originated with McKinley. The senator from Massachusetts, who was perhaps the president's key spokesman on Hawaii in the upper chamber, told a friend: "I have been fighting the battle of the administration for Hawaii, and the speech which they cut off by putting me in secret session was made after consultation with the President and my declaration against adjournment was all done at his request."[35]

The administration's strategy of using Lodge to call attention to Hawaii's military role and simultaneously embarrassing the Senate opponents of annexation seriously calls into question the president's sincerity regarding his use of the war measure argument. If McKinley had been convinced that Hawaii had to be acquired in order to prosecute the war, then he probably would have placed a military protectorate over the islands in May or June, when he seriously considered seizing the islands.[36] He decided against the protectorate, however, and waited until Hawaii could be acquired by some less objectionable means. Because the president used the war measure argument as a political tactic to discredit foes of annexation and then awaited the outcome of the July vote in the Senate (by which time Spain had been virtually defeated), it seems evident that McKinley did not believe Hawaii had to be annexed to carry on the war.

The administration did not succeed in its attempt to impress upon Congress the military urgency for annexing Hawaii. Evidence of this can be seen in the speeches minimizing the military need for possessing Hawaii, delivered by a number of congressional annexationists in mid-1898. Commercial rather than military reasons seem to have been uppermost in the thinking of annexationists on Capitol Hill. Representative Charles H. Grosvenor of Ohio, a close friend of McKinley and the chairman of the Republican party organization in the House, declared: "I advocate the adoption of this resolution [for Hawaiian annexation] upon a ground wholly distinct from any question of war necessity. I believe that the growth of the commerce of this country, independent of anything which is to result from this war, is in very large part bound up in the acquisition of this half-way house to the great markets of the East by way of the Pacific."[37] Grosvenor's view is especially noteworthy since he was, in the words of the *New York Times*, a "leader of the annexationists" in the House. Grosvenor's view was not an isolated opinion. Of the fifty-nine members of the lower house who delivered speeches in Congress advocating annexation, only ten legislators claimed that the main reason for acquiring Hawaii was to prosecute the war. However, twenty-four members of the House indicated that commercial considerations carried the most weight in their decision to support annexation.[38]

Likewise, the war measure argument was not very influential among annexationists in the upper house. Not one of the six senators who spoke in favor of annexation claimed that the main reason for acquiring Hawaii was to prosecute the war. Instead, they gave an assortment of other reasons for their support of annexation.[39]

The second claim of historians adhering to the war thesis— that the United States acquired Hawaii because of the belief among annexationists that America could not defend her western coastline during the pending war, or afterward, unless she possessed the islands—also fails to sustain close scrutiny. To begin with, a study of the editorial opinions in the leading west coast newspapers suggests that the Pacific coast states were not worried about a Spanish attack;[40] the members of Congress from that area who favored annexation did not express much apprehension that the Pacific coastline would be endangered if Hawaii were not acquired;[41] and the administration, especially after early May, expressed no anxiety about a possible assault.[42] With respect to the matter of defending the Pacific seaboard after the pending war, sixteen of the fifty-nine members of the House who spoke in favor of annexation indicated that the main reason America should possess Hawaii was in order to protect the western coastline in the future.[43] This point, however, requires amplification. The coastal defense argument was not invariably a military one, since four of those sixteen representatives who advanced it did so believing that an American-owned Hawaii would protect future Pacific coast *trade*, as well as the coastline itself.[44] In a strict sense, then, not more than twelve annexationists in the lower house could be said to have advanced a military, as opposed to a partly commercial, coastal defense argument. However, as noted earlier, twenty-four members of that chamber stated that unalloyed commercial considerations were mainly responsible for their decision to support annexation. Not one of the six Senate speakers who urged annexation claimed that the islands should be acquired for future coastal defense.

The foregoing critique of the military interpretation, or the war thesis, should not lead one to conclude that there was no significant connection between the Spanish-American War and the acquisition of the Polynesian archipelago. That connection, however, was an indirect one; it had little to do with either the prosecution of the war, or the defense of the west coast and, curiously, historians adhering to the war thesis have failed to recognize it. Because the Newlands annexation resolution was introduced in Congress on May 4, 1898, just three days after Dewey's engagement at Manila Bay, many historians adhering to the war thesis have attributed both the introduction of the resolution as well as the administration's subsequent push for annexation later in May to the naval battle in the Philippines.[45] Dewey's engagement at Manila Bay may have been instrumental in the timing of the introduction of the Newlands resolution, although more evidence is needed to confirm this point. Nevertheless, it is doubtful that the battle at Manila Bay had much to do with the administration's subsequent push for annexation later in May. Instead, that push can be explained in part by a factor that has been entirely overlooked by the historians subscribing to the war thesis: namely, the fear in Washington that if Hawaii were not annexed until peace terms had been negotiated with Spain, rival powers would demand territorial compensation. Writing to Secretary of State William R. Day from London on May 9, Ambassador John Hay warned about European intervention in the Pacific upon the termination of hostilities with Spain. Hay enclosed a memorandum from Sir Cecil Spring Rice, who was serving as second secretary in the British embassy in Berlin. Unless the United States annexed Hawaii immediately, Spring Rice had told him, the nations of Europe would gain the erroneous impression that Uncle Sam's possession of these islands was an out-growth of the pending war and would demand compensation elsewhere. Germany, for example, would seek concessions in Samoa. The British diplomatist concluded: "America should not allow it to be taken for granted that Hawaii is her share and that if she takes it it gives other people a right to demand 'compensation.' It [Hawaii] was hers by right *before the war* and its acquisition has nothing whatever to do with the war. And to make that clear the acquisition should be at once made perfect, de jure and de facto."[46] Ambassador Hay agreed. His dispatch, which included the Spring Rice memorandum, reached the State Department on May 21. According to Lodge, and the *New York Tribune* as well, it was approximately from this time on that McKinley became anxious to incorporate Hawaii into the Union.[47]

The concern in Washington about precluding foreign—especially German—demands for compensation helps to account only for the administration's decision in late May to expedite passage of the Newlands annexation resolution. The commercial considerations that were largely responsible for the United States' acquisition of the islands remain to be explained.

The commercial interpretation of Hawaiian annexation offered here is not entirely new, since the works of Walter LaFeber and Thomas J. McCormick on late nineteenth-century American foreign policy have sketched the broad outlines of such a view. Unfortunately, while advancing a commercial view of Hawaiian annexation, neither LaFeber nor McCormick refuted the military interpretation. The other major problems with their writings on Hawaiian annexation result from a lack of close argumentation and an absence of sufficient evidence, both of which are needed to sustain a commercial interpretation of America's decision to acquire the islands.[48]

The main reason for the United States' annexation of Hawaii lies in the commercial opportunities that administration leaders, many expansionists in Congress, and some businessmen thought would open in the Far East; Hawaii, they argued, would serve as an American coaling station and naval base facilitating the China trade. Dewey's victory in the Philippines and the prospect of retaining at least a base there may have hastened Hawaiian annexation by calling attention to the need for protecting the Manila foothold, which in turn was useful in safeguarding the potential Chinese market. The commercial linkage among Hawaii, the Philippines, and China did not go unnoticed by the proponents of annexation.[49]

Though the prospect of the United States securing a naval base in the Philippines may have abetted the cause of those who wanted to annex Hawaii, this prospect was immaterial to the outcome of the Hawaiian debate. When the Polynesian archipelago was annexed in mid-1898, the McKinley administration had not yet decided what to do with the Philippines. Besides, the economic considerations that led to the United States' acquisition of Hawaii existed, as we are about to see, virtually independent of the Philippine question.

A key economic factor that helped bring about Hawaiian annexation was the prevalent belief in the late 1890s that the surplus of manufactures, if not marketed overseas, would topple domestic prices, retard economic growth, and possibly spark labor turmoil, even social revolution. In early June 1898, Senator Lodge warned Secretary Day: "We have developed our industries until our home markets can no longer absorb our product. We must have new markets unless we would be visited by declines in wages and by great industrial disturbances, of which signs have not been lacking."[50] Secretary Day shortly thereafter called attention to this situation in a letter to the House of Representatives. "Recently . . . the output of the United States manufacturers . . . has reached the point of large excess above the demands of consumption," he declared. "Under these circumstances it is not surprising that greater interest should be exhibited among our manufacturers, exporters, and economists, in the enlargement of foreign markets for American goods."[51]

Many influential expansionists believed that a potentially

limitless Asian market would help to consume the American surplus and that the annexation of Hawaii would foster and protect that market and the resulting trade. The European market was protected by tariffs while the South American countries were already providing an outlet for American manufacturers. Although these two continents were considered vital to American trade, it was to Asia in general, and to China in particular, that some businessmen and politicians looked with the hope of establishing a vast new market. Senator Lodge prepared a memorandum on the importance of the China trade, a copy of which was sent to Secretary Day on June 6. "It is quite true that we shall gain markets at the conclusion of this war in Cuba and Porto Rico," said Lodge, "and we can undoubtedly add to our share of the South American markets, but all these are small compared with the vast markets furnished by the millions of people in the East."[52] Three days after Day received the trade memorandum from Lodge, the secretary of state sent a communiqué to the House of Representatives extolling the commercial opportunities awaiting American businessmen in China and urging them to act promptly, before the Celestial Empire fell under the domination of the rival powers who were rapidly partitioning her. Day's letter bore a striking resemblance to Lodge's memorandum. "It would seem to be obvious," said the secretary, "that the United States has important interests at stake in the partition of commercial facilities in regions which are likely to offer developing markets for its goods. Nowhere is this consideration of more interest than in its relation to the Chinese Empire." "It would seem to be clear," he continued, "that the present is a golden opportunity for enlarging the channels of commercial intercourse with the [Chinese] Empire." Day urged Congress to appropriate $20,000 to investigate the opportunities for expanding American trade with China.[53] The secretary of state's views were warmly received and amplified somewhat by members of Congress. "The Hawaiian Islands will be the key that will unlock to us the commerce of the Orient, and in a commercial sense make us rich and prosperous," affirmed Representative William Sulzer of New York. This view was shared by many legislators who made similar statements in June and early July.[54]

Some of the enthusiasm about tapping the Chinese market

may have been generated by the dramatic upturn in the American export trade during the spring of 1898. "The war with Spain," observed Chairman Cushman K. Davis of the Senate Foreign Relations Committee, "coincided with the widest industrial and commercial expansion that the United States has ever known."[55] A "phenomenal record," boasted the *New York Tribune* on July 3, was made in the month of May when the United States exported fifty percent more manufactured goods than were imported. In an effort to maintain this spectacular commercial growth the administration sought to disseminate trade information to American manufacturers and exporters. In May President McKinley endorsed the recommendation of Secretary Day that Congress print "a special edition of ten thousand copies" of a State Department report entitled "Review of the World's Commerce" and five thousand copies of a related document entitled "Commercial Relations of the United States with Foreign Countries during the Years 1896 and 1897."[56] While the administration took steps to publicize commercial information, the nation's export trade continued to register unprecedented gains. When the House began its debate on the Newlands annexation resolution during the second week in June, exports of manufactured goods exceeded imports of those articles by the largest margin in American history up to that time. "The export trade of the United States is undergoing a transformation which promises to profoundly influence the whole economic future of the country," announced Secretary Day.[57]

The annexationists' plan for the expansion of America's export trade—particularly with the Orient—called for the construction of an isthmian canal and the laying of a trans-Pacific cable. These measures, coupled with the annexation of Hawaii, would foster and control the lucrative trade with the Far East. Senator Cushman K. Davis spoke at length before an executive session of the upper house in January 1898 about the commercial-strategic relationship among the projected Nicaraguan Canal, Hawaii, and the Orient. According to the *New York Tribune* of January 13, Davis showed that Hawaii lay directly in the path of a straight line drawn from the western terminus of the proposed isthmian canal to China. "The nation which controls Hawaii," he added, "will control that great gateway to commerce, as the guns planted upon

Hawaii would be pointed directly at the mouth of the canal."
Senator William P. Frye of Maine expressed a similar view in an
address delivered in late January 1898 at the annual convention of
the National Association of Manufacturers. Taking the rostrum
shortly after President McKinley had finished a speech calling for
the opening of undeveloped foreign markets for American
manufacturers,[58] Senator Frye told businessmen to "use their
powerful influence on the Congress of the United States" and
persuade that body to build the Nicaraguan Canal and annex
Hawaii in order to penetrate the markets of the East.[59] The
relationship among the potential Asian market, the prospective
canal, and the acquisition of Hawaii was summarized in the
majority report on Hawaiian annexation issued by the Senate
Foreign Relations Committee in March: "Upon the opening of the
Nicaraguan or Panama Canal, practically all of the shipping
bound for Asia, making use thereof, will stop at Honolulu for coal
and supplies."[60] Senator John T. Morgan of Alabama, one of the
nation's leading proponents of Hawaiian annexation, likewise,
argued that the United States needed to possess the islands in
order to have a coaling station along the route from the prospective isthmian canal to the markets of the Orient.[61]

Because a trans-Pacific cable would promote trade by im-
proving communication, annexationists discussed it in conjunc-
tion with the future isthmian canal, the possession of Hawaii, and
the Chinese market. In one of the most revealing passages contained in the trade memorandum Lodge sent to Secretary Day in
early June, the senator observed: "If we hold the island of Luzon
and Hawaii we shall have a cable line to London with only four
relays. . . . Commerce follows the cables, and as we offer the
most direct cable route, so should we offer the most direct
steamship route. With our cheap steel and a foothold at Manila—
which is the greatest commercial and strategic point in the East—
the carrying trade would fall into our hands very largely when the
Nicaraguan Canal is opened, and until that is done would pass to
San Francisco and New York."[62] Hawaii, then, would foster
American trade in the Pacific by serving as a coaling and cable
station and guarding the canal.

The prospect of expanding trade between the mainland and
Hawaii furnished Congress with an additional commercial rea-

son for passing the Newlands annexation resolution. This prospect was noted in the majority report on Hawaiian annexation issued by the House Foreign Affairs Committee in May: "Our trade with the Hawaiian Islands last year amounted to $18,385,000, and with annexation practically the whole trade with the Hawaiian Islands would come to the United States and would rapidly increase."[63] Some annexationists in the Senate expressed a similar view. Both houses of Congress were probably influenced to some extent by public opinion on the west coast, where great interest was shown in expanding the American-Hawaiian trade through annexation.[64]

The economic explanation for Hawaiian annexation is not complete until two important questions are answered. First, why was it incumbent upon the United States to annex Hawaii for commercial reasons when America already had rights to a base at Pearl Harbor? Second, would not the establishment of an American protectorate over Hawaii have afforded the United States all of the commercial advantages to be derived from annexation?

The answer to the first question is that many annexationists thought it was necessary to acquire Hawaii in order to give the United States *permanent* rights to Pearl Harbor. American rights to that harbor derived from an amendment that was added in 1884 to the Hawaiian reciprocity treaty.[65] Because of increasing opposition to reciprocity, especially from American sugar interests, the abrogation of that treaty was possible. In 1897 the beet sugar interests joined with the American Sugar Refining Company in an attempt to remove the Hawaiian reciprocity clause from the Dingley tariff and nearly succeeded in doing so. If this attempt had been successful, the reciprocity treaty would have been "as dead as a herring," declared Francis M. Hatch, the Hawaiian minister in Washington.[66]

There was some chance, too, that the Hawaiian government might abrogate the reciprocity treaty. The government headed by President Sanford B. Dole was alarmed about the growing number and influence of Orientals in Hawaii, a situation that resulted largely from the sugar economy and the reciprocity treaty upon which that economy depended. The insular republic was willing to allow the treaty to remain in force only as long as annexation could be expected. In other words, the Hawaiian government viewed reciprocity as a step toward annexation, and opposition to the former was interpreted as opposition to the latter as well. Just prior to the 1897 tariff debate, Minister Hatch was instructed by his government to warn Washington officials that if annexation was not desired, Hawaii would denounce the reciprocity treaty and the Pearl Harbor lease.[67]

In response to the claim of some anti-annexationists in Congress that the reciprocity treaty conferred ownership of Pearl Harbor upon the United States, the Hawaiian government asserted that the Pearl Harbor amendment to the treaty had not transferred sovereignty over the harbor to Uncle Sam and offered two documents in support of that case. The first was a note from Henry A. P. Carter, who had served as the resident Hawaiian minister in Washington, to then Secretary of State Thomas F. Bayard. The second was Bayard's reply to Carter. "The question of Hawaiian jurisdiction," wrote Carter, "is left untouched by the article . . . and as no special jurisdiction is stipulated for in the article inserted by the Senate, it cannot be inferred from anything in the article that it was the intention of the Senate to invade the autonomous jurisdiction of Hawaii and to transfer the absolute property in, and jurisdiction over, the harbor to the United States." Secretary Bayard agreed with Carter's interpretation. "No ambiguity or obscurity in the amendment is observable," stated Bayard, "and I can discern therein no subtraction from Hawaiian sovereignty over the harbor to which it relates."[68] If these documents failed to prove that sovereignty was not transferred to the United States, they at least challenged the view that America's rights to Pearl Harbor were permanent.

The Senate Foreign Relations Committee affirmed in its majority report on Hawaiian annexation issued in March 1898 that America's rights to Pearl Harbor derived from the reciprocity treaty, which "is terminable by either party upon a year's notice." "Only annexation will maintain American control in Hawaii," concluded the report.[69] In May the House Foreign Affairs Committee stated in its majority report on Hawaiian annexation:

The grant of this harbor to our Government is part of a reciprocity treaty. After that treaty had been ratified, but before the ratification had been exchanged, the Hawaiian minister and the Secretary of State of the United

States exchanged notes which declared that our rights in Pearl Harbor would cease whenever the reciprocity treaty was terminated. That treaty may be terminated upon one year's notice by either party. . . . With the Japanese element in the ascendant and the Government under Japanese control, the [reciprocity] treaty would be promptly terminated, and with it our special rights.[70]

"Annexation, and that alone," the report stated, "will securely maintain American control in Hawaii." Representative Francis G. Newlands of Nevada, author of the joint resolution that brought Hawaii into the Union, reminded the House in June that the United States did not have "a perpetual right" to use Pearl Harbor. "Our rights there are secured by a reciprocity treaty terminable at the will of either party," he declared. The only way to safeguard America's claim to Pearl Harbor, asserted Newlands, was to annex the Hawaiian Islands.[71] There were at least six other members of the lower chamber who expressed the view that America's rights to Pearl Harbor were based on the reciprocity treaty, a fact which they said necessitated the annexation of Hawaii in order to secure those rights permanently.

Senator Stephen M. White conceded for the purpose of argument that America's rights to Pearl Harbor were terminable with the reciprocity treaty, but he questioned the necessity of annexing the entire Hawaiian archipelago in order to gain permanent American coaling rights to that harbor. This implacable foe of annexation asked his fellow senators why the United States could not merely enter into a "supplemental agreement" with the Hawaiian republic insuring the permanent availability of a coaling station at Pearl Harbor. White was answered by Senator Joseph B. Foraker of Ohio, who correctly observed that the only offer that the Hawaiian government had made to the United States was to cede all of her territory. Likewise, annexationists on Capitol Hill were not interested in a partial cession of Hawaiian territory to the United States. Pearl Harbor could not be defended adequately, they argued, unless Uncle Sam annexed all of Hawaii. America must possess Honolulu and the island of Oahu, said Representative Marion De Vries, otherwise "Pearl Harbor is defenseless and useless." "It would be idle to talk of annexing the capital of Hawaii without annexing all the islands," he concluded.[72]

The alternative of establishing an American protectorate over Hawaii, in lieu of annexation, was considered briefly and rejected in the majority report on Hawaiian annexation issued by the House Foreign Affairs Committee in May. "A protectorate imposes responsibility without control," declared the committee. "Annexation imposes responsibility, but will give full power of ownership and absolute control."[73] Representative Newlands opposed an American protectorate over the islands because the Hawaiian government would probably reject it, and even if that government consented, the international complications arising from such an arrangement would place the United States in a difficult position.[74] As an American protectorate Hawaii would remain free to conduct her own foreign affairs—and to become involved in disputes with other nations. The United States, as Hawaii's protector, could then possibly become embroiled with whatever nation that might make demands upon the island republic. The prevailing sentiment in the House Foreign Affairs Committee and in the lower chamber was that no arrangement short of annexation would avoid international complications and protect America's interests in Hawaii.

Thus historians seem to have exaggerated the role played by the Spanish-American War in overcoming the opposition to Hawaiian annexation—though the matter of precluding possible foreign demands for compensation in the postwar settlement, which they have overlooked, was of some importance in overcoming that opposition. On the other hand, commercial considerations, such as the fear of the economic consequences of the manufacturing surplus, the appeal of the Asian market, the concern about the economic partitioning of China by rival powers, the dramatic upturn in American foreign trade in mid-1898, and the hope of enlarging the American-Hawaiian commerce, were more decisive in bringing about the defeat of the anti-annexationists.

Conclusion

It has been argued here that the anti-annexationists' struggle in the 1890s against the acquisition of Hawaii was based upon a reverence for America's republican tradition and an inveterate hostility to colonialism. The opposition of the sugar and labor interests to the annexation of the northern Pacific archipelago was by no means inconsiderable; it was secondary in importance, however.

Few of the anti-imperialists were irreconcilably antagonistic to the incorporation of the islands into the Union. Most of the opponents of annexation seemed to sense that at some time in the future Hawaii would probably become American territory but they remained hopeful that such an event could be postponed, if not entirely averted.

These hopes were dashed not so much by the military exigencies arising out of the war with Spain, as Bailey and others have claimed, but rather by the fear that Hawaii had to be annexed quickly to preclude possible foreign demands for compensation, and especially by the accelerated European partitioning of China in the spring of 1898—a partitioning that augured the loss of a vast potential market in the Far East for the surplus of American manufactures. Amid this charged atmosphere the reasoned warnings of the anti-imperialists seemed overdrawn. Although McKinley's treaty would not have been ratified in mid-1898, these events and fears made the passage of the Newlands measure a virtual certainty.

Yet why, over the years, was there such stubborn resistance to acquiring the Polynesian archipelago? To most anti-annexationists far more was at issue than the absorption of one small group of islands in the Pacific into the body politic. Generally, they believed that if Hawaii were annexed other accessions of distant territory would follow. To the domestic sugar interests this meant that in addition to having to compete with all grades of the Hawaiian product, the output of the Cuban and Philippine cane fields might further reduce the profits of the mainland producers if these former Spanish colonies were transferred to the United States. In addition to fearing the migration of Hawaii's Oriental toilers to the west coast and the reestablishment of virtual slavery as a result of annexation, American workingmen were concerned about having to contend with the products made by cheap native labor on the other islands that Uncle Sam might covet. Most importantly, however, the anti-imperialists were certain that Hawaii's acquisition constituted the "entering wedge" of a new imperialistic policy. For them the annexation of the insular nation symbolized America's loss of innocence. The opponents of empire viewed the United States as the archetype of the virtuous republic—a secularized "City upon a Hill." The possession of Hawaii signified the abandonment of America's time-honored mission of exemplifying the workings of self-government and augured the drift into colonialism with all its attendant embroilments and injustices. Because the Hawaiian controversy was the first to raise the specter of imperialism before the American public, the debate had about it a sense of poignancy that accounts for the relentless opposition to annexation from 1893 to 1898.

After Hawaii was brought into the Union it was easier to acquire other dependencies even though the difficult process of treaty ratification was involved. This point is illustrated by the fact that the Hawaiian debate of the 1890s lasted more than *five years* and was terminated by the approval of a joint resolution because a treaty would not pass the Senate. However, within approximately *seven months* of the passage of the Newlands measure the United States acquired Guam, the Philippines, Puerto Rico, and Wake Island. When the Hawaiian controversy is viewed in this manner it becomes evident that the "Great Debate" over empire did not begin in 1898, as so many historians have assumed, but in 1893.

By focusing upon the years 1898–1900 historians of American anti-imperialism have been examining only the most dramatic and advanced stage of the crusade against empire, while largely ignoring the vast body of evidence connected with the formative stage of that crusade. Some writers, while assessing the attitudes of the anti-imperialists, have drawn hasty and erroneous conclusions based only upon a small portion of the evidence, namely, what the foes of empire may have said during the contest over the ratification of the Treaty of Paris in 1898–99. If the New Left-oriented scholars had devoted more attention to the Hawaiian controversy of 1893–98, the chances are they would not have arrived at such one-sided verdicts about the racial and commercial views of the anti-imperialists, who, as it turns out, were neither militant trade expansionists nor wholesale xenophobes. The more traditional academicians, with the exception of E. Berkeley Tompkins and a few others, have likewise fallen into the error of treating the struggle against colonialism in the 1890s as though it started with the opposition to Philippine annexation in late 1898. By paying greater notice to the Hawaiian case, historians would put themselves on firmer ground when reaching conclusions about the nature of American anti-imperialism in the late nineteenth century.

Hawaii is ours. As I look back upon the first steps in this miserable business, and as I contemplate the means used to complete the outrage, I am ashamed of the whole affair.

– GROVER CLEVELAND
Letter to Richard Olney
8 July 1898

Notes

INTRODUCTION

1. Earlier episodes concerning the acquisition of overseas dependencies did not occasion much alarm in the United States. The attempt of President Franklin Pierce to annex Hawaii in 1854 was defeated by King Kamehameha IV; therefore, the United States Senate did not have a chance to deliberate on the issue of acquiring the islands. The United States' acquisition of the Midway Islands in 1867 did not cause a stir. Those uninhabited islands were mere flyspecks of land that were occupied summarily by an American naval officer. No treaty was concluded and no congressional debate took place. Because Alaska was situated on the North American continent and was sparsely populated, anti-expansionists in the 1890s tended not to regard this acquisition as an act of imperialism.

2. Alfred T. Mahan, "Hawaii and Our Future Sea Power," *The Forum*, 15 (March 1893): 1.

3. Message of December 18, 1893, James D. Richardson, ed., *A Compilation of the Messages and Papers of the Presidents, 1789-1897*, 9: 461.

4. *Congressional Record*, 55 Cong., 2 sess., Appendix, p. 597 (June 21, 1898).

5. U.S., Department of Commerce and Labor, *Statistical Abstract of the United States*, p. 555.

6. This writer found no monograph, either published or in manuscript form, which focused on the opposition to Hawaiian annexation. The subject is treated peripherally in such major works as: Thomas A. Bailey, "The United States and Hawaii during the Spanish-American War," *American Historical Review*, 36 (April 1931): 553-54, 558; Robert L. Beisner, *Twelve Against Empire: The Anti-Imperialists, 1898-1900*, pp. 26, 31, 73, 76, 104, 194-95, 207-8; Charles S. Campbell, *The Transformation of American Foreign Relations, 1865-1900*, pp. 186 ff., 292-95; John A. S. Grenville and George Berkeley Young, *Politics, Strategy, and American Diplomacy: Studies in Foreign Policy, 1873-1917*, pp. 103, 106-16; David Healy, *U.S. Expansionism: The Imperialist Urge in the 1890s*, pp. 215-16, 220, 223, 231; Walter LaFeber, *The New Empire: An Interpretation of American Expansion, 1860-1898*, pp. 147-48, 203-9, 363, 366, 368-69; Ernest R. May, *Imperial Democracy: The Emergence of America as a Great Power*, pp. 15-16, 20-23, 123, 243; Julius W. Pratt, *Expansionists of 1898: The Acquisition of Hawaii and the Spanish Islands*, pp. 122-204 passim, 225, 280, 293, 321-26; William A. Russ, Jr., *The Hawaiian Revolution (1893-94)*, pp. 114-63 passim, 177-81, 203-6, 211-12, 222-32, 245-50, 281-322 passim, 339-48, 350-51; idem, *The Hawaiian Republic (1894-98) and Its Struggle to Win Annexation*, pp. 109, 208, 219-27, 232-33, 259-60, 293-379 passim; Sylvester K. Stevens, *American Expansion in Hawaii, 1842-1898*, pp. 231-53 passim, 256-67, 278-95 passim; Merze Tate, *The United States and the Hawaiian Kingdom: A Political History*, pp. 195-223, 228-58 passim, 262-63, 279-80, 282, 285, 288-92, 300-306; idem, *Hawaii: Reciprocity or Annexation*, pp. 245-54; E. Berkeley Tompkins, *Anti-Imperialism in the United States: The Great Debate, 1890-1920*, pp. 27-62, 95-118.

7. LaFeber, *The New Empire*, pp. 200-201, 412-16; Christopher Lasch, "The Anti-Imperialists, the Philippines, and the Inequality of Man," *Journal of Southern History*, 24 (August 1958): 321, 325-26; Thomas J. McCormick, "A Commentary on 'The Anti-

Imperialists and Twentieth Century American Foreign Policy,'" *Studies on the Left*, 3, no.
1 (1962): 28–33, and *China Market: America's Quest for Informal Empire, 1893-1901*, pp.
105-6; William Appleman Williams, *The Tragedy of American Diplomacy*, see Chapter I,
"Imperial Anticolonialism"; idem, *The Contours of American History*, pp. 366-68.

8. Bailey, "The United States and Hawaii during the Spanish-American War," p. 560.

9. Thomas B. Reed, "Empire Can Wait," *The Illustrated American*, 22 (December 4,
1897): 713-14.

10. *The Oxford English Dictionary* (1933), s.v. "Imperialism." According to the
prefatory pages of Volume One of the *OED*, the definition of the word "imperialism,"
which appears in Volume Five, was written between 1899 and 1901. Emphasis is in the
original.

1. OPPOSITION AT THE CLOSE OF
HARRISON'S ADMINISTRATION

1. Lorrin A. Thurston was a second-generation descendant of Asa Thurston, one
of the original New England missionary sires who landed in Hawaii in 1820. Like a
number of other Americans of similar background living in Hawaii, he was a dual citizen of the insular nation and the United States. Although not known for his tact, he
was one of the most able and energetic promoters of Hawaiian annexation to represent the provisional government in Washington, where he served intermittently
between 1893 and 1898. His lengthy and biased account of the deposition of
Liliuokalani and the annexation movement that followed, entitled *Memoirs of the
Hawaiian Revolution*, is an indispensable primary source for historians of American-
Hawaiian foreign relations. See Allen Johnson and Dumas Malone, eds., *Dictionary of
American Biography* (22 vols., N.Y.. Charles Scribner's Sons, 1928-58), 9: 517-18.

2. The protocols and stenographic notes for all seven conferences are in *Protocol—
First Conference between Hawaiian Commissioners and Secretary of State*, February 4,
1893, in the diplomatic correspondence of the Department of State, National Archives,
Washington, D.C. The present writer has relied upon Ralph S. Kuykendall's edited
compilation of these materials, in that author's "Negotiation of the Hawaiian Annexation
Treaty of 1893," Fifty-first *Annual Report* of the Hawaiian Historical Society for the Year
1942 (September 1943), pp. 5–64.

3. Protocol of the Third Conference between the secretary of state and Mr.
Thurston, Chairman of the Hawaiian Commission, Thursday, February 9, 1893, in
Kuykendall, "Negotiation of the Hawaiian Annexation Treaty of 1893," p. 46.

4. Minutes of Meeting Held February 10, 1893, at 4 P.M., Wormley's Hotel,
Washington, D.C., ibid., pp. 51–52.

5. Thurston to Dole, February 9, 1893, Foreign Office and Executive File (hereafter
cited as F.O. and Ex.), 1893, State Archives of Hawaii (hereafter cited as A.H.), Honolulu,
H.I. Thurston told Dole: "He [Foster] informed us on Thursday that he was instructed by
the President to say that the President and Cabinet had made up their minds to annex the
Islands; that they were willing to do so on as nearly the lines that we asked as was
possible, . . . They have made up their minds to act immediately, . . ." Thurston's letter,
which depicts Harrison as an unequivocal advocate of the acquisition of Hawaii in early
February 1893, contradicts, if it does not refute, the view that that Republican administration "continued to remain noncommittal" with the commissioners from the islands and that
the president was "overly cautious in pursuing annexation." The notion that Harrison was a
reluctant annexationist is argued unconvincingly in George W. Baker, "Benjamin Harrison

and Hawaiian Annexation: A Reinterpretation," *Pacific Historical Review*, 33 (August 1964): 306, 309.

6. Minutes of Meeting Held February 10, 1893, at 4 P.M., Wormley's Hotel, Washington, D.C., in Kuykendall, "Negotiation of the Hawaiian Annexation Treaty of 1893," p. 51.

7. The accord contained seven articles which provided for the cession of the Hawaiian Islands, including all public buildings, "to the United States forever"; the extension to Hawaii within one year of the laws of the United States respecting "imports, the internal revenue, [and] commerce and navigation"; the prohibition of the further immigration of Chinese laborers to the islands as well as from there to the American mainland; the assumption by the United States of the Hawaiian debt, not to exceed $3,250,000; the payment of an annuity of $20,000 to Liliuokalani for life and a total disbursement of $150,000 to Princess Kaiulani provided that the latter "submits to the authority of the United States." The terms of the annexation compact appear in U.S. Department of State, *Papers Relating to the Foreign Relations of the United States, 1894*, Appendix II, pp. 197–202.

8. *New York Herald*, February 6, 1893, p. 3.

9. John W. Foster, *Diplomatic Memoirs*, 2: 168.

10. *New York Tribune*, February 25, 1893, p. 6.

11. Thurston to William H. Dimond, February 22, 1893, F.O. and Ex., 1893, A.H.

12. Neumann headed a royalist delegation (comprising himself, Prince David Kawananakoa, and E. C. MacFarlane) sent to the United States by Liliuokalani to negotiate for the queen's reinstatement, and, failing that, to arrange for financial considerations for her and Crown Princess Kaiulani. Liliuokalani, *Hawaii's Story by Hawaii's Queen*, p. 390; Thurston to Dole, March 10, 1893, F.O. and Ex., 1893, A.H.

13. William De Witt Alexander, *History of Later Years of the Hawaiian Monarchy and the Revolution of 1893*, pp. 76–77.

14. *New York Herald*, January 30, 1893, p. 3; January 31, 1893, p. 5; February 6, 1893, p. 3; February 25, 1893, p. 11; February 1, 1893, p. 5.

15. Ibid., January 31, 1893, p. 5.

16. Pettigrew quoted in the *San Francisco Examiner*, January 31, 1893, p. 1; Gray in the *New York Herald*, February 6, 1893, p. 3.

17. Thurston to Antone Rosa, March 16, 1893, *Foreign Relations, 1894*, Appendix II, p. 478.

18. George F. Pearce, "Assessing Public Opinion: Editorial Comment and the Annexation of Hawaii—A Case Study," *Pacific Historical Review*, 43 (August 1974): 330.

19. See the press surveys appearing in the *New York Herald*, February 8, 1893, p. 6; February 9, 1893, p. 5; February 10, 1893, p. 3; February 12, 1893, p. 18; and February 13, 1893, p. 5.

20. The *New York Herald*, which claimed to have the largest daily circulation in the United States in 1893 (190,500), sent Charles Nordhoff, the well-known journalist, to the islands to investigate the deposition of Liliuokalani and the annexation movement. While in Hawaii during the spring and early summer of 1893 he became well acquainted with Commissioner Blount. Nordhoff's long dispatches, which were printed in the *Herald* and excerpted in many other American newspapers, were regarded as authoritative by a number of leading anti-annexationists, including Gresham. Nordhoff corresponded with the secretary of state and Carl Schurz in the fall of 1893 regarding Hawaiian matters. At that time the *Herald* frequently anticipated the administration's unfolding Hawaiian policy while vigorously attacking annexation. Commissioner William De Witt Alexander

referred to the *Herald* as "our greatest enemy" in a letter to President Dole. See Alexander to Dole, November 19, 1893, quoted by Lorrin A. Thurston, *Memoirs of the Hawaiian Revolution*, p. 341.

21. *New York Evening Post*, February 3, 1893, quoted by William M. Armstrong, *E. L. Godkin and American Foreign Policy, 1865-1900*, p. 177.

22. *Albany Times* as quoted by the *New York Herald*, February 10, 1893, p. 3; *Seattle Post-Intelligencer*, February 23, 1893, quoted by Richard H. Olson, "Imperialism and the Pacific Northwest Press, 1893-1900" (Ph.D. diss., University of Idaho, 1976), p. 42.

23. Matilda Gresham, *Life of Walter Quintin Gresham, 1832-1895*, 2: 684-85.

24. Foster believed that Gresham was primarily responsible for Cleveland's prevention of a Senate vote. Foster, *Diplomatic Memoirs*, 2:168.

25. Schurz to Cleveland, February 27, 1893, Frederic Bancroft, ed., *Speeches, Correspondence and Political Papers of Carl Schurz*, 5: 128.

26. Harrison to Cyrus C. Hines, February 3, 1893, Benjamin Harrison Papers, Presidential Papers Microfilm, Series 1, reel 38, frame 34,102, Manuscript Division, Library of Congress.

2. CLEVELAND'S WITHDRAWAL OF THE TREATY FROM THE SENATE

1. James D. Richardson, ed., *A Compilation of the Messages and Papers of the Presidents, 1789-1897*, 8: 327; 500-501.

2. Archibald Hopkins to Thurston, December 29, 1892, in Lorrin A. Thurston, *Memoirs of the Hawaiian Revolution*, p. 243.

3. *New York Herald*, February 2, 1893, p. 5; Richard D. Weigle, "The Sugar Interests and American Diplomacy in Hawaii and Cuba, 1893-1903" (Ph.D. diss., Yale University, 1939), pp. 100-10.

4. Richardson, ed., *Messages and Papers of the Presidents*, 9: 393.

5. *New York Tribune*, March 10, 1893, p. 1. For Secretary Foster's view see John W. Foster, *Diplomatic Memoirs*, 2: 168. Thurston's and Castle's views are found in Thurston, *Memoirs of the Hawaiian Revolution*, pp. 559-60, and William R. Castle Diary, entry for March 9, 1893 (p. 29), manuscript, Hawaiian Collection, University of Hawaii Library. Mrs. Gresham's opinion appears in Matilda Gresham, *Life of Walter Quintin Gresham, 1832-1895*, 2: 741. See also the *New York Herald*, March 10, 1893, p. 5.

6. Gresham's wife did not deny the charge in her biography of the secretary of state. She stated: "If my husband was actuated only by resentment towards President Harrison, the Republican leaders, and the Republican Party, he had the satisfaction of knowing that he embarrassed them greatly and that he exposed much of their cant and hypocrisy about a free ballot and a fair count." Gresham, *Life of Walter Quintin Gresham*, 2: 738-39. See also Allan Nevins, *Grover Cleveland: A Study in Courage*, p. 553.

7. Robert M. McElroy, *Grover Cleveland: The Man and the Statesman*, 2: 177.

8. Thurston to Dole, March 10, 1893, Foreign Office and Executive File (hereafter cited as F.O. and Ex.), 1893, State Archives of Hawaii (hereafter cited as A.H.), Honolulu, H.I.

9. Gresham to Blount, March 11, 1893, U.S. Department of State, *Papers Relating to the Foreign Relations of the United States, 1894*, Appendix, II, p. 567.

10. Both quoted by the *Literary Digest*, 6 (March 18, 1893): 554.

11. *San Francisco Chronicle*, March 20, 1893, p. 3.

12. Quoted by the *Literary Digest*, 6 (March 18, 1893): 554.

13. Smith to Dole, March 10, 1893, and April 6, 1893, F.O. and Ex., 1893, A.H.

14. Dole to Thurston, July 19, 1893, ibid.

15. Cleveland to Schurz, March 19, 1893, Frederic Bancroft, ed., *Speeches, Correspondence and Political Papers of Carl Schurz*, 5: 133–34.

16. Mary H. Krout, *Hawaii and a Revolution*, pp. 138–39.

17. Nevins, *Grover Cleveland*, p. 549. Two other historians who subscribe to this view of Cleveland as being consistently opposed to imperialism in general and Hawaiian annexation in particular are Julius W. Pratt, *Expansionists of 1898: The Acquisition of Hawaii and the Spanish Islands*, p. 209; and E. Berkeley Tompkins, *Anti-Imperialism in the United States: The Great Debate, 1890–1920*, p. 39.

18. Nevins, ed., *Letters of Grover Cleveland, 1850–1908*, pp. 491–92.

19. Weigle, "The Sugar Interests and American Diplomacy," p. 112, n. 45.

3. OPPOSITION FROM AMERICAN SUGAR INTERESTS

1. *The Nation*, 56 (March 2, 1893): 151. Thurston's remarks appear in Thurston to Dole, April 7, 1893, Foreign Office and Executive File (hereafter cited as F.O. and Ex.), 1893, State Archives of Hawaii (hereafter cited as A.H.), Honolulu, H.I.

2. Thurston to Dole, ibid. Thurston also claimed to have persuaded the anti-annexationist editors of the *New York World* and the *Chicago Herald* and *Post* that the Hawaiian sugar planters were not responsible for the deposition of the queen. See also Julius W. Pratt, *Expansionists of 1898: The Acquisition of Hawaii and the Spanish Islands*, p. 160, n. 34.

3. The *San Francisco Examiner* conducted an extensive poll in late 1892 on the attitudes of the major Hawaiian sugar planters toward possible annexation to the United States and found that the sentiment was clearly against the proposition. *San Francisco Examiner*, November 21, 1892, pp. 1–3. The opposition of the Hawaiian sugar planters to annexation, both immediately before and after the Revolution of 1893, is treated persuasively and at length in Thurston to Robert McCurdy (member of the Illinois state legislature), February 3, 1893, F.O. and Ex., 1893, A.H. Thurston's view has been substantiated in a detailed and fully documented discussion of the Hawaiian sugar planters' attitudes toward annexation in 1892 and 1893 which appears in Richard D. Weigle, "The Sugar Interests and American Diplomacy in Hawaii and Cuba, 1893–1903" (Ph.D. diss., Yale University, 1939), pp. 60–91; and by the same author, "Sugar and the Hawaiian Revolution," *Pacific Historical Review*, 16 (February 1947): 41–58.

4. William R. Castle Diary, entry for January 28, 1893 (p. 4), manuscript, Hawaiian Collection, University of Hawaii Library, Honolulu, H.I.

5. The interview appeared in an unknown New York newspaper and was excerpted in the *Hawaiian Star*, April 7, 1893, p. 3, New York dateline, March 23, 1893.

6. *San Francisco Chronicle*, May 4, 1893, p. 2. See also the *Hawaiian Star*, April 21, 1893, p. 2.

7. Jacob Adler, *Claus Spreckels: The Sugar King in Hawaii*, p. 233.

8. *New York Herald*, May 13, 1893, p. 3.

9. *San Francisco Chronicle*, July 27, 1893, p. 4.

10. *Hawaiian Star*, September 19, 1893, p. 5.

11. W. D. Alexander to A. C. Alexander, May 23, 1893, quoted by Ralph S. Kuykendall, *The Hawaiian Kingdom: The Kalakaua Dynasty, 1874–1893*, 3: 626.

12. Stevens to Alexander, July 16, 1893, F.O. and Ex., 1893, A.H.

13. *San Francisco Bulletin*, n.d., quoted by Adler, *Claus Spreckels*, p. 248.

14. Thurston to Dole, November 20, 1893, Lorrin A. Thurston, *Memoirs of the Hawaiian Revolution*, p. 347.

15. It should be noted that Henry Oxnard's brother, Robert, was a director of Spreckels' Western Sugar Refinery Company. Welch & Co. (correspondent's personal name does not appear on the letter) to Thurston, January 3, 1898, Francis M. Hatch Papers, Letters, 1898 (M-58), A.H. This letter gives an excellent account of the connection between Spreckels' beet sugar interests and the sugar trust.

16. *Omaha Bee*, February 5, 1893, pp. 4–5.

17. *Louisiana Planter*, 10 (February 18, 1893): 105, quoted by Weigle, "The Sugar Interests and American Diplomacy," p. 107.

18. Stenographic Report of Second Conference (February 7, 1893, 10 A.M.), reprinted in Ralph S. Kuykendall, ed., "Negotiation of the Hawaiian Annexation Treaty of 1893," Fifty-first *Annual Report* of the Hawaiian Historical Society for the Year 1942, p. 36. In a speech delivered at the Washington (D.C.) City Club on March 7, 1893, Commissioner Thurston claimed that the Hawaiian planters were forced into agreeing to give Spreckels and the sugar trust one-half of any bounty that might be paid under the McKinley tariff to growers in the islands in the event that annexation should occur. According to Thurston, Spreckels and the sugar trust told the Hawaiian planters: "If you don't like these terms[,] eat your sugar." *New York Herald*, March 8, 1893, p. 7.

19. Weigle, "The Sugar Interests and American Diplomacy," p. 117.

20. *New York Times*, February 18, 1893, p. 1. See also the *San Francisco Chronicle*, February 17, 1893, p. 1.

21. *Omaha Bee*, February 1 and 7, 1893, quoted by Weigle, "The Sugar Interests and American Diplomacy," p. 99.

22. There were two major reasons why Spreckels and Oxnard, as California beet sugar producers, did not want to compete with Hawaiian-grown cane sugar. First, a large part of the product from the islands was so pure in content as to require no refining. This sugar, known as "grocery grade," simply needed to be granulated before being sold. Second, field labor in Hawaii was paid about fifty cents per day while such workers in California earned about $2.00 per day. Annexation might reduce the disparity in wages but it would not eliminate it. George T. Surface, *The Story of Sugar*, pp. 128–29; Thomas J. Osborne, "Claus Spreckels and the Oxnard Brothers: Pioneer Developers of California's Beet Sugar Industry, 1890–1900," *Southern California Quarterly*, 54 (Summer 1972): 121, 124.

23. Compiling statistics from U.S. Department of State, *Papers Relating to the Foreign Relations of the United States, 1894*, Appendix II, pp. 1081–1185, 1110–36, Weigle found that various San Francisco stockholders contributed "a large amount" of the total $13,526,800 that Americans had invested in Hawaiian sugar plantations. He suggested, with good reason, that this financial stake of California businessmen explains the passage in January 1893 of a resolution favoring Hawaiian annexation by the San Francisco Chamber of Commerce. Senator Charles N. Felton of California received a telegram in Washington from the San Francisco Chamber of Commerce notifying him of this action and requesting him to communicate this information to Congress. Weigle, "The Sugar Interests and American Diplomacy," pp. 57, 100.

24. Edith Dobie, *The Political Career of Stephen Mallory White: A Study of Party Activities under the Convention System*, 2: 192.

25. Thurston to Dole, April 7, 1893, F.O. and Ex., 1893, A.H.

4. IDEOLOGICAL DETERRENTS TO HAWAIIAN ANNEXATION

1. *New York Herald*, April 24, 1893, p. 6. The *San Francisco Argonaut*, a major Republican weekly, responded in a similar vein. See *San Francisco Argonaut*, 33 (November 20, 1893): 1.

2. *Cleveland Plain Dealer*, quoted by the *New York Herald*, April 28, 1893, p. 15; *Brooklyn Citizen*, quoted by the *Literary Digest*, 6 (March 18, 1893): 554; *Pittsburg (Kansas) Dispatch*, quoted by the *New York Herald*, May 8, 1893, p. 6; *St. Paul Dispatch*, quoted by the *Literary Digest*, 6 (March 18, 1893): 554; *Pen Yan Democrat* and *Toledo Bee*, quoted by the *New York Herald*, April 28, 1893, p. 15.

3. *St. Paul Dispatch*, March 10, 1893, quoted by the *Literary Digest*, 6 (March 18, 1893): 554; Carl Schurz, "Manifest Destiny," *Harper's New Monthly Magazine*, 87 (October 1893): 739–45. A cogent rebuttal to these anti-imperialist arguments was offered by Simeon E. Baldwin, "The Historic Policy of the United States as to Annexation," *Yale Review*, 2 (August 1893): 133–58. Interestingly, Baldwin, a Yale Law School professor, became an anti-imperialist at the close of the Spanish-American War.

4. *St. Paul Dispatch*, March 10, 1893, quoted by the *Literary Digest*, 6 (March 18, 1893): 554.

5. *New York Herald*, July 22, 1893, p. 5.

6. *Brooklyn Eagle*, March 10, 1893, quoted by the *Literary Digest*, 6 (March 18, 1893): 554; *San Francisco Argonaut*, 32 (April 24, 1893): 1; *New York Herald*, March 17, 1893, p. 6.

7. Schurz, "Manifest Destiny," pp. 740, 743. Interestingly, Schurz, like numerous other anti-imperialists, was not opposed to the acquisition of territory on the North American continent, such as Canada. The United States should "look for territorial expansion only to the north [Canada]," he said, "where some day a kindred people may freely elect to cast their lot with this republic . . ." Ibid., p. 746.

8. Gresham to Schurz, October 6, 1893, vol. XLI, Walter Q. Gresham Papers, Manuscript Division, Library of Congress; Rhodes quoted by E. Berkeley Tompkins, *Anti-Imperialism in the United States: The Great Debate, 1890–1920*, p. 52; Coudert in *New York Herald*, November 12, 1893, p. 4.

9. Webster to Timoteo Halilio and William Richards, December 19, 1842, *Senate Executive Documents*, 52 Cong., 2 sess., No. 77 (Serial 3062), pp. 40–41; see also President John Tyler's statement of December 30, 1842, ibid., pp. 35–37.

10. *New York Herald*, February 23, 1893, p. 6.

11. George T. Curtis, "Is It Constitutional?" *North American Review*, 156 (March 1893): 282, 284.

12. Thomas M. Cooley, "Grave Obstacles to Hawaiian Annexation," *The Forum*, 15 (June 1893): 392.

13. Ibid., pp. 393, 394.

14. This spectrum of opinion is sampled and quoted in the press surveys appearing in the *New York Herald* during the months of January and February, 1893.

15. *Congressional Record*, 53 Cong., 2 sess., pp. 703–4 (January 11, 1894).

16. James Schouler, "A Review of the Hawaiian Controversy," *The Forum*, 16 (February 1894): 671, 673.

17. Gresham to Noble C. Butler, November 23, 1893; to John Overmeyer, July 25, 1894; to Thomas F. Bayard, December 17, 1893; all from box 48, Gresham Papers.

18. See the following editions of the *New York Herald*: April 17, 1893, p. 5; April 24, 1893, p. 6; May 5, 1893, p. 7; May 6, 1893, p. 4; May 13, 1893, p. 3.

19. Quoted by ibid., May 10, 1893, p. 10.

20. *San Francisco Argonaut*, 32 (April 24, 1893): 1.

21. Schurz, "Manifest Destiny," p. 742.

22. George W. Merrill, "The Annexation of Hawaii," *The Californian Illustrated Magazine*, 3 (March 1893): 507.

23. Quoted by the *Literary Digest*, 6 (March 18, 1893): 554.

24. Quoted by the *New York Herald*, March 1, 1893, p. 12; March 3, 1893, p. 4.

25. Christopher Lasch, "The Anti-Imperialists, the Philippines, and the Inequality of Man," *Journal of Southern History*, 24 (August 1958): 324–26.

26. J. Rogers Hollingsworth, *The Whirligig of Politics: The Democracy of Cleveland and Bryan*, pp. 149–50. Hollingsworth stated: "The starting point in the thinking of many anti-imperialists, as in that of the imperialists, was their neo-Darwinian outlook. . . . It was not at all uncommon for the anti-imperialists to be more impressed with the Darwinian view of society than with the natural rights philosophy of the Declaration of Independence." The author of these statements footnoted Lasch as his authority. See also Robert L. Beisner, *Twelve Against Empire: The Anti-Imperialists, 1898–1900*, pp. 160, 232–33. Beisner asserted that "most anti-imperialists . . . were as disdainful of 'inferior races' as the expansionists" (p. 160) and that the anti-imperialists "can be condemned as racists" (p. 232). James P. Shenton expressed views quite similar to Hollingsworth and Beisner, "Imperialism and Racism," Donald Sheehan and Harold C. Syrett, eds., *Essays in American Historiography: Papers Presented in Honor of Allan Nevins*, pp. 232–33.

27. Martin Diamond, Winston Mills Fisk, and Herbert Garfinkel, *The Democratic Republic: An Introduction to American National Government*, p. 6.

28. Infra, p. 61; supra, p. 35.

5. STRATEGIC AND ECONOMIC OBJECTIONS TO HAWAIIAN ANNEXATION

1. Alfred T. Mahan, "Hawaii and Our Future Sea Power," *The Forum*, 15 (March 1893): 8.

2. *New York Herald*, March 8, 1893, p. 7.

3. George W. Merrill, "The Annexation of Hawaii," *The Californian Illustrated Magazine*, 3 (March 1893), 508.

4. Carl Schurz, "Manifest Destiny," *Harper's New Monthly Magazine*, 87 (October 1893): 744; Gresham to Schurz, October 6, 1893, vol. XLI, Walter Q. Gresham Papers, Manuscript Division, Library of Congress (hereafter cited as L. C.).

5. Quoted by the *New York Herald*, May 9, 1893, p. 9.

6. Ibid., May 18, 1893, p. 5; April 24, 1893, p. 6; July 22, 1893, p. 5.

7. Merze Tate, "Great Britain and the Sovereignty of Hawaii," *Pacific Historical Review*, 31 (November 1962): 348.

8. Memorandum of discussion between Gresham and British Ambassador Sir Julian Pauncefote, dated March 16, 1893, *Memoranda of Conversations with the Secretary of State, 1893–1898*, Miscellaneous Archives, Records of the Department of State, Record Group 59, National Archives.

9. Instead, the Japanese government indicated its approval of the United States' possible annexation of Hawaii. Gazo Tateno, the Japanese minister at Washington, told Gresham that "his government would be pleased to see the sovereignty of the United States extended over them [the Hawaiian Islands]." Memorandum of discussion between

Gresham and Japanese Minister Gazo Tateno, dated March 16, 1893, *Memoranda of Conversations with the Secretary of State, 1893-1898*. See also William A. Russ, Jr., *The Hawaiian Revolution, (1893-94)* pp. 159-63.

10. *New York Herald*, April 14, 1893, p. 5; April 7, 1893, p. 8. Fujii's statement was made to Nordhoff in Honolulu.

11. Blount to Gresham, July 17, 1893, U.S. Department of State, *Papers Relating to the Foreign Relations of the United States, 1894*, Appendix II, p. 569.

12. Fujii to Dole, March 23, 1893, enclosed in Hatch to Day, May 22, 1897, Notes from the Hawaiian Legation in the United States to the Department of State, IV, Record Group 59, National Archives Microfilm Publication T 160, roll 4.

13. E. L. Godkin, "The Hawaiian Fiasco," *The Nation*, 56 (February 2, 1893): 154; anonymous, "Hawaii and British Interests," ibid. (May 18, 1893), p. 362.

14. Quoted by E. Berkeley Tompkins, *Anti-Imperialism in the United States: The Great Debate, 1890-1920*, p. 48.

15. *New York Herald*, April 24, 1893, p. 6.

16. *New York Herald*, March 9, 1893, p. 7.

17. *Congressional Record*, 52 Cong., 2 sess., pp. 980, 999 (January 31, 1893).

18. Merrill, "The Annexation of Hawaii," pp. 508-9.

19. Excerpts from these newspapers were quoted in the press surveys appearing in the following editions of the *New York Herald*, March 1, 1893, p. 5; April 27, 1893, p. 9; April 29, 1893, p. 9; May 8, 1893, p. 6; May 12, 1893, p. 9.

20. Thomas J. McCormick, "A Commentary on 'The Anti-Imperialists and Twentieth-Century American Foreign Policy,'" *Studies on the Left*, 3, no. 1 (1962): 28-29. Perhaps the earliest expression of this view appeared in William Appleman Williams, *The Tragedy of American Diplomacy*, pp. 16-50 passim.

21. Lloyd C. Gardner, Walter F. LaFeber, and Thomas J. McCormick, *Creation of the American Empire: U.S. Diplomatic History*, pp. 226-27.

22. Walter LaFeber, *The New Empire: An Interpretation of American Expansion, 1860-1898*, pp. 200-201, 412, 416; Thomas J. McCormick, *China Market: America's Quest for Informal Empire, 1893-1901*, p. 7.

23. McCormick, "A Commentary on 'The Anti-Imperialists,'" p. 29.

24. Message of December 6, 1886, James D. Richardson, ed., *A Compilation of the Messages and Papers of the Presidents, 1789-1897*, 8: 500-501.

25. Schurz, "Manifest Destiny," pp. 744-45.

26. Gresham to Schurz, October 6, 1893, vol. XLI, Gresham Papers. Regarding Schurz's article, the secretary of state said: "I think it will do a great deal of good. . . . It is the best article of the kind that I have seen, and I sincerely hope to see something else from your pen upon the same subject." Contemporary historian James Ford Rhodes told Schurz that the latter's essay would "have a large influence and do a great deal of good." Quoted by Tompkins, *Anti-Imperialism in the United States*, p. 52. Also, Charles Nordhoff wrote to Schurz congratulating him on his "excellent article." Nordhoff to Schurz, October 10, 1893, vol. CIX, Carl Schurz Papers, Manuscript Division, L.C.

27. Like Senator Stephen M. White, George W. Merrill opposed Hawaiian annexation and was greatly concerned about expanding American trade in the Pacific Ocean. Merrill was one of the few prominent anti-annexationists to promote the building of a submarine cable between Hawaii and the American mainland. See supra, p. 45.

28. McCormick, "A Commentary on 'The Anti-Imperialists,'" p. 29.

29. Quoted by the *New York Herald*, April 29, 1893, p. 9.

30. Nordhoff, ibid., July 22, 1893, p. 5; May 6, 1893, p. 4.

6. CLEVELAND'S DECISION TO REJECT
THE HAWAIIAN TREATY

1. Blount to Gresham, July 17, 1893, U.S. Department of State, *Papers Relating to the Foreign Relations of the United States, 1894*, Appendix II, pp. 594, 599. See also *House Executive Documents*, 53 Cong., 2 sess., No. 47 (Serial 3224), p. 128.

2. Gresham to Schurz, September 14, 1893, vol. CIX, Carl Schurz Papers, Manuscript Division, Library of Congress (hereafter cited as L.C.).

3. Hastings to Thurston, September 8, 1893, Foreign Office and Executive File, 1893, State Archives of Hawaii.

4. Olney to Gresham, October 9, 1893, vol. XLI, Walter Q. Gresham Papers, Manuscript Division, L.C.

5. Gresham to Cleveland, October 18, 1893, *Foreign Relations, 1894*, Appendix II, p. 463.

6. Memorandum, dated February 1901, manuscript, box 1, Letters, Richard Olney Papers, Massachusetts Historical Society, Boston.

7. Gresham to Willis, October 18, 1893, *Foreign Relations, 1894*, Appendix II, p. 464.

8. Willis to Gresham, November 16, 1893, *House Executive Documents*, 53 Cong., 2 sess., No. 70 (Serial 3224), p. 2.

9. Matilda Gresham, *Life of Walter Quintin Gresham, 1832-1895*, 2: 776.

10. Mary H. Krout, *Hawaii and a Revolution*, p. 21.

11. Thurston to Dole, November 14, 1893, Lorrin A. Thurston, *Memoirs of the Hawaiian Revolution*, p. 326.

12. Telegram, Thurston to Dole, November 15, 1893, ibid., pp. 334-35.

13. The quotation appears in Gresham to Cleveland, October 18, 1893, *Foreign Relations, 1894*, Appendix II, p. 460. Cf. Thurston to Dole, November 14, 1893, Thurston, *Memoirs of the Hawaiian Revolution*, p. 327. Cf. Gresham's account of the conversation appearing in memorandum, dated November 14, 1893, p. 2, *Memoranda of Conversations with the Secretary of State, 1893-1898*, Miscellaneous Archives, Records of the Department of State, Record Group 59, National Archives (hereafter cited as N.A.).

14. Thurston to Dole, November 14, 1893, Thurston, *Memoirs of the Hawaiian Revolution*, p. 328. Cf. memorandum, dated November 14, 1893, p. 3, *Memoranda of Conversations with the Secretary of State, 1893-1898*.

15. Ibid. Also, this was the view expressed by Cleveland in his special Hawaiian message of December 18, 1893. See James D. Richardson, ed., *A Compilation of the Messages and Papers of the Presidents, 1789-1897*, 9: 471-72.

16. Gresham to Noble C. Butler, November 23, 1893, Letterbook, box 48, Gresham Papers.

17. To John Overmeyer, Gresham wrote: "It seems that you would have the United States pursue an imperial policy. How long would popular government survive under such a policy? If Hawaii should be annexed, your argument would apply with equal force in favor of the annexation of other islands in the Pacific and South Pacific. A free Government can not pursue an imperial policy." Gresham to Overmeyer, July 25, 1894, ibid. The secretary of state told Ambassador Thomas F. Bayard: "If we enter upon a career of acquisition of distant territory, governing it as Great Britain and other European powers govern their dependencies, our republic will not long endure." Gresham to Bayard, December 17, 1893, ibid. Gresham rejected Hawaiian annexation on patently anti-imperialist grounds when he stated to another correspondent: "I cannot escape the belief that if our Government, departing from the sound, honest and patriotic teachings and

warnings of its founders and earlier statesmen, enters upon a career of foreign acquisition and colonization, the results will be disastrous. Such a policy is essentially an imperial one. . . . This is the first time it has been seriously maintained that we should leave our continent and annex remote regions. Popular government will not long survive under such a policy." Gresham to Thomas G. Shearman, March 8, 1895, ibid. Historians Thomas G. Paterson, J. Garry Clifford, and Kenneth J. Hagan have argued, despite the existence of strong evidence to the contrary such as that just presented, that Gresham was "an expansionist willing to annex territories if legal political processes were observed." Thomas G. Paterson, J. Garry Clifford, and Kenneth J. Hagan, *American Foreign Policy: A History*, p. 175.

18. Bayard to Gresham, November 25, 1893, quoted by William A. Russ, Jr., *The Hawaiian Revolution (1893-94)*, p. 287.

19. A. B. Farquhar to Cleveland, November 13, 1893, Grover Cleveland Papers, Presidential Papers Microfilm, Series 2, reel 80, frame 21,688, Manuscript Division, L.C. For other letters of commendation regarding Gresham's letter to Cleveland dated October 18, 1893, see: Charles Nordhoff to Gresham, November 13, 1893, vol. XLI, Gresham Papers; Robert Duval to Gresham, November 15, 1893, ibid.; Oliver T. Morton to Gresham, November 17, 1893, ibid.; and J. J. Abercrombe to Gresham, November 18, 1893, ibid.

20. *The Nation*, 57 (November 16, 1893): 389.

21. *San Francisco Chronicle*, n.d., quoted by the *Literary Digest*, 8 (December 2, 1893): 96; see the statement by Murat Halstead quoted by the *New York Herald*, November 16, 1893, p. 10; *New York Tribune*, n.d., quoted by the *Literary Digest*, 8 (November 18, 1893): 59; *Chicago Inter Ocean*, quoted by ibid. (November 25, 1893), p. 77.

22. *New York Herald*, November 16, 1893, p. 10.

23. Quoted by the *Literary Digest*, 8 (November 18, 1893): 59-60.

24. Quoted by the *Literary Digest*, 8 (November 25, 1893): 77.

25. Nordhoff to Gresham, December 9, 1893, Cleveland Papers Microfilm, Series 2, reel 81, frame 22,410.

26. *New York Herald*, November 20, 1893, p. 6; *New York Sun*, December 5, 1893, cited by Russ, *The Hawaiian Revolution*, pp. 285-86. For Thurston's rebuttal see Thurston to Gresham, December 5, 1893, Notes from the Hawaiian Legation in the United States to the Department of State, IV, Record Group 59, National Archives Microfilm Publication T 160, roll 4. This dispatch is printed in *House Executive Documents*, 53 Cong., 2 sess., No. 48 (Serial 3224), pp. 171-76. For Stevens' rebuttal see the *Congressional Record*, 53 Cong., 2 sess., pp. 191 ff. (December 13, 1893).

27. Richardson, ed., *Messages and Papers of the Presidents*, 9: 441-42.

28. Senators Joseph N. Dolph of Oregon, William P. Frye of Maine, and George F. Hoar of Massachusetts did most of the talking on behalf of annexation and against restoration. *Congressional Record*, 53 Cong., 2 sess., pp. 19-30 (December 5, 1893). Senators Roger Q. Mills of Texas and George Gray of Delaware spoke against annexation and in favor of restoration. Ibid., pp. 61-73 (December 6, 1893). Hoar's resolution is found in ibid., p. 19 (December 5, 1893). For the charge that Hoar was seeking partisan advantage see the *New York Herald*, December 7, 1893, p. 8.

29. *Congressional Record*, 53 Cong., 2 sess., pp. 220-21 (December 13, 1893).

30. Telegram, Admiral John Irwin to the Secretary of the Navy, December 4, 1893, Ciphers Received, No. 1, p. 323, Records of the Department of the Navy, Record Group 45, N.A. The telegram is printed in *House Executive Documents*, 53 Cong., 2 sess., No. 48 (Serial 3224), p. 509.

31. Memorandum, dated February 1901, Letters, box 1, Olney Papers. The Gresham draft, which was written with the assistance of John Bassett Moore, recommended that Cleveland continue to seek the queen's reinstatement. Gerald G. Eggert, *Richard Olney: Evolution of a Statesman*, p. 187. The Olney draft, on the other hand, urged that the president abandon the cause of Liliuokalani, giving her refusal to accept the conditions laid down by the chief executive as the reason for doing so. Furthermore, the attorney general stipulated that the contending parties in Hawaii should settle the matter of who should rule in the islands. If anything remained to be done regarding Hawaii, said Olney, Congress should take "such action . . . as its wisdom may advise and its more extended powers may render practicable." Richard Olney, "Suggestions for President's Message of December 18, 1893, Concerning Hawaii," p. 17, Scrapbook, box 4, Richard Olney Papers, Manuscript Division, L.C.

32. Message of December 18, 1893, Richardson, ed., *Messages and Papers of the Presidents*, 9: 461, 468–72.

33. Quoted by the *New York Herald*, December 20, 1893, p. 5. The president's statement also received editorial compliments from other Democratic organs such as *The Nation*, the *St. Louis Republic*, the *Omaha World-Herald*, the *Philadelphia Times*, and the *Nashville American*. See *The Nation*, 57 (December 21, 1893): 460; newspaper survey in the *New York Herald*, December 20, 1893, p. 5; *Literary Digest*, 8 (December 23, 1893): 7.

34. *New York World*, December 19, 1893, quoted by the *Literary Digest*, 8 (December 23, 1893): 6. Commissioner Alexander had talked with the editor of the *World* and probably played some role in bringing about the changed outlook of that newspaper. Russ, *The Hawaiian Revolution*, pp. 292–93.

35. Quoted by the *Literary Digest*, 8 (December 23, 1893): 146.

36. Quoted by the *New York Herald*, December 20, 1893, p. 5.

37. Voorhees to Cleveland, December 18, 1893, Cleveland Papers Microfilm, Series 2, reel 81, frames 22,621 and 22,622.

38. Straus to Cleveland, December 23, 1893, ibid., frame 22,765.

39. Bayard to Gresham, December 28, 1893, vol. XLI, Gresham Papers; Bristow to Gresham, December 19, 1893, ibid.; White to Gresham, December 24, 1893, ibid.

40. Allan Nevins, *Grover Cleveland: A Study in Courage*, p. 561.

41. Russ, *The Hawaiian Revolution*, pp. 350–51.

42. The recommendation appears in Olney, "Suggestions for President's Message of December 18, 1893, Concerning Hawaii," p. 17.

7. CONGRESSIONAL RESISTANCE TO HAWAIIAN ANNEXATION

1. Alexander to Dole, December 17, 1893, Foreign Office and Executive File (hereafter cited as F.O. and Ex.), 1893, State Archives of Hawaii (hereafter cited as A.H.), Honolulu, H.I.

2. *Congressional Record*, 53 Cong., 2 sess., pp. 375–76 (December 18, 1893). Since all three of these documents dealt mainly with the administration's intention of restoring the Hawaiian queen, it seems likely that Boutelle was attempting to show that Gresham planned to use military force to reinstate the fallen monarch. If this impression could be conveyed to the House, the administration's Hawaiian policy would appear vulnerable on constitutional grounds since Congress had not given its consent, as the Constitution required (Article I, section 8), for an act of war.

3. Ibid., p. 399 (December 19, 1893).

4. Ibid., p. 1814 (February 2, 1894), p. 2001 (February 7, 1894); printed in *House Miscellaneous Documents*, 53 Cong., 2 sess., No. 44 (Serial 3229).

5. *Congressional Record*, 53 Cong., 2 sess., p. 1814 (February 2, 1894).

6. Rayner to Gresham, January 1, 1894, vol. XLI, Walter Q. Gresham Papers, Manuscript Division, Library of Congress. Emphasis in original.

7. *Congressional Record*, 53 Cong., 2 sess., p. 513 (January 6, 1894).

8. Ibid., p. 1810 (February 2, 1894).

9. Ibid., p. 1821.

10. Ibid., p. 1831 (February 3, 1894).

11. Ibid., Appendix, pp. 440–42 (February 2, 1894), p. 446 (February 3, 1894).

12. *Congressional Record*, 53 Cong., 2 sess., pp. 1890-91 (February 5, 1894).

13. Ibid., p. 1959 (February 6, 1894).

14. Ibid., pp. 1968–69.

15. Ibid., p. 2007 (February 7, 1894).

16. Quoted by the *Literary Digest*, 8 (February 15, 1894): 367.

17. *New York Times*, February 8, 1894, p. 4.

18. Quoted by ibid., p. 368.

19. The reactions of Republican and independent papers to passage of the McCreary resolution are found in ibid., pp. 367–68.

20. *Congressional Record*, 53 Cong., 2 sess., p. 434 (December 20, 1893); *Senate Reports*, 53 Cong., 2 sess., No. 227 (Serial 3180), p. 1.

21. *Senate Miscellaneous Documents*, 53 Cong., 2 sess., No. 29 (Serial 3167).

22. *Congressional Record*, 53 Cong., 2 sess., p. 707 (January 11, 1894).

23. Ibid., p. 1220 (January 23, 1894).

24. Ibid., p. 1308 (January 24, 1894); printed in *Senate Miscellaneous Documents*, 53 Cong., 2 sess., No. 48 (Serial 3167).

25. *Congressional Record*, 53 Cong., 2 sess., p. 1308 (January 24, 1894).

26. Ibid., p. 1578 (January 29, 1894).

27. Ibid., p. 2086 (February 12, 1894), and p. 2129 (February 13, 1894).

28. Ibid., p. 2314 (February 20, 1894).

29. For example, Senators John W. Daniel of Virginia, George Gray of Delaware, and David Turpie of Indiana were not irreconcilably opposed to Hawaiian annexation.

30. *Congressional Record*, 53 Cong., 2 sess., Appendix, p. 481 (February 21, 1894).

31. *Senate Reports*, 53 Cong., 2 sess., No. 227 (Serial 3180), pp. 1–36.

32. The Democratic members of the committee, aside from John T. Morgan (that is, Senators Matthew C. Butler of South Carolina, David Turpie of Indiana, John W. Daniel of Virginia, and George Gray of Delaware) refused to accept the report's endorsement of Stevens' conduct. Butler and Turpie appended a separate statement approving Hawaiian annexation in principle but disavowing the proposition at that particular time due to the current internal dissension in the islands. Ibid., pp. 35–36. The Republican members of the Committee on Foreign Relations (that is, Senators John Sherman of Ohio, William P. Frye of Maine, Joseph N. Dolph of Oregon, and Cushman K. Davis of Minnesota) approved Morgan's "essential findings," but derided Cleveland for appointing Blount and equipping him with paramount authority, as well as for attempting to reinstate the native monarch. Ibid., pp. 33–34.

33. The views of the *Philadelphia Record*, the *New York Evening Post*, and the *Detroit Free Press* are quoted by the *Literary Digest*, 8 (March 8, 1894): 455.

34. *Congressional Record*, 53 Cong., 2 sess., p. 5499 (May 31, 1894).

35. Ibid., p. 5500.

36. Ibid., p. 5499.

37. It is pertinent to note that Cleveland was able to influence the wording of the Senate's pronouncement on Hawaii in a way that was very important to him. Two days before the upper house voted on Turpie's resolution the president wrote to Senator William F. Vilas of Wisconsin, stating: "The thing I care the most about is the declaration that the *people* of the islands instead of the *Provisional Government* should determine the policy, etc. . . . Can you not nail the endorsement of the Provisional Government, by putting in its place the more American and Democratic reference to the *People* as the source of power and control?" Cleveland to Vilas, May 29, 1894, Allan Nevins, ed., *Letters of Grover Cleveland: 1850-1908*, p. 353 (emphasis in original). Cleveland's request was granted as the substitute Turpie resolution, which passed the Senate on May 31, 1894, and stated: "That of right it belongs wholly to the people of the Hawaiian Islands to establish and maintain their own form of government and domestic polity; . . ." *Congressional Record*, 53 Cong., 2 sess., p. 5499 (May 31, 1894).

38. *Literary Digest*, 9 (June 16, 1894): 187.

39. In a conversation held on August 2, 1894, Secretary Gresham told H. A. Widemann (a spokesman for Liliuokalani): "You will encounter no opposition from this Government. We claim no right to meddle in the domestic affairs of your country." Memorandum dated August 2, 1894, p. 4, *Memoranda of Conversations with the Secretary of State, 1893-1898*, Miscellaneous Archives, Records of the Department of State, Record Group 59, National Archives. Three days later Gresham stated to Samuel Parker (who accompanied Widemann to Washington): "The attitude of this Government ought to be understood at Honolulu. Our warships were sent there not to uphold the provisional government or its successor, but to afford protection to such of our own citizens as did not participate in the local strifes." Memorandum dated August 5, 1894, p. 4, ibid

40. Willis to Gresham, January 11, 1895, *House Executive Documents*, 53 Cong., 3 sess., No. 282 (Serial 3324), pp. 3-4; Willis to Gresham, January 11, 1895, and telegram, same to same, January 30, 1895 (Honolulu, H.I.), February 6, 1895 (San Francisco, Ca.), U.S. Department of State, *Papers Relating to the Foreign Relations of the United States, 1894*, Appendix II, pp. 1393-94, 1396-97.

41. For the text of the president's message of January 9, 1895, and the accompanying documents, see James D. Richardson, ed., *A Compilation of the Messages and Papers of the Presidents, 1789-1897*, 9: 559-60; *Senate Executive Documents*, 53 Cong., 3 sess., No. 31 (Serial 3275), pp. 1-2; *House Executive Documents*, 53 Cong., 3 sess., No. 1, Pt. 1 (Serial 3294), pp. 1378-79; and the *Congressional Record*, 53 Cong., 3 sess., p. 768 (January 9, 1895), and pp. 822-23 (January 10, 1895). Section IV of the reciprocity treaty of 1875 required the consent of the United States in order for the Hawaiian government to lease or otherwise dispose of its territory to another foreign power. William M. Malloy, ed., *Treaties, Conventions, International Acts, Protocols and Agreements between the United States of America and Other Powers, 1776-1909*, 1: 917.

42. *Congressional Record*, 53 Cong., 3 sess., p. 1167 (January 21, 1895); printed in *Senate Miscellaneous Documents*, 53 Cong., 3 sess., No. 60 (Serial 3281).

43. *Congressional Record*, 53 Cong., 3 sess., p. 628 (January 4, 1895).

44. The most vociferous advocates of a cable connecting Hawaii with the United States were, with few exceptions, annexationists. See, for example, the speeches of Senators Eugene Hale of Maine, ibid., pp. 1817-19 (February 6, 1895); Orville H. Platt of Connecticut, ibid., pp. 1826, 1828; William P. Frye of Maine, ibid., p. 1828; John T. Morgan of Alabama, ibid., p. 1949 (February 8, 1895); and Henry Cabot Lodge, ibid., pp. 1983-84

(February 9, 1895). The leading opponents of the cable measure were anti-annexationists. See, for example, the speeches of Senators Donelson Caffery of Louisiana, ibid., p. 1895 (February 7, 1895); and George Gray of Delaware, ibid., p. 1981 (February 9, 1895).

45. The amendment is printed in *Senate Reports*, 53 Cong., 3 sess., No. 834 (Serial 3289). For the Senate vote on the cable measure, see the *Congressional Record*, 53 Cong., 3 sess., p. 1986 (February 9, 1895). The vote was 36 yeas to 25 nays, with 26 abstentions.

46. Cleveland to Bayard, February 13, 1895, Nevins, ed., *Letters of Grover Cleveland*, pp. 377-78.

8. THE CAMPAIGN AGAINST
THE TREATY OF 1897

1. William O. Smith to Hawaiian Minister of Foreign Affairs Henry E. Cooper, March 26, 1897, Foreign Office and Executive File (hereafter cited as F.O. and Ex.), 1897, State Archives of Hawaii (hereafter cited as A.H.). Enclosed in this communication was a memorandum of an interview of Hatch and Smith with McKinley, March 25, 1897.

2. Hatch to Cooper, March 27, 1897, F.O. and Ex., 1897, A.H.

3. *Journal of the Executive Proceedings of the Senate of the United States of America*, vol. XXXI, Pt. 1, p. 230 (July 14, 1897); John Bassett Moore, *A Digest of International Law. . .* , 1: 503; John W. Foster, *Diplomatic Memoirs*, 2: 173. For the text of the treaty see *Senate Reports*, 55 Cong., 2 sess., No. 681 (Serial 3622), pp. 96-97.

4. Hatch to Cooper, July 1, 1897, F.O. and Ex., 1897, A.H. Minister Hatch stated: "Nothing however is more certain than this—that our sugars would have been put on the dutiable list if the President had not come forward with annexation."

5. White to Andrew Gillison, June 22, 1897, vol. XLVI, Stephen Mallory White Papers, Special Collections Department, Stanford University Library, Stanford, Ca.

6. Ripley to Gage, October 14, 1897, cited by Richard D. Weigle, "The Sugar Interests and American Diplomacy in Hawaii and Cuba, 1893-1903" (Ph.D. diss., Yale University, 1939), p. 142; Alameda Sugar Company to Secretary Wilson, November 1, 1897, quoted in ibid. The resolution passed by the Association of Beet Sugar Manufacturers is discussed in ibid.

7. "Sugar Trust and Annexation," December 27, 1897, F.O. and Ex., 1897, A.H. It should be kept in mind that in accordance with the reciprocity treaty with Hawaii only unrefined sugar from the islands could enter the United States duty free. Under annexation all grades of Hawaiian sugar would be entitled to free entry and, therefore, the island planters would have an incentive to start their own refining operations.

8. It is pertinent to note that in San Francisco, where Spreckels' business operations were headquartered and, therefore, where one might expect his influence to be greatest, the mercantile community was practically unanimous in its support of annexation. See, for example, Memorial of the Chamber of Commerce of San Francisco, California, urging the prompt annexation of the Hawaiian Republic, July 5, 1897, Records of the Committee on Foreign Relations, 55 Cong., 1 sess., Records of the United States Senate, Record Group 46, National Archives (hereafter cited as N.A.). Both the *San Francisco Chronicle* and the *Examiner* favored annexation on the ground that it would benefit the city's commerce. *Literary Digest*, 15 (June 26, 1897): 243; *San Francisco Chronicle*, December 11, 1897, p. 6.

9. Weigle, "The Sugar Interests and American Diplomacy," p. 140.

10. Resolutions of the Chamber of Commerce of Los Angeles setting forth how the annexation of Hawaii will be detrimental to the beet sugar interests of Southern California,

December 15, 1897, Records of the Committee on Foreign Relations, 55 Cong., 2 sess., Records of the United States Senate, Record Group 46, N.A. The resolutions were passed by the Los Angeles Chamber of Commerce on December 8, 1897; Resolution of the Board of Trade of Los Angeles, California, opposing the annexation of Hawaii to the United States, January 19, 1898, Petitions and Memorials, Resolutions of State Legislatures, and Related Documents which Were Tabled, 55 Cong., 2 sess., Records of the United States Senate, Record Group 46, N.A.; *Los Angeles Times*, June 18, 1897, p. 6.

11. Weigle, "The Sugar Interests and American Diplomacy," pp. 144-45.

12. See Petition from the citizens of Nebraska protesting against the annexation of Hawaii, February 11, 1898; Resolutions of the Nebraska Beet Sugar Association in opposition to annexation of Hawaii, February 7, 1898; Protest of the faculty and students of the Nebraska State University against ratification of the proposed treaty providing for the annexation of Hawaii, March 7, 1898; Memorial from the American Sugar Growers Society protesting against annexation of Hawaii, January 5, 1898; all of which are found in Records of the United States Senate, 55 Cong., 2 sess., Record Group 46, N.A.

13. Cited by Weigle, "The Sugar Interests and American Diplomacy," pp. 143-44.

14. See Hatch's projected tabulations, dated January 12, 1898, showing how senators would probably vote on the Hawaiian annexation treaty, Annexation Documents (M-58), Francis M. Hatch Papers, A.H.

15. The *Louisiana Planter* and the *New Orleans Daily Picayune* are cited by Weigle, "The Sugar Interests and American Diplomacy," p. 143. Regarding Hatch's view that Louisiana's senators opposed annexation, see his projected tabulations, dated January 12, 1898, showing how senators would probably vote on the Hawaiian annexation treaty, Annexation Documents (M-58), Hatch Papers, A.H. Senator McEnery's views are found in the *Congressional Record*, 55 Cong., 2 sess., p. 6303 (June 24, 1898). See also George F. Pearce, "Assessing Public Opinion: Editorial Comment and the Annexation of Hawaii—A Case Study," *Pacific Historical Review*, 43 (August 1974): 336.

16. For Wilson's letter, see *Senate Documents*, 55 Cong., 2 sess., No. 63 (Serial 3592); *Congressional Record*, 55 Cong., 2 sess., p. 666 (January 17, 1898); *New York Times*, January 18, 1898, p. 1. For reactions to Wilson's letter, see Weigle, "The Sugar Interests and American Diplomacy," p. 146.

17. As in the early 1890s, affiliates of the trust opposed annexation in 1897-98. The business connection between the Spreckelses, the Oxnards, and the trust is discussed in Welch & Co. to Lorrin A. Thurston, January 3, 1898, Letters, 1898 (M-58), Hatch Papers, A.H.

18. White to E. S. Leake, the *San Francisco Call*, January 22, 1898, vol. XLVII, White Papers. In this letter White said that Senators Gorman, Murphy, and Aldrich supported the annexation treaty and this was "proof enough" that the sugar trust was behind the project. However, of these three legislators only Gorman voted for the Newlands joint resolution in July 1898. Aldrich and Murphy were among those not voting on the Newlands measure, although they both said they favored it. *Congressional Record*, 55 Cong., 2 sess., p. 6712 (July 6, 1898). Regarding the claim that the trust opposed annexation see the *Washington Evening Star*, January 15-19, 1898, newspaper clippings (M-58), Hatch Papers, A.H. Senator Morgan also thought the trust opposed annexation. See Hatch to Cooper, July 21, 1897, F.O. and Ex., 1897, A.H.

19. Henry T. Oxnard's statement appears in the *New Orleans Daily Picayune*, January 28, 1898, quoted by Weigle, "The Sugar Interests and American Diplomacy," p. 147. Historian Merze Tate asserted that the trust opposed McKinley's annexation treaty in her book, *The United States and the Hawaiian Kingdom: A Political History*, p. 282. Senator

Lodge's view appears in Lodge to Stephen O'Meara, January 11, 1898, Letterbook No. 12, Henry Cabot Lodge Papers, Massachusetts Historical Society, Boston.

20. John C. Appel, "American Labor and the Annexation of Hawaii: A Study in Logic and Economic Interest," *Pacific Historical Review*, 23 (February 1954): 5, 7.

21. *Coast Seamen's Journal* (November 3, 1897), p. 6; ibid. (December 15, 1897), p. 7.

22. Appel, "American Labor and the Annexation of Hawaii," p. 6.

23. Samuel Gompers, "Should Hawaii Be Annexed?" *American Federationist*, 4 (November 1897): 216. See also Philip S. Foner, *History of the Labor Movement in the United States: From the Founding of the American Federation of Labor to the Emergence of American Imperialism*, 2: 407.

24. *Proceedings* of the Seventeenth Annual Convention of the American Federation of Labor, held at Nashville, Tennessee, December 13-21, 1897, p. 60; *San Francisco Call*, December 15, 1897, newspaper clipping in Scrapbook No. 4 (M-144), Lorrin A. Thurston Papers, A.H.; Thurston to Dole, December 23, 1897, F.O. and Ex., 1897, A.H.

25. *Coast Seamen's Journal* (December 8, 1897), p. 6.

26. Gompers, "Should Hawaii Be Annexed?" pp. 215-16; *Coast Seamen's Journal* (January 12, 1898), p. 7; Appel, "American Labor and the Annexation of Hawaii," p. 7.

27. Ronald Radosh, "American Labor and the Anti-Imperialist Movement: A Discussion," *Science and Society*, 28 (Winter 1964): 93-100.

28. *Coast Seamen's Journal* (November 3, 1897), p. 7. See also Appel, "American Labor and the Annexation of Hawaii," pp. 10-11.

29. See, for example, the *American Federationist*, 4 (November 1897): 215-17.

30. As mentioned earlier, historian Thomas J. McCormick and others regard the anti-imperialists as militant trade expansionists. See that author's "A Commentary on 'The Anti-Imperialists and Twentieth Century American Foreign Policy,'" *Studies on the Left*, 3, no. 1 (1962): 28.

31. Radosh, "American Labor and the Anti-Imperialist Movement: A Discussion," p. 93; also by that author, *American Labor and United States Foreign Policy*, p. 6.

32. Gompers, "Should Hawaii Be Annexed?" p. 215. In addition to perusing Gompers's article in the *American Federationist*, the present writer examined that portion of the labor leader's correspondence which appeared in Letterbooks, vols. XX-XXII (May 19, 1897-March 15, 1898), Samuel Gompers Papers, Library of Congress Microfilm, 1967.

33. *New York Times*, January 28, 1898, p. 2; *New York Tribune*, January 28, 1898, p. 2.

34. An explanatory note is in order. Admittedly, these statements are from only one person in each category, but Frye and Gompers were major leaders of the imperialists and anti-imperialists, respectively, and, therefore, their views were something more than isolated opinions. Also, it might be said that these remarks were made in different contexts; that is, that Frye, unlike Gompers, was addressing himself to a larger topic than just Hawaiian annexation. While this is true, it is also a fact that Frye rarely, if ever, either spoke or wrote about the acquisition of Hawaii without alluding to the expansion of American commerce with the Orient and the rest of the world. However, this writer has seen no evidence in either Gompers's published writings or correspondence indicating that before the fall of 1898 he shared Frye's vision of an overseas commercial empire for the United States. So although the contexts are different, these two quotations suggest major differences in the commercial views of Gompers and Frye during the Hawaiian annexation debate of 1897-98.

35. *New York Times*, June 18, 1897, p. 1. Theodore Roosevelt, an ardent expansionist, also subscribed to this view. See Roosevelt to Alfred T. Mahan, December 11 and 13, 1897, Elting E. Morison and John M. Blum, eds., *The Letters of Theodore Roosevelt*, 1: 741.

36. Shortly after McKinley's inauguration in 1897 Schurz met with him in New York to

discuss the wisdom of appointing annexationist Harold M. Sewall of Maine as minister to Hawaii. The president assured Schurz that annexation was not in the offing, saying "you may be sure that there will be no jingo nonsense under my administration." Later, at a White House dinner on July 1, 1897, Schurz queried the chief executive about the annexation project then underway. McKinley replied, rather evasively it would seem, that the treaty had been sent to the Senate merely to test public opinion on the issue. Claude Moore Fuess, *Carl Schurz: Reformer, 1829-1906*, pp. 349-50. For Senator White's statement see the *New York Times*, June 17, 1897, p. 1.

37. Stephen M. White, "The Proposed Annexation of Hawaii," *The Forum*, 23 (August 1897): 723-36; John Sherman, *Recollections of Forty Years in the House, Senate and Cabinet: An Autobiography*, 2: 1216.

38. *The American Monthly Review of Reviews*, 17 (January 1898): 77.

39. Thomas B. Reed, "Empire Can Wait," *The Illustrated American*, 22 (December 4, 1897): 714.

40. E. L. Godkin, "The Momentous Decision," *The Nation*, 65 (December 16, 1897): 468-69.

41. James Bryce, "The Policy of Annexation for America," *The Forum*, 24 (December 1897): 395. Bryce's essay was discussed in *The Nation*, 65 (December 2, 1897): 432; *The American Monthly Review of Reviews*, 17 (January 1898): 75; *The Outlook*, 58 (January 8, 1898): 109-10; and *Harper's Weekly*, 42 (July 9, 1898); 659. See also William A. Russ, Jr., *The Hawaiian Republic (1894-98) and Its Struggle to Win Annexation*, p. 200.

42. *New York Times*, January 25, 1898, p. 1.

43. George S. Boutwell, "Hawaiian Annexation," an address before the Boot and Shoe Club of Boston, December 22, 1897, p. 7, George Sewall Boutwell Pamphlets, Massachusetts Historical Society, Boston, Mass. These pamphlets are kept in a special file apart from the George Sewall Boutwell Papers.

44. Speech of Moorfield Storey as Chairman of the National Democratic Convention, September 30, 1897, p. 20, Moorfield Storey Papers, Manuscript Division, Library of Congress, Washington, D.C.

45. *Pittsburgh Dispatch*, January 30, 1898, cited by E. Berkeley Tompkins, *Anti-Imperialism in the United States: The Great Debate, 1890-1920*, p. 101; Russ, *The Hawaiian Republic*, p. 221.

46. For Schurz's view see, "'Cold Facts' and Hawaii," *Harper's Weekly*, 42 (February 12, 1898): 147. *New York Times*, January 13, 1898, p. 6.

47. Daniel Agnew, "Unconstitutionality of the Hawaiian Treaty," *The Forum*, 24 (December 1897): 461-63.

48. E. L. Godkin, "How Are We to Govern Hawaii?" *The Nation*, 65 (December 2, 1897): 432-33.

49. White, "The Proposed Annexation of Hawaii," pp. 730, 735; Dubois's statement was quoted in the Honolulu *Pacific Commercial Advertiser*, November 19, 1897, a copy of which was enclosed in Sewall to Sherman, No. 80, November 20, 1897, Despatches from United States Ministers in Hawaii, XXX, Record Group 59, National Archives Microfilm Publication T 30, roll 30; Prince A. Morrow, "Leprosy and Hawaiian Annexation," *North American Review*, 165 (November 1897): 582.

50. Longfield Gorman, "The Administration and Hawaii," *North American Review*, 165 (September 1897): 379. See also Schurz, "'Cold Facts' and Hawaii," p. 147; *Los Angeles Times*, June 18, 1897, p. 6; *San Francisco Call*, October 24, 1897, newspaper clipping in Scrapbook No. 4 (M-144), Thurston Papers, A.H.; *Coast Seamen's Journal* (February 2, 1898), p. 2.

51. Senator Henry Cabot Lodge was anxious to annex Hawaii in order to promote

American trade with the Orient. In late 1897 he wrote to one correspondent: "The recent seizures by great European powers of commanding points in [sic] Chinese coasts makes the importance of [Hawaiian] annexation more imperative than ever." Lodge to Alfred C. Vinton, December 17, 1897, Letterbook No. 12, Lodge Papers. See also Cushman K. Davis to Frank B. Kellogg and Cordenio A. Severance, December 27, 1897, box 9, Cushman K. Davis Papers, Minnesota Historical Society, St. Paul, Minn.; and John T. Morgan, "The Duty of Annexing Hawaii," *The Forum*, 25 (March 1898): 13.

52. Schurz, "Hawaii and the Partition of China," *Harper's Weekly*, 42 (January 22, 1898): 75.

53. Schurz, " 'Cold Facts' and Hawaii," p. 147.

54. Boutwell, "Hawaiian Annexation," pp. 8–9.

55. *Senate Documents*, 55 Cong., 2 sess., No. 82 (Serial 3593), p. 13; ibid., No. 28 (Serial 3590), pp. 1–3.

56. Cf., supra, pp. 45–48.

57. White, "The Proposed Annexation of Hawaii," pp. 725–26. President Dole reportedly said during his visit to the United States in early 1898 that there was no immediate threat of a Japanese takeover of Hawaii. He also refuted the notion that Japanese soldiers were immigrating to the Polynesian archipelago in the guise of contract workers. See *New York Times*, January 24, 1898, p. 5.

58. Senator Cushman K. Davis, Chairman of the Committee on Foreign Relations, was one of the many expansionists to advance the claim that Hawaii had to be annexed to protect the future isthmian canal. See the *New York Tribune*, January 13, 1898, p. 4; White, "The Proposed Annexation of Hawaii," p. 726; White to Truman L. Crowder, January 25, 1898, and White to Edward W. Smith, February 5, 1898, vol. XLVII, White Papers.

59. Richard E. Welch, Jr., *George Frisbie Hoar and the Half-Breed Republicans*, pp. 208–9; *Congressional Record*, 55 Cong., 2 sess., p. 45 (December 6, 1897).

60. Memorial of the Sacramento Federated Trades Council against the Annexation of Hawaii, December 14, 1897, Petitions and Memorials, Resolutions of State Legislatures, and Related Documents which Were Tabled, 55 Cong., 2 sess., Records of the United States Senate, Record Group 46, N.A.

61. The anti-imperialists fought in vain for an open session. The expansionists claimed that the European partitioning of China necessitated the secret debate on Hawaii. *New York Times*, January 11, 1898, p. 5. Other sources of information that the writer has relied upon include the White Papers, the diplomatic correspondence of Hawaiian Minister Hatch, and the *New York Times*.

62. *New York Times*, January 13, 1898, p. 3; *The Outlook*, 58 (January 22, 1898): 208; *Congressional Record*, 55 Cong., 2 sess., p. 788 (January 20, 1898); *New York Times*, March 14, 1898, p. 3.

63. For Pettigrew's resolution, see *Congressional Record*, 55 Cong., 2 sess., p. 1173 (January 28, 1898); *New York Times*, January 29, 1898, p. 2; Morgan's amendment, *Congressional Record*, 55 Cong., 2 sess., p. 1495 (February 7, 1898); Teller as quoted in the *New York Times*, February 8, 1898, p. 3. For the remaining speeches by Senate anti-imperialists see ibid., February 9, 1898, p. 3; February 15, 1898, p. 3; February 16, 1898, p. 3; and February 17, 1898, p. 3.

64. Hatch to Cooper, March 6, 1898, F.O. and Ex., 1898, A.H.; *New York Times*, February 21, 1898, p. 4.

65. Welch, *George Frisbie Hoar and the Half-Breed Republicans*, p. 209.

66. Hatch to Cooper, March 3, 1898; and same to Dole, March 6, 1898, both of which are in F.O. and Ex., 1898, A.H. The *Congressional Record* is replete with references during the summer of 1898 to McKinley's pending treaty in the Senate. See, for example, *Con-*

gressional Record, 55 Cong., 2 sess., p. 6308 (June 24, 1898); pp. 6518, 6521, 6524, 6528 (June 30, 1898); pp. 6588–89 (July 1, 1898); pp. 6667, 6671 (July 5, 1898); p. 6707 (July 6, 1898); and Appendix, pp. 592, 595 (June 21, 1898).

67. For Congressman Lewis's resolution see the *Congressional Record*, 55 Cong., 2 sess., p. 664 (January 15, 1898). For the tabling of his resolution see ibid., p. 904 (January 22, 1898), and pp. 1104–5 (January 27, 1898). The vote was 143 yeas to 101 nays, with 103 abstentions.

68. Johnson in ibid., pp. 2031–34 (February 22, 1898); for Grosvenor's rebuttal, see ibid., pp. 5876–79 (June 14, 1898).

69. Foster, *Diplomatic Memoirs*, 2: 173.

70. *New York Times*, June 17, 1897, p. 2; *Los Angeles Times*, June 18, 1897, p. 1; Hatch to Attorney General William O. Smith, December 10, 1897, Letters, 1897 (M–58), Hatch Papers, A.H.

71. The charge that Democratic partisanship was an important reason for the defeat of McKinley's annexation treaty appears in Foster, *Diplomatic Memoirs*, 2: 174. For the Democratic Party platform of 1896, see Kirk H. Porter and Donald B. Johnson, comps., *National Party Platforms, 1840–1960*, pp. 97–100. Harold Baron argues convincingly that the Democratic Party was not an anti-imperialist party in the late nineteenth century. See that writer's "Anti-Imperialism and the Democrats," *Science and Society*, 21 (Summer 1957): 222. William Jennings Bryan's view of Hawaiian annexation is treated in Kendrick A. Clements, "William Jennings Bryan and Democratic Foreign Policy, 1896–1915" (Ph.D. diss., University of California, Berkeley, 1970), p. 45. Democratic Party pressure to dissuade White from opposing annexation is treated in Curtis E. Grassman, "Prologue to Progressivism: Senator Stephen M. White and the California Reform Impulse, 1875–1905" (Ph.D. diss., University of California, Los Angeles, 1970), pp. 380–81; Edith Dobie, *The Political Career of Stephen Mallory White: A Study of Party Activities under the Convention System*, p 202. In addition to Morgan, the Democratic senators supporting Hawaiian annexation included Gorman of Maryland, Money of Mississippi, Murphy of New York, Pettus of Alabama, Rawlins of Utah, and Turpie of Indiana. *New York Times*, January 15, 1898, p. 1.

72. Hatch to Cooper, March 3, 1898, F.O. and Ex., 1898, A.H.

73. Same to same, December 22, 1897, F.O. and Ex., 1897, A.H.; Lodge to Stephen O'Meara, January 11, 1898, Letterbook No. 12, Lodge Papers.

9.   THE DEFEAT OF THE ANTI-ANNEXATIONISTS

1. For the Morgan resolution, see the *Congressional Record*, 55 Cong., 2 sess., p. 2853 (March 16, 1898). Documents supporting that resolution appear in *Senate Reports*, 55 Cong., 2 sess., No. 681 (Serial 3622), pp. 27–37.

2. Hatch to Cooper, April 14, 1898, Foreign Office and Executive File (hereafter cited as F.O. and Ex.), 1898, State Archives of Hawaii (hereafter cited as A.H.). Near the end of this twelve-page epistle Hatch observed: "It will not be safe to under-rate the activity, or the power, of the interests which are arrayed against us in this fight. They work in methods which we cannot, have agents throughout the entire country, and exert a power which it is going to be very difficult indeed to overcome."

3. Same to same, May 13, 1898, ibid. It should be noted that before the anti-imperialists swung their full weight against the new joint resolution, they offered an alternative to annexation—a scheme for the neutralization of the islands. According to this

plan a "free marine zone" would be created around the archipelago, enabling all nations to use Honolulu for commercial purposes. Congressman Henry U. Johnson of Indiana introduced, unavailingly, a proposal to that effect. *Congressional Record*, 55 Cong., 2 sess., p. 4747 (May 9, 1898). For additional information on the neutralization alternative see typed, undated, unsigned memorandum, box 19, Edward A. Atkinson Papers, Massachusetts Historical Society, Boston. The letters in this collection indicate that the neutralization plan was formulated primarily by Horace Kenney, treasurer of The American Industries Company. Edward A. Atkinson, industrialist and economist, worked with Kenney on the project. Representative Johnson of Indiana was persuaded by Kenney to introduce the neutralization resolution in Congress. See Kenney to Atkinson, March 31, 1898, ibid.

4. Schurz to McKinley, May 9, 1898, Frederic Bancroft, ed., *Speeches, Correspondence and Political Papers of Carl Schurz*, 5: 466. In a Senate speech Stephen M. White of California quoted a lengthy excerpt from a statement denouncing Hawaiian annexation made by former Secretary Sherman on May 15 to a correspondent for the *New York World*. See White's address in the *Congressional Record*, 55 Cong., 2 sess., Appendix, p. 604 (June 22, 1898). Sherman expressed his opposition to Hawaiian annexation on anti-imperialist grounds in a number of press interviews in the late spring and early summer of 1898. See newspaper clippings, vol. DCXIII, Scrapbook, 1897–1898, John Sherman Papers, Library of Congress (hereafter cited as L.C.). Former President Cleveland's statement appears in the *New York Times*, June 22, 1898, pp. 6–7.

5. For the majority report of the Foreign Affairs Committee see "Annexation of the Hawaiian Islands," *House Reports*, 55 Cong., 2 sess., No. 1355, Pt. 1 (Serial 3721), p. 7; *Congressional Record*, 55 Cong., 2 sess., p. 4989 (May 17, 1898). For the minority report of that committee see *House Reports*, ibid., Pt. 2, pp. 1–2.

6. Lodge to Roosevelt, May 31, 1898, Henry Cabot Lodge and Charles F. Redmond, eds., *Selections from the Correspondence of Theodore Roosevelt and Henry Cabot Lodge, 1884–1918*, 1: 302. The Speaker's opposition was applauded in an unsigned article, "How the Speakership Looks Now," *The Nation*, 66 (June 30, 1898): 493. Reed's resistance to annexation was also commended by *The Outlook*, 59 (June 25, 1898): 453.

7. Tyler Dennett, *Americans in Eastern Asia: A Critical Study of United States Policy in the Far East in the Nineteenth Century*, p. 624. Details of the debate can be found in the *Congressional Record*.

8. See, for example, the *Congressional Record*, 55 Cong., 2 sess., p. 5975 (June 15, 1898); pp. 6229–30 (June 22, 1898); p. 6258 (June 23, 1898); pp. 6351, 6355 (June 27, 1898); pp. 6483, 6486 (June 29, 1898); pp. 6523, 6527 (June 30, 1898). For an expression of this view outside of Congress see George B. Merrill, "Thirty Years After: Supplemental Notes on Hawaii," *Overland Monthly*, 32 (July 1898): 64–65.

9. For expressions of Senator Caffery's view see the *Congressional Record*, 55 Cong., 2 sess., p. 5977 (June 15, 1898); p. 6188 (June 21, 1898); p. 6229 (June 22, 1898); pp. 6352, 6354 (June 27, 1898); pp. 6483, 6486 (June 29, 1898); p. 6528 (June 30, 1898); p. 6625 (July 2, 1898); pp. 6641, 6644, 6648 (July 4, 1898); pp. 6702, 6706 (July 6, 1898); Appendix, pp. 568, 571 (June 15, 1898); p. 597 (June 21, 1898). For evidence of the anti-imperialists' fear that the annexation of Hawaii would lead to other acquisitions see the *Congressional Record*, 55 Cong., 2 sess., p. 6188 (June 21, 1898); p. 6352 (June 27, 1898); p. 6483 (June 29, 1898); p. 6531 (June 30, 1898); p. 6642 (July 4, 1898); pp. 6702, 6706 (July 6, 1898); Appendix, p. 569 (June 15, 1898); p. 607 (June 22, 1898). For an expression of this view outside of Congress see David Starr Jordan, "Lest We Forget," an address delivered before the graduating class of 1898 at Leland Stanford Jr. University on May 25, 1898, printed copy, p. 24, David Starr Jordan File, Bancroft Library, University of California, Berkeley.

10. *Congressional Record*, 55 Cong., 2 sess., p. 6143 (June 20, 1898). See also ibid., Appendix, pp. 597–98 (June 21, 1898); p. 609 (June 22, 1898).

11. *Congressional Record*, 55 Cong., 2 sess., p. 6149 (June 20, 1898). See also ibid., p. 6310 (June 24, 1898); p. 6482 (June 29, 1898); p. 6518 (June 30, 1898); Appendix, pp. 594–95 (June 21, 1898).

12. *Congressional Record*, 55 Cong., 2 sess., pp. 6148, 6151 (June 20, 1898). Interestingly, Senator Cushman K. Davis of Minnesota, a vigorous exponent of Hawaiian annexation, stated privately that he was greatly concerned that passage of the Newlands measure might cripple senatorial prerogative. To his law partners he wrote: "It may be that those who are opposing the [Newlands] resolutions upon Constitutional grounds may come to me with a proposition to let them drop, and advise and consent to the treaty instead. If this proposition is made, I shall accept it, because I have been exceedingly reluctant all through to proceed by way of resolutions. While I have little doubt of their Constitutionality, I dislike very much to see the treaty making prerogatives of the Senate maimed by that method of procedure." Davis to Frank B. Kellogg and Cordenio A. Severance, June 30, 1898, box 9, Cushman K. Davis Papers, Minnesota Historical Society, St. Paul, Minn.

13. *Congressional Record*, 55 Cong., 2 sess., p. 6518 (June 30, 1898).

14. Allen's statement appears in ibid., p. 6651 (July 4, 1898). For White's statement, see ibid., Appendix, p. 594 (June 21, 1898). The same point was stressed by Senator William Lindsay of Kentucky and others. See, especially, the *Congressional Record*, 55 Cong., 2 sess., p. 6671 (July 5, 1898). Turley's statement appears in the *Congressional Record*, 55 Cong., 2 sess., p. 6332 (June 25, 1898).

15. See, for example, ibid., p. 5937 (June 14, 1898); p. 5998 (June 15, 1898); p. 6141 (June 20, 1898); p. 6189 (June 21, 1898); and p. 6486 (June 29, 1898).

16. Bate's remark appears in ibid., p. 6521 (June 30, 1898). For the other racial comments see ibid., p. 6618 (July 2, 1898); and p. 6189 (June 21, 1898).

17. Ibid., pp. 6709–10 (July 6, 1898). Bacon's amendment was defeated by a vote of 20 yeas to 42 nays, with 27 abstentions.

18. See, for example, ibid., p. 5982 (June 15, 1898); Appendix, pp. 669–70 (June 13, 1898); p. 566 (June 11, 1898).

19. Transcript of the Secret Debate in the Senate on the Annexation of Hawaii, May 31, 1898 (Sen. 55 B–C4), pp. 45, 58–59, 148, Records of the United States Senate, Record Group 46, National Archives (hereafter cited as N.A.). This important document was not declassified and made available by the federal government until 1969. It has been neither cited nor mentioned in the literature dealing with Hawaiian annexation.

20. *Congressional Record*, 55 Cong., 2 sess., p. 5840 (June 13, 1898).

21. Ibid., p. 5992 (June 15, 1898); p. 6348 (June 25, 1898); p. 6635 (July 4, 1898); pp. 6671–72 (July 5, 1898); Appendix, p. 533 (June 11, 1898).

22. Dole's interview appears in the *Congressional Record*, 55 Cong., 2 sess., pp. 6621–22 (July 2, 1898). For the excerpt from Hoshi's journal article see ibid., p. 6001 (June 15, 1898). Cf., Toru Hoshi, "The New Japan," *Harper's New Monthly Magazine*, 95 (November 1897): 890–98. Senator Davis's charge appeared in "Report on the Joint Resolution for the Annexation of Hawaii," in *Senate Reports*, 55 Cong., 2 sess., No. 681 (Serial 3622), pp. 38–39. Minister Hoshi's response was quoted in the *Congressional Record*, 55 Cong., 2 sess., Appendix, pp. 599–600 (June 21, 1898). Hoshi quoted Sherman in the *Congressional Record*, 55 Cong., 2 sess., Appendix, p. 600 (June 21, 1898). In June 1897 Secretary Sherman had told United States Minister Edwin Dun at Tokyo that the talk of Japanese designs upon Hawaii was based upon "mischievous reports" that "were not credited here [Washington] and needed no denial." Sherman to Dun, telegram, June 25, 1897, Diplomatic Instructions of the Department of State, Japan, IV, Record Group 59,

National Archives Microfilm Publication M 77, roll 107, pp. 426-27. Because of this communication and other corroborating evidence the present writer does not think that the McKinley administration regarded Japan as a serious threat to Hawaii's sovereignty. However, Washington was concerned that if the islands remained independent they would be a source of friction in American-Japanese relations.

23. John Hay to William R. Day, May 9, 1898, General Correspondence, 1898, box 8, William R. Day Papers, L.C. See the undated, typewritten, two-page memorandum prepared by Cecil Spring Rice that was enclosed with the letter. That Britain did not covet Hawaii in the late 1890s has been shown by Merze Tate, "Great Britain and the Sovereignty of Hawaii," *Pacific Historical Review*, 31 (November 1962): 327-48.

24. For White's statement see *Congressional Record*, 55 Cong., 2 sess., Appendix, p. 617 (July 6, 1898). The charge that White represented the trust is discussed in Stephen M. White to Editor of the *San Francisco Chronicle*, June 9, 1898, vol. LIII, Stephen Mallory White Papers, Special Collections Department, Stanford University Library, Stanford, Ca.

25. Allen's statement appears in the *Congressional Record*, 55 Cong., 2 sess., p. 6705 (July 6, 1898). For Clark's view see *ibid.*, p. 5793 (June 11, 1898). Actually, Clark exaggerated somewhat. Representative Charles H. Grosvenor of Ohio, one of the leading expansionists in the House, presented letters supporting Hawaiian annexation written by the officers of the six major railroad brotherhoods. Ibid., p. 5874 (June 14, 1898). Gompers's letter appears in ibid., pp. 6350-51 (June 27, 1898). Pettigrew's amendment appears in ibid., p. 6709 (July 6, 1898).

26. The views of Morrill and Pettigrew appear in ibid., p. 6143 (June 20, 1898); p. 6612 (July 2, 1898). For White's view see ibid., Appendix, p. 615 (July 6, 1898). For expressions of the view that the home market ought to be developed before the overseas market see the *Congressional Record*, 55 Cong., 2 sess., pp. 6269-70 (June 23, 1898); p. 6355 (June 27, 1898). McEnery's view appears in ibid., p. 6304 (June 24, 1898). For Bate's view see ibid., p. 6526 (June 30, 1898).

27. Cf. supra, pp. 45-48, 93-95, 101-2.

28. *Congressional Record*, 55 Cong., 2 sess., p. 6000 (June 15, 1898); pp. 6142-44 (June 20, 1898); p. 6703 (July 6, 1898); Appendix, p. 595 (June 21, 1898); p. 533 (June 11, 1898).

29. The substitute measure, which pledged the United States to maintain Hawaii's independence, was defeated by a vote of 96 yeas to 204 nays, with 53 not voting and two answering "present." *Congressional Record*, 55 Cong., 2 sess., p. 6018 (June 15, 1898). For the House vote on the Newlands resolution see ibid., p. 6019. Forty-nine congressmen abstained and six answered "present."

30. Ibid., p. 6712 (July 6, 1898).

31. Cleveland to Olney, July 8, 1898, box 6, Richard Olney Papers, Manuscript Division, L.C.

32. Thomas A. Bailey, "The United States and Hawaii during the Spanish-American War," *American Historical Review*, 36 (April 1931): 560. The more specialized works advancing Bailey's thesis include Michael J. Devine, "John W. Foster and the Struggle for the Annexation of Hawaii," *Pacific Historical Review*, 46 (February 1977): 49-50; Allen Lee Hamilton, "Military Strategists and the Annexation of Hawaii," *Journal of the West*, 15 (April 1976): 81, 89-90; Julius W. Pratt, *Expansionists of 1898: The Acquisition of Hawaii and the Spanish Islands*, p. 317; William A. Russ, Jr., *The Hawaiian Republic (1894-98) and Its Struggle to Win Annexation*, pp. 300, 305, 372; Merze Tate, *The United States and the Hawaiian Kingdom: A Political History*, pp. 311, 315. For general works emphasizing the role of the Spanish-American War in bringing about the annexation of Hawaii see Samuel Flagg Bemis, *A Diplomatic History of the United States*, p. 462; Alexander De-

Conde, *A History of American Foreign Policy*, 1: 302; Robert H. Ferrell, *American Diplomacy: A History*, pp. 358–59; Paul S. Holbo, "Economics, Emotion, and Expansion: An Emerging Foreign Policy," in H. Wayne Morgan, ed., *The Gilded Age*, pp. 219, 221; Richard W. Leopold, *The Growth of American Foreign Policy*, p. 183; Ernest R. May, *Imperial Democracy: The Emergence of America as a Great Power*, p. 243; Frederick Merk, *Manifest Destiny and Mission in American History: A Reinterpretation*, pp. 255–56; H. Wayne Morgan, *William McKinley and His America*, pp. 295–96; Armin Rappaport, *A History of American Diplomacy*, p. 186; Daniel M. Smith, *The American Diplomatic Experience*, p. 196; Harold and Margaret Sprout, *The Rise of American Naval Power, 1776–1918*, pp. 242–43; Richard W. Van Alstyne, *American Diplomacy in Action*, p. 678.

33. Bailey, "The United States and Hawaii during the Spanish-American War," pp. 557, 559.

34. The Senate Finance Committee, which was considering a war revenue bill, had decided previously that any discussion of the Hawaiian annexation rider that Lodge was attempting to attach to the revenue bill, or any discussion of Hawaii's role in the pending war, should take place in closed session in order to insure the secrecy necessary to wage the war. Lodge called attention to Hawaii's role in the war, and indirectly to his annexation rider, by claiming that unless the islands were acquired the United States would have no naval base in the Pacific from which to send supplies and reinforcements to Dewey in the Philippines. Transcript of the Secret Debate in the Senate on the Annexation of Hawaii, pp. 1-3, 33.

35. Lodge to George [H. Lyman?], June 2, 1898, Letterbook No. 15, Lodge Papers, Massachusetts Historical Society, Boston.

36. Henry Cabot Lodge to Theodore Roosevelt, May 31, 1898, and June 15, 1898, in Lodge and Redmond, eds., *Selections from the Correspondence of Theodore Roosevelt and Henry Cabot Lodge*, 1: 302, 315; Lodge to Brooks Adams, June 20, 1898, Letterbook No. 15, Lodge Papers; *New York Tribune*, June 5, 1898, p. 1.

37. *Congressional Record*, 55 Cong., 2 sess., p. 5879 (June 14, 1898).

38. The twenty-four representatives who indicated that the United States needed to annex Hawaii primarily for commercial reasons included: John A. Barham of Ca.; Samuel S. Barney of Wis.; Edwin C. Burleigh of Me.; Samuel M. Clark of Iowa; Charles F. Cochran of Mo.; John B. Corliss of Mich.; Amos J. Cummings of N.Y.; Marion De Vries of Ca.; Henry R. Gibson of Tenn.; Frederick H. Gillett of Mass.; Joseph V. Graff of Ill.; Charles H. Grosvenor of Ohio; William A. Hepburn of Iowa; John F. Lacey of Iowa; Philip B. Low of N.Y.; James R. Mann of Ill.; Daniel W. Mills of Ill.; John M. Mitchell of N.Y.; James Norton of S.C.; Theobald Otjen of Wis.; George W. Ray of N.Y.; Edwin R. Ridgely of Kans.; William Alden Smith of Mich.; Thomas H. Tongue of Oreg. For their speeches, see the *Congressional Record*, 55 Cong., 2 sess. (1898).

39. The six senators who spoke in favor of Hawaiian annexation included: Eugene Hale of Me.; George F. Hoar of Mass.; William E. Mason of Ill.; Edmund W. Pettus of Ala.; Joseph L. Rawlins of Utah; and Henry M. Teller of Colo. Hoar wanted the United States to acquire Hawaii in order to prevent the islands from being taken by Japan. Pettus urged annexation for unspecified military reasons; however, he made no mention of the pending war. Teller favored annexation mainly for commercial reasons. Hale, Mason, and Rawlins recommended the acquisition of Hawaii without explaining why.

40. See the *Seattle Post-Intelligencer*, May 6, 1898, p. 4; the *Portland Oregonian*, May 4, 1898, p. 4; the *San Francisco Chronicle*, June 8, 1898, p. 6; the *San Francisco Examiner*, May 4, 1898, p. 6; the *San Jose Mercury*, quoted in the *Los Angeles Times*, June 13, 1898, p. 9; the *Los Angeles Times*, May 19, 1898, p. 7; the *San Diego Union*, May 1, 1898, p. 4.

41. Bailey has implied that because fourteen of the sixteen members of Congress from

the Pacific coast states voted for annexation, the coastal defense argument, particularly as it pertained to future wars, must have carried top priority with the west coast delegation on Capitol Hill. See Bailey, "The United States and Hawaii during the Spanish-American War," p. 559. This view, however, does not comport with the evidence. The present writer was able to locate speeches and comments made by only six members of Congress from the Pacific seaboard states who voted for annexation, and their remarks clearly indicated that their votes were based more on commercial than on military considerations. Representative John A. Barham of California is quoted in the *Congressional Record*, 55 Cong., 2 sess., p. 5911 (June 14, 1898). The remarks of Representative Marion De Vries of California appear in ibid., Appendix, p. 656. The views of Representatives Samuel G. Hilborn of California and James Hamilton Lewis of Washington appear in the *Congressional Record*, 55 Cong., 2 sess., p. 5927 (June 14, 1898), and ibid., Appendix, pp. 535–36 (June 11, 1898). For the view of Senator George C. Perkins of California, see the *San Francisco Examiner*, May 28, 1898, p. 2. Representative Thomas H. Tongue of Oregon is quoted in the *Congressional Record*, 55 Cong., 2 sess., Appendix, p. 534 (June 11, 1898).

42. That the Navy Department was not exercised over the specter of a Spanish invasion of the Pacific coast was revealed in its decision to order virtually all war vessels of any consequence (including the *Charleston*, the *Monadnock*, the *Monterey*, and the *Oregon*) away from that coastline. Senator White of California, after having visited the Navy and War Departments, told one of his constituents that the military policymakers in Washington were "convinced that we [those residing along the western coastline] are in no danger." "Especially is this the case," said White, "since the Philippine incident, and the danger of privateers etc. is not regarded as serious." White to Judge J. N. Phillips, May 11, 1898, vol. 52, p. 884, White Papers.

43. The sixteen representatives who urged annexation mainly on the grounds that an American-owned Hawaii was essential to the future safety of the west coast included: Robert Adams, Jr. of Pa.; Jacob H. Bromwell of Ohio; Jonathan P. Dolliver of Iowa; Daniel Ermentrout of Pa.; Edward L. Hamilton of Mich.; Charles L. Henry of Ind.; Robert R. Hitt of Ill.; Freeman T. Knowles of S. Dak.; Francis G. Newlands of Nev.; Horace B. Packer of Pa.; Richard Wayne Parker of N.J.; Charles E. Pearce of Mo.; Joseph B. Showalter of Pa.; Horace G. Snover of Mich.; James F. Stewart of N.J.; William Sulzer of N.Y.

44. The four representatives included Newlands, Packer, Pearce, and Sulzer.

45. See, e.g., Bailey, "The United States and Hawaii during the Spanish-American War," pp. 556, 560; Bemis, *A Diplomatic History of the United States*, p. 462; Pratt, *Expansionists of 1898*, pp. 319–20; Russ, *The Hawaiian Republic*, pp. 287–88, 300, 303, 305; Sprout and Sprout, *The Rise of American Naval Power*, p. 242; Tate, *The United States and the Hawaiian Kingdom*, pp. 298, 300, 315.

46. The memorandum by Spring Rice was enclosed in Hay to William R. Day, May 9, 1898, General Correspondence, 1898, box 8, Day Papers.

47. Lodge to Paul Dana, June 1, 1898, Letterbook No. 15, Lodge Papers; *New York Tribune*, May 28, 1898, p. 1.

48. Both LaFeber and McCormick assert, rather than demonstrate, that Hawaii was annexed in 1898 primarily to enable the United States to develop trade with the Orient. Their works do not follow closely the course of the Hawaiian debate in Congress during the crucial months of May and June 1898; nor do they treat adequately the key parliamentary role played by Senator Henry Cabot Lodge. If these writers had paid more attention to the congressional debate over Hawaii in mid-1898, the chances are that they would not have virtually ignored an additional commercial argument for annexation—namely, the contention that Uncle Sam's possession of the Polynesian archipelago would increase the American-Hawaiian trade.

49. George F. Hoar, *Autobiography of Seventy Years*, 2: 308; Lodge to Louis Amonson, May 3, 1898, and Lodge to Theodore Roosevelt, May 24, 1898, Letterbook No. 14, Lodge Papers; *Wall Street Journal*, May 5, 1898, p. 2; *Commercial and Financial Chronicle*, May 21, 1898, p. 977.

50. Lodge to William R. Day, June 6, 1898, memorandum, General Correspondence, 1898, box 9, Day Papers.

51. "A Communication from the Secretary of State Submitting a Recommendation for an Appropriation for a Commercial Commission to China," *House Documents*, 55 Cong., 2 sess., No. 536 (Serial 3692), p. 2.

52. Lodge to Day, June 6, 1898, memorandum, General Correspondence, 1898, box 9, Day Papers.

53. "A Communication from the Secretary of State Submitting a Recommendation for an Appropriation for a Commercial Commission to China," pp. 3, 5. This writer has not located evidence which indisputably links Day's plans to increase the China trade, as outlined in the above letter, with Hawaiian annexation. Unless or until more documentation turns up, Day's views will have to be inferred from circumstantial evidence. Because he seemed to be influenced by Lodge's memorandum of June 6, which connected the expansion of Asian commerce with the acquisition of Hawaii (see note 62), it seems likely that the secretary of state shared, at least to some extent, Lodge's views regarding the commercial importance of the Polynesian archipelago.

54. For Sulzer's comment see the *Congressional Record*, 55 Cong., 2 sess., p. 5906 (June 14, 1898). Other expressions of this view appear in ibid. (under varying dates), pp. 5782, 5829, 5835, 5840, 5879, 5896, 5909, 5911, 5916, 5928, 5932, 5973, 5983, 5989, 6008, 6009, 6018, 6347; Appendix, pp. 500, 512, 534, 548, 562, 566, 578, 582, 656.

55. "The Foreign Relations of the United States," an address by Cushman K. Davis before the alumni of the University of Pennsylvania, June 12, 1900, box 13, Notes and Transcripts of Lectures and Speeches, Davis Papers.

56. "Commercial Relations of the United States with Foreign Countries during the Years 1896 and 1897," *House Documents*, 55 Cong., 2 sess., No. 483 (Serial 3694), p. 15.

57. "A Communication from the Secretary of State Submitting a Recommendation for an Appropriation for a Commercial Commission to China," p. 1.

58. Charles A. Moore to John A. Porter, January 14, 1898, William McKinley Papers, Presidential Papers Microfilm (Washington, D.C., 1961), series 3, reel 59. President McKinley's reasons for wanting to annex Hawaii are difficult to ascertain. He tended to speak either cryptically or in generalities about insular expansion, saying on one occasion that Hawaii was annexed because of "manifest destiny." His official papers reveal very little specific information about why he wanted Hawaii annexed. Thus McKinley's view regarding this matter will have to be surmised from circumstantial evidence. His address before the National Association of Manufacturers in January 1898 indicates that he was concerned about opening undeveloped foreign markets to American commerce while he was trying to get Hawaii annexed by treaty. The fact that his general statement was given more precise meaning by Senator Frye (speaking shortly after McKinley), who connected American commercial expansion with Hawaiian annexation, suggests that the president and the senator may have been working in tandem at the N.A.M. conference. Secretary Day's letter to the House of Representatives, dated June 9, indicates that two days before the commencing of the House debate on the Newlands annexation resolution the administration was notifying the lower chamber that "the present is a golden opportunity for enlarging the channels of commercial intercourse with the [Chinese] Empire." (See note 53) Finally, since Representative Grosvenor of Ohio was regarded as a close friend and frequent companion of McKinley, the president may have shared Grosvenor's opinion that Hawaii should be annexed primarily for commercial reasons. Although the above

evidence is fragmentary and proves little if anything, it does suggest that McKinley was mindful of the commercial aspects of the Hawaiian question at the same time that he was trying to acquire the islands.

59. *New York Tribune*, January 28, 1898, p. 2.

60. "Report on the Joint Resolution for the Annexation of Hawaii," p. 16.

61. John T. Morgan, "What Shall We Do With the Conquered Islands?" *North American Review*, 166 (1898): 644, 649.

62. Lodge to Day, June 6, 1898, memorandum, General Correspondence, 1898, box 9, Day Papers.

63. "Annexation of the Hawaiian Islands," *House Reports*, 55 Cong., 2 sess., No. 1355, Part I (Serial 3721), p. 5.

64. See, e.g., the *Portland Oregonian*, May 23, 1898, p. 4; the *Seattle Post-Intelligencer*, June 5, 1898, p. 4.

65. U.S. Department of State, *Papers Relating to the Foreign Relations of the United States, 1894*, Appendix II, p. 171. See Article II of the treaty.

66. Hatch to Henry E. Cooper, July 21, 1897, F.O. and Ex., 1897, A.H.

67. William O. Smith to Hatch, November 12, 1896, Letters, 1896 (M-58), Francis M. Hatch Papers, A.H.

68. Carter to Bayard, September 23, 1887, Notes from the Hawaiian Legation in the United States to the Department of State, III, Record Group 59, National Archives Microfilm Publication T 160, roll 3; Bayard to Carter, September 23, 1887, Notes to the Foreign Legation, Hawaii, III, Record Group 59, General Records of the Department of State, N.A.

69. "Report on the Joint Resolution for the Annexation of Hawaii," p. 31.

70. "Annexation of the Hawaiian Islands," p. 4.

71. *Congressional Record*, 55 Cong., 2 sess., p. 5830 (June 13, 1898).

72. Ibid., Appendix, p. 608 (July 6, 1898). For Foraker's reply, see the *Congressional Record*, 55 Cong., 2 sess., p. 6334 (June 25, 1898). Hawaii was unwilling to make a partial cession of her territory to the United States most likely because that would have left her in the predicament she had been in as an independent insular nation, that is, vulnerable to Japanese domination. Hawaii's Japanese population had been expanding rapidly in numbers and influence, and Tokyo had shown increasing concern about the rights of her nationals in the island republic. Unless the United States took complete possession of Hawaii, Japan could eventually pressure the Polynesian archipelago into granting the franchise to her Japanese residents and then Nippon might dominate the island republic. For evidence of Hawaii's growing fear of Japanese domination at home and, ultimately, of being controlled by Japan, see William O. Smith to Hatch, November 12, 1896, Letters, 1896 (M-58), Hatch Papers. De Vrie's argument appears in ibid., Appendix, p. 656 (June 14, 1898).

73. "Annexation of the Hawaiian Islands," p. 4.

74. *Congressional Record*, 55 Cong., 2 sess., p. 5830 (June 13, 1898).

Selected Bibliography

Manuscript Sources

UNITED STATES OFFICIAL PAPERS, NATIONAL ARCHIVES, WASHINGTON, D.C.

Record Group 45, Records of the Department of the Navy
Ciphers Received, vol. 1 (November 5, 1888 to December 14, 1897).
Ciphers Sent, vol. 1 (October 27, 1889 to May 31, 1898).
Confidential Official Correspondence, vols. 1 and 2 (September 1893 to January 1897).
Record Group 46, Records of the United States Senate
Petitions and Memorials Relating to the Annexation of Hawaii that Were Presented to the Senate Foreign Relations Committee, 55 Congress, 2 session.
Petitions and Memorials, Resolutions of State Legislatures, and Related Documents which Were Tabled, 55 Congress, 2 session.
Transcript of the Secret Debate in the Senate on the Annexation of Hawaii, May 31, 1898, 55 Congress, 2 session.
Record Group 59, General Records of the Department of State
Miscellaneous Archives, *Memoranda of Conversations with the Secretary of State, 1893-1898.*
Microcopy M 77, Diplomatic Instructions, Hawaii, 1893-1898, Japan, 1893-1898.
Microcopy M 99, Notes to Foreign Legations in the United States from the Department of State, Hawaii, 1887-1898.
Microcopy M 144, Despatches from United States Consuls in Honolulu, Hawaii, 1893-1898.
Microcopy T 30, Diplomatic Despatches, Hawaii, 1893-1898.
Microcopy T 160, Notes from the Hawaiian Legation in the United States to the Department of State, 1887-1898.
Record Group 84, Records of the Foreign Service Posts of the Department of State
Miscellaneous Letters Received, Hawaii, 1896-1898.
Miscellaneous Letters Sent, Hawaii, 1897-1898.

PROVISIONAL GOVERNMENT AND REPUBLIC OF HAWAII OFFICIAL PAPERS, STATE ARCHIVES OF HAWAII, HONOLULU.

Foreign Office and Executive File, 1893, 1897, 1898.
Letterbook of the Executive Council of the Provisional Government, 1893.

PRIVATE PAPERS

Atkinson, Edward A. Papers. Massachusetts Historical Society, Boston.
Bayard, Thomas F. Papers. Manuscript Division, Library of Congress.

Boutwell, George Sewall. Pamphlets and Papers. Massachusetts Historical
    Society, Boston.
Castle, William R. Diary. Hawaiian Collection, University of Hawaii Library,
    Honolulu.
Cleveland, Grover. Papers. Presidential Papers Microfilm, Manuscript Division,
    Library of Congress.
Davis, Cushman K. Papers. Minnesota Historical Society, St. Paul.
Day, William R. Papers. Manuscript Division, Library of Congress.
Foster, John W. Papers. Manuscript Division, Library of Congress.
Gompers, Samuel. Papers. Manuscript Division, Library of Congress Microfilm.
Gordon, Hanford Lennox. Papers. Minnesota Historical Society, St. Paul.
Gresham, Walter Q. Papers. Manuscript Division, Library of Congress.
Harrison, Benjamin. Papers. Presidential Papers Microfilm, Manuscript Divi-
    sion, Library of Congress.
Hatch, Francis M. Papers. State Archives of Hawaii, Honolulu.
Jordan, David Starr. Speeches and Miscellaneous Writings, Bancroft Library,
    University of California, Berkeley.
Lodge, Henry Cabot. Papers. Massachusetts Historical Society, Boston.
Long, John D. Papers. Massachusetts Historical Society, Boston.
Morgan, John T. Papers. Manuscript Division, Library of Congress.
Olney, Richard. Papers. Manuscript Division, Library of Congress.
————. Papers. Massachusetts Historical Society, Boston.
Reed, Thomas B. Papers. Bowdoin College Library, Brunswick, Maine.
Schurz, Carl. Papers. Manuscript Division, Library of Congress.
Sherman, John. Papers. Manuscript Division, Library of Congress.
Spooner, John C. Papers. Manuscript Division, Library of Congress.
Stevens, John L. Papers. Maine Historical Society, Portland.
Storey, Moorfield. Papers. Manuscript Division, Library of Congress.
Thurston, Lorrin A. Papers. State Archives of Hawaii, Honolulu.
White, Stephen M. Papers. Department of Special Collections, Stanford Univer-
    sity Library, Stanford.

UNPUBLISHED MANUSCRIPTS AND CONFERENCE PAPERS

Clements, Kendrick A. "William Jennings Bryan and Democratic Foreign
    Policy, 1896–1915." Ph.D. dissertation, University of California, Berkeley,
    1970.
Cordray, William W. "Claus Spreckels of California." Ph.D. dissertation, Uni-
    versity of Southern California, 1955.
Grassman, Curtis E. "Prologue to Progressivism: Senator Stephen M. White and
    the California Reform Impulse, 1875–1905." Ph.D. dissertation, University of
    California, Los Angeles, 1970.
Hendrickson, Kenneth E., Jr. "The Public Career of Richard F. Pettigrew of
    South Dakota, 1846–1926." Ph.D. dissertation, University of Oklahoma, 1962.
Lanier, Osmos, Jr. "Anti-Annexationists of the 1890s." Ph.D. dissertation, Uni-
    versity of Georgia, 1965.

Megargee, Richard. "The Diplomacy of John Bassett Moore: Realism in American Foreign Policy." Ph.D. dissertation, Northwestern University, 1963.

Morgan, William M. "Strategic Factors in Hawaiian Annexation." Ph.D. dissertation, Claremont Graduate School, 1980.

Nagasawa, Arthur. "The Governance of Hawaii from Annexation to 1908: Major Problems and Developments." Ph.D. dissertation, University of Denver, 1968.

Olson, Richard H. "Imperialism and the Pacific Northwest Press, 1893-1900." Ph.D. dissertation, University of Idaho, 1976.

Osborne, Thomas J. "What Was the Main Reason for the Annexation of Hawaii in July, 1898?" M. A. thesis, Claremont Graduate School, 1968.

————. "Trade or War? America's Annexation of Hawaii Reconsidered." Paper presented at the seventieth annual meeting of the Pacific Coast Branch of the American Historical Association, Flagstaff, Arizona, August 12, 1977.

Weigle, Richard D. "The Sugar Interests and American Diplomacy in Hawaii and Cuba, 1893-1903." Ph.D. dissertation, Yale University, 1939.

Published Sources

OFFICIAL PAPERS

United States
    52 Congress, 2 session. *Senate Executive Document 77*
                            [Serial 3062].
    53 Congress, 2 session. *Senate Miscellaneous Document 29*
                            [Serial 3167].
                        Senate Miscellaneous Document 48
                            [Serial 3167].
                        Senate Report 227 [Serial 3180].
                        House Executive Document 47
                            [Serial 3224].
                        House Executive Document 48
                            [Serial 3224].
                        House Executive Document 70
                            [Serial 3224].
                        House Miscellaneous Document 44
                            [Serial 3229].
    53 Congress, 3 session. *Senate Executive Document 31*
                            [Serial 3275].
                        Senate Miscellaneous Document 60
                            [Serial 3281].
                        Senate Report 834 [Serial 3289].
                        House Executive Document 1, Part 1
                            [Serial 3294].
                        House Executive Document 282
                            [Serial 3324].

55 Congress, 2 session. *Senate Document 23* [Serial 3559].
        Senate Document 28 [Serial 3590].
        Senate Document 63 [Serial 3592].
        Senate Document 82 [Serial 3593].
        Senate Report 681 [Serial 3622].
        House Document 536 [Serial 3692].
        House Report 1355, Parts 1 and 2
        [Serial 3721].
Congressional Record, 52 Congress, 2 session; 53 Congress, 2 session; 53 Congress, 3 session; 55 Congress, 2 session.
Department of Commerce and Labor. *Statistical Abstract of the United States.* Washington, D.C.: Government Printing Office, 1908.
Department of State. *Papers Relating to the Foreign Relations of the United States.* Washington, D.C.: Government Printing Office, 1861-.
Journal of the Executive Proceedings of the Senate of the United States of America. Washington, D.C.: Government Printing Office, 1909.

CONTEMPORARY NEWSPAPERS

Anaheim Gazette. 1897.
Hawaiian Star. 1893.
Los Angeles Times. 1893, 1897, 1898.
New York Herald. 1893.
New York Times. 1893, 1894, 1897, 1898.
New York Tribune. 1893, 1898.
Omaha Bee. 1893.
Portland Oregonian. 1898.
St. Louis Post-Dispatch. 1893, 1897.
San Diego Union. 1898.
San Francisco Chronicle. 1893, 1897, 1898.
San Francisco Examiner. 1892, 1893, 1898.
Seattle Post-Intelligencer. 1898.
The periodicals *Literary Digest* and *Public Opinion* were used to gain additional coverage of newspaper editorial commentary on the anti-annexationist movement.

CONTEMPORARY PERIODICALS

American Federationist
American Monthly Review of Reviews
The Argonaut
Atlantic Monthly
The Californian Illustrated Magazine
Coast Seamen's Journal
Commercial and Financial Chronicle
The Forum
Harper's New Monthly Magazine

Harper's Weekly
The Illustrated American
The Independent
Journal of American Politics
Journal of Commerce
Munsey's Magazine
The Nation
The New Time
North American Review
The Outlook
Overland Monthly
Yale Review

BOOKS AND PAMPHLETS

Acheson, Sam Hanna. *Joe Bailey: The Last Democrat*. New York: The Macmillan Co., 1932.

Adler, Jacob. *Claus Spreckels: The Sugar King in Hawaii*. Honolulu: The University Press of Hawaii, 1966.

Alexander, William De Witt. *History of Later Years of the Hawaiian Monarchy and the Revolution of 1893*. Honolulu: Hawaiian Gazette Co., 1896.

Armstrong, William M. *E. L. Godkin and American Foreign Policy*. New York: Bookman Associates, 1957.

Bancroft, Frederic, ed. *Speeches, Correspondence and Political Papers of Carl Schurz*. 6 vols. New York: G. P. Putnam's Sons, 1913.

Beisner, Robert L. *Twelve Against Empire: The Anti-Imperialists, 1898 1900*. New York: McGraw-Hill Book Co., 1968.

Bemis, Samuel Flagg, ed. *The American Secretaries of State and Their Diplomacy*. 10 vols. New York: Alfred A. Knopf, 1927–29.

———. *A Diplomatic History of the United States*. 5th ed. New York: Holt, Rinehart and Winston, Inc., 1965.

Blakey, Roy G. *The United States Beet-Sugar Industry and the Tariff*. New York: Columbia University Press, 1912.

Boutwell, George S. *Reminiscences of Sixty Years in Public Affairs*. 2 vols. New York: McClure, Phillips & Co., 1902.

Bradley, Harold W. *The American Frontier in Hawaii: The Pioneers, 1789-1843*. Reprint ed. Gloucester, Mass.: Peter Smith, 1968.

Campbell, Charles S. *The Transformation of American Foreign Relations, 1865-1900*. New York: Harper & Row, Publishers, 1976.

Chester, Edward W. *Sectionalism, Politics, and American Diplomacy*. Metuchen, N.J.: The Scarecrow Press, 1975.

Clark, Champ. *My Quarter Century of American Politics*. 2 vols. New York: Harper & Brothers, 1920.

Coletta, Paolo E. *William Jennings Bryan*. 3 vols. Lincoln, Nebr.: University of Nebraska Press, 1964-69.

———, ed. *Threshold to American Internationalism: Essays on the Foreign Policies of William McKinley*. New York: Exposition Press, 1970.

Conroy, Hilary. *The Japanese Frontier in Hawaii, 1868-1898.* University of California Publications in History, Vol. 46. Berkeley: University of California Press, 1953.

Daws, Gavan. *Shoal of Time: A History of the Hawaiian Islands.* Honolulu: The University Press of Hawaii, 1968.

DeConde, Alexander. *A History of American Foreign Policy.* 3rd ed. 2 vols. New York: Charles Scribner's Sons, 1978.

Dennett, Tyler. *Americans in Eastern Asia: A Critical Study of United States Policy in the Far East in the Nineteenth Century.* Reprint ed. New York: Barnes & Noble, Inc., 1963.

Dennis, Alfred L. P. *Adventures in American Diplomacy, 1896-1906.* New York: E. P. Dutton & Co., 1928.

Devine, Michael J. *John W. Foster: Politics and Diplomacy in the Imperial Era, 1873-1917.* Athens, Ohio: Ohio University Press, 1980.

Diamond, Martin; Fisk, Winston Mills; and Garfinkel, Herbert. *The Democratic Republic: An Introduction to American National Government.* 2nd ed. Chicago: Rand McNally & Co., 1970.

Dobie, Edith. *The Political Career of Stephen Mallory White: A Study of Party Activities under the Convention System.* Stanford University Series in History, Economics, and Political Science, vol. 2. Palo Alto: Stanford University Press, 1927.

Dole, Sanford B. *Memoirs of the Hawaiian Revolution.* Andrew Farrell, ed. Honolulu: Advertiser Publishing Co., 1936.

Dulles, Foster Rhea. *America in the Pacific: A Century of Expansion.* Reprint ed. New York: Da Capo Press, 1969.

Eggert, Gerald G. *Richard Olney: Evolution of a Statesman.* University Park, Pa.: The Pennsylvania State University Press, 1974.

Ferrell, Robert H. *American Diplomacy: A History.* 3rd ed. New York: W. W. Norton & Co., 1975.

Foner, Philip S. *History of the Labor Movement in the United States.* 4 vols. New York: International Publishers, 1947-65.

Foster, John W. *Diplomatic Memoirs.* 2 vols. Boston: Houghton Mifflin Co., 1909.

———. *American Diplomacy in the Orient.* Reprint ed. New York: Da Capo Press, 1970.

Fowler, Dorothy Ganfield. *John Coit Spooner: Defender of Presidents.* New York: University Publishers, 1961.

Fuess, Claude Moore. *Carl Schurz: Reformer (1829-1906).* Reprint ed. Port Washington, N.Y.: Kennikat Press, 1963.

Gardner, Lloyd C.; LaFeber, Walter F.; and McCormick, Thomas J. *Creation of the American Empire: U.S. Diplomatic History.* Chicago: Rand McNally & Co., 1973.

Grenville, John A. S., and Young, George Berkeley. *Politics, Strategy, and American Diplomacy: Studies in Foreign Policy, 1873-1917.* New Haven: Yale University Press, 1966.

Gresham, Matilda. *Life of Walter Quintin Gresham*. 2 vols. Chicago: Rand McNally & Co., 1919.

Griswold, A. Whitney. *The Far Eastern Policy of the United States*. Reprint ed. New Haven: Yale University Press, 1962.

Hart, Albert B. *The Foundations of American Foreign Policy*. Reprint ed. New York: Da Capo Press, 1970.

Healy, David. *U.S. Expansionism: The Imperialist Urge in the 1890s*. Madison: The University of Wisconsin Press, 1970.

Hoar, George F. *Autobiography of Seventy Years*. 2 vols. New York: Charles Scribner's Sons, 1903.

Hofstadter, Richard. "Manifest Destiny and the Philippines." *America in Crisis: Fourteen Crucial Episodes in American History*. Daniel Aaron, ed. New York: Alfred A. Knopf, 1952.

——. *Social Darwinism in American Thought*. Boston: Beacon Press, 1968.

Holbo, Paul S. "Economics, Emotion, and Expansion: An Emerging Foreign Policy." In *The Gilded Age*. H. Wayne Morgan, ed. Syracuse: Syracuse University Press, 1970.

Hollingsworth, J. Rogers. *The Whirligig of Politics: The Democracy of Cleveland and Bryan*. Chicago: The University of Chicago Press, 1963.

——, ed. *American Expansion in the Late Nineteenth Century: Colonialist or Anticolonialist?* New York: Holt, Rinehart and Winston, 1968.

Holt, W. Stull. *Treaties Defeated by the Senate: A Study of the Struggle between the President and Senate over the Conduct of Foreign Relations*. Baltimore: The Johns Hopkins University Press, 1933.

Iriye, Akira. *Across the Pacific: An Inner History of American-East Asian Relations*. New York: Harcourt, Brace & World, 1967.

——. *Pacific Estrangement: Japanese and American Expansion, 1897-1911*. Cambridge: Harvard University Press, 1972.

James, Henry. *Richard Olney and His Public Service*. Reprint ed. New York: Da Capo Press, 1971.

Johnson, Allen, and Malone, Dumas, eds. *Dictionary of American Biography*. 22 vols. New York: Charles Scribner's Sons, 1928-58.

Jones, Eliot. *The Trust Problem in the United States*. New York: The Macmillan Co., 1921.

Jordan, David Starr. "Lest We Forget." An Address Delivered before the Graduating Class of 1898, Leland Stanford, Jr. University on May 25, 1898. Palo Alto: Stanford University Press, 1898.

Krout, Mary H. *Hawaii and a Revolution*. New York: Dodd, Mead and Co., 1898.

Kuykendall, Ralph S. *The Hawaiian Kingdom*. 3 vols. Honolulu: University of Hawaii Press, 1938-67.

LaFeber, Walter. *The New Empire: An Interpretation of American Expansion, 1860-1898*. New York: Cornell University Press, 1963.

Leopold, Richard W. *The Growth of American Foreign Policy*. New York: Alfred A. Knopf, 1962.

Liliuokalani. *Hawaii's Story by Hawaii's Queen*. Boston: Lee and Shepard, 1898.

Lodge, Henry Cabot, and Redmond, Charles F., eds. *Selections from the Correspondence of Theodore Roosevelt and Henry Cabot Lodge, 1884-1918*. Reprint ed. 2 vols. New York: Da Capo Press, 1971.

McCall, Samuel W. *The Life of Thomas Brackett Reed*. Boston: Houghton Mifflin Co., 1914.

McCormick, Thomas J. *China Market: America's Quest for Informal Empire, 1893-1901*. Chicago: Quadrangle Books, 1967.

McElroy, Robert M. *Grover Cleveland: The Man and the Statesman*. 2 vols. New York: Harper & Brothers Publishers, 1923.

Mahan, Alfred T. *The Interest of America in Sea Power*. Reprint ed. Port Washington, N.Y.: Kennikat Press, 1970.

Malloy, William M., ed. *Treaties, Conventions, International Acts, Protocols and Agreements Between the United States of America and Other Powers, 1776-1909*. Reprint ed. 4 vols. New York: Greenwood Press, 1968.

May, Ernest R. *Imperial Democracy: The Emergence of America as a Great Power*. New York: Harcourt, Brace & World, 1961.

———. *American Imperialism: A Speculative Essay*. New York: Atheneum, 1968.

Merk, Frederick. *Manifest Destiny and Mission in American History: A Reinterpretation*. New York: Vintage Books, 1963.

Miller, Richard H., ed. *American Imperialism in 1898: The Quest for National Fulfillment*. The Wiley Problems in American History Series. New York: John Wiley and Sons, 1970.

Moore, John Bassett. *A Digest of International Law . . .* 8 vols. Washington, D.C.: Government Printing Office, 1906.

———. *Four Phases of American Development: Federalism—Democracy—Imperialism—Expansion*. Reprint ed. New York: Da Capo Press, 1970.

Morgan, H. Wayne. *William McKinley and His America*. Syracuse: Syracuse University Press, 1963.

———. *America's Road to Empire: The War with Spain and Overseas Expansion*. The Wiley America in Crisis Series. New York: John Wiley and Sons, 1965.

Morison, Elting E., and Blum, John M., eds. *The Letters of Theodore Roosevelt*. 8 vols. Cambridge: Harvard University Press, 1951-54.

Mosher, Leroy E. *Stephen M. White: Californian, Citizen, Lawyer, Senator*. 2 vols. Los Angeles: The Times-Mirror Co., 1903.

Nevins, Allan. *Grover Cleveland: A Study in Courage*. New York: Dodd, Mead & Co., 1932.

———, ed. *Letters of Grover Cleveland, 1850-1908*. Reprint ed. New York: Da Capo Press, 1970.

Palmer, Julius A., Jr. *Memories of Hawaii and Hawaiian Correspondence*. Boston: Lee and Shepard, 1894.

———. *Again in Hawaii*. Boston: Lee and Shepard, 1895.

Paterson, Thomas G., ed. *American Imperialism & Anti-Imperialism*. Crowell Problem Studies in American History. New York: Thomas Y. Crowell Co., 1973.

———; Clifford, Garry J.; and Hagan, Kenneth J. *American Foreign Policy: A History*. Lexington, Mass.: D. C. Heath and Co., 1977.

Pettigrew, Richard F. *Imperial Washington: The Story of American Public Life from 1870 to 1920*. Chicago: Arno Press and the New York Times, 1922.

Porter, Kirk H., and Johnson, Donald B., comps. *National Party Platforms, 1840-1960*. Urbana: University of Illinois Press, 1961.

Pratt, Julius W. *Expansionists of 1898: The Acquisition of Hawaii and the Spanish Islands*. Reprint ed. Chicago: Quadrangle Books, 1964.

Radosh, Ronald. *American Labor and United States Foreign Policy*. New York: Vintage Books, 1969.

Rappaport, Armin. *A History of American Diplomacy*. New York: The Macmillan Co., 1975.

Reynolds, Clifford P., comp. *Biographical Directory of the American Congress, 1774-1961*. Washington, D.C.: Government Printing Office, 1961.

Richardson, James D. *A Compilation of the Messages and Papers of the Presidents, 1789-1897*. 10 vols. Washington, D.C.: Government Printing Office, 1899.

Robinson, William A. *Thomas B. Reed: Parliamentarian*. New York: Dodd, Mead & Co., 1930.

Russ, William A., Jr. *The Hawaiian Revolution (1803-04)*. Selinsgrove, Pa.: Susquehanna University Press, 1959.

———. *The Hawaiian Republic (1894-98) and Its Struggle to Win Annexation*. Selinsgrove, Pa.: Susquehanna University Press, 1961.

Seager, Robert II, and Maguire, Doris D., eds. *Letters and Papers of Alfred Thayer Mahan*. 3 vols. Annapolis: Naval Institute Press, 1975.

Shenton, James P. "Imperialism and Racism." *Essays in American Historiography: Papers Presented in Honor of Allan Nevins*. Donald Sheehan and Harold Syrett, eds. New York: Columbia University Press, 1960.

Sherman, John. *Recollections of Forty Years in the House, Senate and Cabinet: An Autobiography*. 2 vols. Chicago: The Werner Co., 1895.

Sievers, Harry J. *Benjamin Harrison*. 3 vols. New York: University Publishers, 1952-68.

Smith, Daniel M. *The American Diplomatic Experience*. Boston: Houghton Mifflin Co., 1972.

Sprout, Harold and Margaret. *The Rise of American Naval Power, 1776-1918*. Princeton: Princeton University Press, 1967.

Stevens, Sylvester K. *American Expansion in Hawaii, 1842-1898*. Harrisburg, Pa.: Archives Publishing Co., 1945.

Surface, George T. *The Story of Sugar*. New York: D. Appleton and Co., 1910.

Tansill, Charles C. *The Foreign Policy of Thomas F. Bayard, 1885-1897*. New York: Fordham University Press, 1940.

Tate, Merze. *The United States and the Hawaiian Kingdom: A Political History.* New Haven: Yale University Press, 1965.

———. *Hawaii: Reciprocity or Annexation.* East Lansing: Michigan State University Press, 1968.

Terrill, Tom E. *The Tariff, Politics, and American Foreign Policy, 1874–1901.* Westport, Conn.: Greenwood Press, 1973.

Thurston, Lorrin A. *A Handbook on the Annexation of Hawaii.* St. Joseph, Michigan: A. B. Morse Co., 1897.

———. *Memoirs of the Hawaiian Revolution.* Andrew Farrell, ed. Honolulu: Advertiser Publishing Co., 1936.

Tompkins, E. Berkeley. *Anti-Imperialism in the United States: The Great Debate, 1890–1920.* Philadelphia: University of Pennsylvania Press, 1970.

Treat, Payson J. *Diplomatic Relations between the United States and Japan, 1853–1905.* 3 vols. Stanford: Stanford University Press, 1932–38.

Tuchman, Barbara W. *The Proud Tower: A Portrait of the World before the War, 1890–1914.* New York: The Macmillan Co., 1966.

Van Alstyne, Richard W. *American Diplomacy in Action.* Revised ed. Stanford: Stanford University Press, 1947.

Vogt, Paul L. *The Sugar Refining Industry in the United States.* Philadelphia: University of Pennsylvania Press, 1908.

Weinberg, Albert K. *Manifest Destiny: A Study of Nationalist Expansionism in American History.* Reprint ed. Chicago: Quadrangle Books, 1963.

Welch, Richard E., Jr. *George Frisbie Hoar and the Half-Breed Republicans.* Cambridge: Harvard University Press, 1971.

———. *Imperialists vs. Anti-Imperialists: The Debate Over Expansion in the 1890s.* Itasca, Ill.: F. E. Peacock Publishers, 1972.

Williams, William Appleman. *The Tragedy of American Diplomacy.* 2nd ed., revised. New York: Dell Publishing Co., 1962.

———. *The Contours of American History.* Reprint ed. Chicago: Quadrangle Paperbacks, 1966.

———. *The Roots of the Modern American Empire: A Study of the Growth and Shaping of Social Consciousness in a Marketplace Society.* New York: Vintage Books, 1969.

Young, Marilyn Blatt. "American Expansion, 1870–1900: The Far East." *Towards a New Past: Dissenting Essays in American History.* Barton J. Bernstein, ed. New York: Vintage Books, 1969.

PROCEEDINGS AND REPORTS

Hunter, Charles H. "Statehood and the Hawaiian Annexation Treaty of 1893." Fifty-ninth *Annual Report* of the Hawaiian Historical Society for the Year 1950 (1951), pp. 5–11.

Kuykendall, Ralph S. "Negotiation of the Hawaiian Annexation Treaty of 1893." Fifty-first *Annual Report* of the Hawaiian Historical Society for the Year 1942 (September 1943), pp. 5–64.

Proceedings of the Seventeenth Annual Convention of the American Federation of Labor, held at Nashville, Tennessee, December 13–21, 1897.

JOURNAL ARTICLES

Appel, John C. "American Labor and the Annexation of Hawaii: A Study in Logic and Economic Interest." *Pacific Historical Review* 23 (February 1954): 1–18.

Bailey, Thomas A. "Japan's Protest against the Annexation of Hawaii." *Journal of Modern History* 3 (March 1931): 46–61.

——. "The United States and Hawaii during the Spanish-American War." *American Historical Review* 36 (April 1931): 552–60.

Baker, George W., Jr. "Benjamin Harrison and Hawaiian Annexation: A Reinterpretation." *Pacific Historical Review* 33 (August 1964): 295–309.

Baron, Harold. "Anti-Imperialism and the Democrats." *Science and Society* 21 (Summer 1957): 222–39.

Devine, Michael J. "John W. Foster and the Struggle for the Annexation of Hawaii." *Pacific Historical Review* 46 (February 1977): 29–50.

Dozer, Donald M. "The Opposition to Hawaiian Reciprocity, 1876–1888." *Pacific Historical Review* 14 (June 1945): 157–83.

Hamilton, Allen Lee. "Military Strategists and the Annexation of Hawaii." *Journal of the West* 15 (April 1976): 81–91.

Hammett, Hugh B. "The Cleveland Administration and Anglo-American Naval Friction in Hawaii, 1893–1894." *Military Affairs* 40 (February 1976): 27–32.

Harrington, Fred Harvey. "The Anti-Imperialist Movement in the United States, 1898–1900." *Mississippi Valley Historical Review* 22 (September 1935): 211–30.

——. "Literary Aspects of American Anti-Imperialism, 1898–1902." *New England Quarterly* 10 (December 1937): 650–67.

Holbo, Paul S. "Perspectives on American Foreign Policy, 1890–1916: Expansion and World Power." *The Social Studies* 58 (November 1967): 246–56.

Knoles, George Harmon, ed. "Grover Cleveland on Imperialism." *Mississippi Valley Historical Review* 37 (September 1950): 303–4.

Lasch, Christopher. "The Anti-Imperialists, the Philippines, and the Inequality of Man." *Journal of Southern History* 24 (August 1958): 319–31.

McCormick, Thomas J. "A Commentary on 'The Anti-Imperialists and Twentieth Century American Foreign Policy.'" *Studies on the Left* 3, no. 1 (1962): 28–33.

——. "Insular Imperialism and the Open Door: The China Market and the Spanish-American War." *Pacific Historical Review* 32 (May 1963): 155–69.

McKee, Delber L. "Samuel Gompers, the A.F. of L., and Imperialism, 1895–1900." *The Historian* 21 (February 1959): 187–99.

Nichols, Jeannette P. "The United States Congress and Imperialism: 1861–1897." *Journal of Economic History* 21 (December 1961): 526–38.

Osborne, Thomas J. "Claus Spreckels and the Oxnard Brothers: Pioneer Developers of California's Beet Sugar Industry, 1890–1900." *Southern California Quarterly* 54 (Summer 1972): 117–25.

Pearce, George F. "Assessing Public Opinion: Editorial Comment and the Annexation of Hawaii—A Case Study." *Pacific Historical Review* 43 (August 1974): 324–41.

Pratt, Julius W. "The Hawaiian Revolution: A Re-interpretation." *Pacific Historical Review* 1, no. 3 (1932): 273-94.
———. "The 'Large Policy' of 1898." *Mississippi Valley Historical Review* 19 (September 1932): 219-42.
———. "Collapse of American Imperialism." *American Mercury* 31 (March 1934): 269-78.
Radosh, Ronald. "American Labor and the Anti-Imperialist Movement: A Discussion." *Science and Society* 28 (Winter 1964): 91-100.
Rollins, John W. "The Anti-Imperialists and Twentieth Century American Foreign Policy." *Studies on the Left* 3, no. 1 (1962): 9-24.
Rowland, Donald. "The United States and the Contract Labor Question in Hawaii, 1862-1900." *Pacific Historical Review* 2, no. 3 (1933): 249-69.
———. "The Establishment of the Republic of Hawaii, 1893-1894." *Pacific Historical Review* 4, no. 3 (1935): 201-20.
———. "Orientals and the Suffrage in Hawaii." *Pacific Historical Review* 12 (March 1943): 11-21.
Russ, William A., Jr. "Hawaiian Labor and Immigration Problems before Annexation." *Journal of Modern History* 15 (September 1943): 207-22.
———. "The Role of Sugar in Hawaiian Annexation." *Pacific Historical Review* 12 (December 1943): 339-50.
Tate, Merze. "Great Britain and the Sovereignty of Hawaii." *Pacific Historical Review* 31 (November 1962): 327-48.
———. "The Myth of Hawaii's Swing toward Australasia and Canada." *Pacific Historical Review* 33 (August 1964): 273-93.
———. "Hawaii: A Symbol of Anglo-American Rapprochement." *Political Science Quarterly* 79 (December 1964): 555-75.
———. "Twisting the Lion's Tail over Hawaii." *Pacific Historical Review* 36 (February 1967): 27-46.
Thompson, J. A. "William Appleman Williams and the 'American Empire.' " *Journal of American Studies* 7 (April 1973): 91-104.
Tompkins, E. Berkeley. "The Old Guard: A Study of the Anti-Imperialist Leadership." *The Historian* 30 (May 1968): 366-88.
Tuchman, Barbara W. "Czar of the House." *American Heritage* 14 (December 1962): 32-35, 92-102.
Vevier, Charles. "American Continentalism: An Idea of Expansion, 1845-1910." *American Historical Review* 65 (January 1960): 323-35.
Weigle, Richard D. "Sugar and the Hawaiian Revolution." *Pacific Historical Review* 16 (February 1947): 41-58.
Welch, Richard E., Jr. "Motives and Policy Objectives of Anti-Imperialists, 1898." *Mid-America* 51 (April 1969): 119-29.

Index

Acknowledgments

Generous financial support for this study was provided by the Ford Foundation, the International Studies Association, and Claremont Graduate School. Santa Ana College granted me a sabbatical leave which allowed time for much of the writing of the manuscript.

Librarians and archivists were uniformly kind and helpful. Patricia J. Palmer, former manuscripts librarian in the Special Collections Department at the Stanford University Library, guided me expertly through several large, partially catalogued manuscript collections. Agnes Conrad, Archivist of the State of Hawaii, allowed me to draw upon her vast knowledge of Hawaiian source materials, and handled my numerous requests for the mailing of photocopied documents with unfailing promptness and courtesy. Two government documents librarians—Joyce M. Wilder-Jones of the California State University, Fullerton Library, and Lynda Adams of the University of California, Irvine Library—helped me find my way through a maze of official reports and dispatches dealing with American-Hawaiian foreign relations before annexation. Doris Smedes and Virginia J. Renner, both members of the Huntington Library's Reader Services staff, helped me make good use of that library's excellent rare books and periodicals collections. Santa Ana College librarians Kelley J. Powell and May K. Dunning handled my many requests for interlibrary loan materials. I also wish to acknowledge gratitude for the cooperation and assistance I received from the very fine staffs of the following manuscript repositories and libraries: the Manuscript Division of the Library of Congress; the diplomatic and naval branches of the National Archives; the Massachusetts Historical Society; the Minnesota Historical Society (which altered its schedule significantly to accommodate a travel-weary, out-of-state researcher on a hot Fourth of July weekend in 1975); the Maine Historical Society; the Honnold Library of the Claremont Colleges; the State Library of

Hawaii; the University of Hawaii Library; the Bowdoin College Library; the Bancroft Library at the University of California, Berkeley; and the University Research Library at the University of California, Los Angeles.

This book, begun as a doctoral dissertation, was improved immensely as a result of the criticisms and suggestions offered by other historians. Whatever merit this book possesses is due largely to the exacting standards of Professor Charles S. Campbell, my mentor at Claremont Graduate School, Professors William John Niven and Charles A. Lofgren, of Claremont Graduate School and Claremont Men's College respectively, gave me the benefit of their incisive criticisms and helpful suggestions; as did Professors Richard E. Welch, Jr., of Lafayette College, Robin W. Winks of Yale University, and Donald D. Johnson of the University of Hawaii at Manoa.

The *Pacific Historical Review* has kindly allowed me to use, in abbreviated form, material from an earlier article of mine appearing in that journal.

Finally, friends and relatives provided generous support. Dr. and Mrs. Richard Sneed, and especially Charles F. Penhallow, saw to it that I was well cared for while researching parts of this book in Honolulu. My mother, Dorothy M. Osborne, to whom this book is dedicated, typed and proofed numerous drafts of the manuscript and helped in countless other ways. Throughout the lengthy process of bringing this study to completion, I was sustained by my devoted and understanding wife, Ginger T. Osborne, who, in addition to supplying needed encouragement, gave me the benefit of her clear thinking and sound advice on matters of composition. Without her unwavering support this endeavor would not have been possible.

THOMAS J. OSBORNE, a specialist in 20th century American foreign relations, achieved his Ph.D. at Claremont Graduate University in 1979. This native Californian has won fellowships from the Ford Foundation, the National Endowment for the Humanities and from the University of California Institute on Global Conflict and Cooperation.

A member of the International History Honor Society, Osborne spent a year as visiting faculty on the Manoa campus of the University of Hawaii. Today, Professor Osborne coordinates the Honors Program and teaches at Santa Ana College where in 1988 he was the recipient of the Distinguished Faculty Award and, in 1997, merited the President of the Board of Trustee's Award.

He was selected by the Kettering Foundation to participate in Dartmouth's Conference on Soviet-American Relations and on the National Board of Directors of the Beyond War Foundation. In 1991 - 1992, Osborne completed conflict resolutions studies at Harvard Law School.

Tom and his wife, Ginger, a psychology professor, live in Laguna Beach and surf the Pacific with sons Brooks and Todd.